A QUESTION OF SEX

A Question of Sex

FEMINISM, RHETORIC, AND DIFFERENCES THAT MATTER

Kristan Poirot

University of Massachusetts Press
Amherst & Boston

ISBN 978-1-62534-089-4 (paper); 088-7 (hardcover)

Designed by Jack Harrison
Set in Adobe Minion Pro
Printed and bound by the Maple-Vail Book Manufacturing Group

Library of Congress Cataloging-in-Publication Data
Poirot, Kristan, 1976–
A question of sex : feminism, rhetoric, and differences that matter / Kristan Poirot.
    pages cm
Includes bibliographical references and index.
ISBN 978-1-62534-089-4 (pbk. : alk. paper) —
ISBN 978-1-62534-088-7 (hardcover : alk. paper)
1. Feminism—United States. 2. Sex differences. 3. Sex. 4. Feminist theory.
I. Title.
HQ1410.P65 2014
305.420973—dc23
                2014005980

British Library Cataloguing-in-Publication Data
A catalogue record for this book is available from the British Library.

Sex . . . is situational; it is explicable only within the context of battles over gender and power.

THOMAS LAQUEUR, *Making Sex*

Contents

Preface

IN MY OFFICE I have hanging a *Life* magazine cover from 1971. The cover presents an image of a woman, presumably a feminist, holding a sign that says "EVE WAS FRAMED," standing next to another, semi-nude woman, presumably Eve, holding an apple. Above these images the cover reads "The 'Woman Problem'—Then and Now." As I started to conceptualize this project many years ago, feminism's "woman problem" was not simply one centered on the necessity for feminism to intervene in sex politics; rather, as I began to think of the relationship between feminist history and the "woman problem," I saw feminist commitments to "woman" itself as a problem. For me, feminism's "woman problem" was one founded on its historical commitment to an ontologically stable female subject; it was a problem framed by exclusion and the constitutive limits of identity politics, and I thought it necessary to consider seriously what possibilities were foreclosed by these exclusions. I was persuaded by a variety of critiques of identity politics, and I wanted to provide clear historical evidence that the failures of feminism were due in large part to activists' naïve identity commitments.

Over time my views changed. I realized that my initial biases and conclusions were somewhat superficial. Feminism's "woman problem" was much more complex than I had previously thought. Eventually I came to believe that the question of woman belies questions of feminism's relationship to those systems that constitutively contoured woman variously yet continuously over time; it sidesteps questions of sex, difference, and identity, always assuming that the feminist politics of differentiation and identification are stable, even if the specific articulations of womanly difference are not. My engagement with feminism needed not to place emphasis on the woman problem, but instead to consider questions of differentiation and identification as context-bound problems to which feminist activism inevitably responds. I wanted to keep in question sex itself in order to remain mindful of identity—sex, gender, race, or otherwise—not as a fact of human difference, but as the effect of a contingent process of recognition and identification. And while my questions and style of engagement were necessarily academic, I hoped to communicate a commitment to feminism more broadly—to theories and movements that highlight the role of sex and gender in order to make the world a better place.

I open these prefacing remarks with this shift in thinking to highlight and make concrete the various personal and professional influences that have undoubtedly helped shape my conclusions in this book. Countless conversations with mentors, colleagues, and friends pushed me to consider different sides of the questions that I wanted to ask, (re)directing my conceptual thinking at times and reminding me of the importance of movements, material politics, and history at others. I feel extraordinarily fortunate to be surrounded by such a diverse set of wickedly smart friends and colleagues who have influenced this project for the better.

My affinity for public address, feminist history, and struggles in U.S. political contexts emerges most clearly from my doctoral work at the University of Georgia. Bonnie J. Dow directed my doctoral dissertation on lesbian sexuality and the "second wave," introduced me to feminist (rhetorical) history, and offered revision suggestions that undoubtedly enhanced the appeal of this project. Her influences on it are innumerable and undeniable, and I am grateful for her mentorship, friendship, and continued support. John Murphy's work, astute advice, and friendship have shaped my approach to rhetorical criticism in very clear ways. I owe much to his direct critique of my first attempts to grapple with identification and the circulation of Sojourner Truth's speech, and to his persistent calls to think about context in expansive and novel ways. Bonnie and John were not my sole faculty influences from UGA, however; I would be remiss not to mention the pivotal role of Celeste Condit, Michelle Ballif, and Kevin DeLuca in my intellectual development.

My ideas about feminism and U.S. politics are also shaped by an awesome set of feminist academics from graduate school and beyond who inspire my commitment to women's/gender movements. Tasha Dubriwny, graduate school "BFF" and current colleague at Texas A&M, shapes my views about feminism and what it means to be a feminist academic. Her friendship is invaluable, and her insights have directly impacted every chapter in this book. Lesli Pace inspired me as a graduate student, and continues to do so as feminist scholar and teacher; I am grateful for her thoughts and support over the years. Finally, a number of others, including Shevaun Watson, Kristy Maddux, Angela Hudson, Joan Wolf, Claire Katz, Claudia Nelson, Jennifer Mease, Cara Wallis, Rebecca Gill, Kirsten Pullen, and Jennifer Jones Barbour, were conversational springboards for ideas, early readers of chapters, and supportive colleagues for this project. They offered not only encouragement and friendship but also astute responses to my writing and ideas about feminism, history, and rhetoric.

While certain people were more clearly engaging my interests in feminist rhetorical history, another group of people pushed my conceptual thinking in useful ways. Conversations with John Muckelbauer and Daniel Smith, probably more than any others, shifted my thinking about Judith Butler's theories and the role of identification and recognition in feminist politics. Many of the conceptual impulses in this book are a direct result of discussions with them about a great number of subjects. Pat Gehrke, Kenneth Rufo, Jim Aune, and Erik Doxtader also contributed directly and indirectly to the theoretical disposition of this book and/or reminded me in various ways that this project was worth pursuing.

Beyond these specific intellectual contributions, I want to acknowledge the practical contributions by individuals and institutions that helped advance the research for and writing of this book. An earlier version of chapter 2 was published as "(Un)Making Sex, Making Race: Nineteenth-Century Liberalism, Difference, and the Rhetoric of Elizabeth Cady Stanton" in the *Quarterly Journal of Speech* 96 (2010): 185–208. Similarly, a much shortened version of chapter 4 appeared as "Domesticating the Liberated Woman: Containment Rhetorics of Second Wave Radical/Lesbian Feminism," *Women's Studies in Communication* 32 (2009): 263–92. I am thankful for the anonymous reviewers of these essays and their editors, John Louis Lucaites and Cindy Griffin, for their efforts to make my ideas and arguments relevant and interesting to rhetorical scholars. Similarly, the anonymous reviewers for the completed monograph, the book's editor Brian Halley, and the editing staff of the University of Massachusetts Press (Carol Betsch, Mary Bellino, and Amanda Heller) deserve thanks for their hard work in moving this project forward toward publication.

The University of Georgia, Texas A&M University, and the University of South Carolina provided financial assistance for this project, for which I am very grateful. With this financial assistance, I was able to persuade a few graduate students to help complete archival research, source and citation checking, as well as content review. I am very thankful that John Higgins, Eleanor Lockhart, and Isaac Holyoak agreed to do such time-consuming work.

I must also acknowledge the love, support, and care that I received from friends and family. My mother and father, Julie and Michael Permenter, and my grandparents, Janice and Jerry Poirot, offered free child care at much-needed times and were also consistent sources of emotional support through this process. My siblings, Amanda (and Dustin), Ryan, Sara, Sam, and Emily, cared for and entertained my son on many occasions in order to allow time for me to research and write, and I am fortunate to have them in my life. Matt Woods also offered free child care, excellent food, and fine wine, and served as a formidable debate "opponent." Toward the end of my work on this book, I was welcomed into another family whose unconditional love and acceptance continue to surprise me. Thank you, Marguerite, Ory, Laura, and Andy Durand, Michelle and Mike Brookover, and Stephanie and Andrew O'Donnell for celebrating our political differences and the sense of accomplishment that completing this project has brought to me.

Last but certainly not least, to my immediate family, Jeff, Eli, Bethany, and Joshua, I owe too much to express here. My husband pushes me to write more clearly, lifts me up when I doubt myself, continues to make sure that I don't take myself too seriously, and never stops challenging me to grow intellectually and emotionally as a feminist, woman, wife, and mother. He is truly my partner, for better or for worse. Our children are the smartest, funniest, and most surprising gang in town, and their existence makes my life, this job, and the world much more fun and interesting.

A QUESTION OF SEX

Introduction

QUESTIONS OF SEX

IN 1994 EVE Ensler brought her off-Broadway production *The Vagina Monologues* to the stage for the first time. Through a series of vignettes, which ranged from teary descriptions of the wonders of childbirth to climactic reclamations of "cunt," Ensler's *Monologues* quickly gained national prominence as a frank, and possibly even strategically crass, feminist intervention into sex politics. Ensler gathered material for the production by interviewing more than two hundred women about their bodies, and in these interviews women narrated their experiences of sex, abuse, menstruation, masturbation, gynecological exams, prostitution, rape, pregnancy, orgasm, and the like.[1] The willingness of women to share the most intimate details about their lives may have surprised some, but according to Ensler, "the story of [a woman's] vagina is the story of [her] life, and women want to talk about their lives."[2] Acclaimed for its rendering of taboo topics about women's bodies as both "visible and speakable," *The Vagina Monologues* spawned the V-Day movement, wherein countless women across the world perform the monologues in an effort to "end violence against women and girls."[3] In more ways than one, V-Day celebrations have become a mainstay in a global feminist campaign against rape, assault, and abuse, and while many value the *Monologues'* intervention, others contend that it places too much emphasis on the sexed body. The direct intervention of *The Vagina Monologues* into discursive and material practices tied to sexed-female anatomy, in other words, is not without controversy. And this controversy is centered precisely on the *question of sex* and its role in feminist activism.

Ensler's first theatrical interrogation of sex and its function in women's lives surfaced alongside a complementary set of academic interventions into sex—ones that aimed to change fundamentally how feminists (and others) conceptualized the "nature" of sex difference. Building from the observations of Michel Foucault's *History of Sexuality,* an array of scholarship emerged in the early 1990s that problematized previously unquestioned conceptual and cultural understandings of sex as a simple description of difference between two distinct types of bodies. The historian Thomas Laqueur, for example, argued that the contemporary notion of incommensurable biological sexes is a relatively new cultural invention, demonstrating that this familiar two-sex understanding of difference is the result of a rhetorical shift in post-Enlightenment identity politics and not a product of more accurate scientific descriptions.[4] A few years later, Anne Fausto-Sterling, a biologist, maintained the existence of five biological sexes, thus positing the model of two exclusive sexes as more normative than natural.[5] Judith Butler went even further, troubling the sex-gender / nature-nurture divide by arguing that both sex and gender are performative categories of identity.[6] Like Ensler's *Monologues,* these histories and theories pointed to the role of culture in the production of sex, insisting that we must no longer understand sex as a fact of human difference. And when we learned that sex was no longer a biological given, we found ourselves amid what Nathan Stormer calls a "scholarly revolution" that radically historicized the sexed subject.[7]

This scholarly sex revolution prompted at least two paths for feminist considerations of the role of sex in the public sphere. On the one hand, these theories offered useful interpretive frames for scholarship committed to understanding a number of contemporary cases of sex/gender bending. From Dennis Rodman to Caster Semenya, *The Birdcage* to Lady Gaga, people have been making some serious sex/gender trouble and getting a lot of mainstream media attention for doing so. Debating the *facts of sex,* interlocutors in these public narratives celebrate and censure drag, medicalize and socialize transgenderism, and attempt to decide the requisite physiological characteristics of "male" and "female." Should sports require sex testing? Should "Gender-Identity Disorder" be included in the *DSM-V*? And how do we make sense of "straight" men dressed in female drag? A revolution in the ivory tower and the streets alike, sex/gender subversion went mainstream, and scholars across the humanities and social sciences attempted to make sense of it all. And for some of these scholars, it was those theories of the scholarly sex revolution—theories that *gendered* sex—that shifted the debate from the *facts of sex* to *questions of gender* and its relationship to the production of sex and sexual difference.

John M. Sloop's *Disciplining Gender,* for example, tackles the questions that emerge from this late twentieth- and early twenty-first-century explosion of attention to sex/gender trouble. Arguing that a quick glance at the 1990s might yield a certain optimism about the state of gender affairs—a belief that "public understandings of gender, sex, and sexuality have changed 'for the better' "—Sloop demonstrates that the transgressions of the 1990s and beyond were positioned in such a way that they refined, rather than subverted, "dominant assumptions about human bodies and sexual desire."[8] Gender trouble, we learn, brings gender discipline—consequences that reaffirm bi-gender sexual systems and reassert sex as an ontological category. Sloop's wariness of the status of sex certainty is no small matter; for those people who do not quite fit within a bi-gender heteronormative framing of identity, the material consequences are often nothing short of ridicule, assault, and even death.

Sloop was not alone in his concern about how sex is persistently rendered as a fact of human difference, and indeed, sex as an ontological distinction was a central position for many contemporary feminist and/or queer theorists. As I discuss in more detail later on, the sex revolution celebrated sex fluidity through the centralization of *gender* as feminism's crucial concern and mechanism for radical social change. For some, *gender* replaced sex in such a way that when sex emerged in public narratives—feminist or otherwise—it was deemed necessarily problematic.[9] The reception of Ensler's *Monologues* is a prime case in point, as it is just as likely to be censured for reducing women (and others) to their sexed anatomy as it is celebrated for its marshaling of resources committed to ending violence against women and girls. As Jenae S. put it on the blog FBomb:

> Women are more than vaginas; I am more than my vagina. The *Vagina Monologues* presents the idea that all women have vaginas so all women can associate with anyone else who possesses one. It's the idea that a vagina is the one thing that connects all women. But what about women who don't possess a vagina? What about men who have a vagina? In the world of the *Vagina Monologues* trans people do not exist. If you have a vagina you're a woman, if not you're a man, it doesn't seem to matter how one chooses to define their gender. It is not life experiences or emotions that make a woman; it's just anatomy.[10]

However illusory, the status of sex as an ontological certainty is so compelling that it supplants any subversive attempt to address sex directly and fight the problems that result from sex/gender norms. Put simply, any feminist *question of sex* was really always already a *question of gender,* and seeing it as such was necessary to counter the hegemonic articulations of sex certainty.

Although a number of people shared this general wariness toward sex certainty—resisting the assumed fact of sex with persistent questions of gender—others reminded feminists of the importance of the materiality of sex in women's lives. The second revelation inspired by the scholarly sex revolution, in other words, departed from the renewed sense of the importance of gender as a critical term and held that sexed matter could not be ignored. For example, the well-known critique against Butler's *Gender Trouble*—What about the body, Judy?—encapsulated an anxiety about sex contingency as well as a desire to keep the fact(s) of (biological) sex separate from the abstract musings of a feminist philosopher. Arguably, the cries of a "ludic feminism,"[11] arguments that "women deserve better,"[12] and lamentations of a "feminism without women"[13] that first emerged in the 1990s as a response to Butler and others positioned feminism as the movement that historically had been necessarily invested in the fact of sexed female specificity. And those who cried the loudest were often firmly committed feminists themselves, as they were reticent to throw sex in with gender's fluidity and, as I argue, questionability.[14] For them, sex was a blank slate, but a slate nonetheless, and the play of social construction lay in the realm of gender and did not describe the corporeal matters of sex. As a result, sex was a *necessary* difference of matter that did matter, and any *question of sex* was supplanted by the *fact of sex* over and over again.

The critics of Butler and others, however, were not the only ones who insisted that feminism had historically required the sexed female subject. Butler herself argued that there is a common belief that feminism must ground itself in the "sexed specificity of the female body,"[15] and similarly Fausto-Sterling argues that "second-wave feminists . . . did not question the realm of physical sex; it was the psychological and cultural meanings of these differences—gender—that was at issue."[16] Arguably, then, although the two prominent responses to the scholarly revolution worked divergently to adamantly insist on and yet pointedly challenge any claim of the facticity of sex, those on both sides of the question of sex and feminism share the assumption that feminism itself has historically sought to ground itself in the female subject. Feminism is understood as a movement that champions the fact of sex, while it intervenes in gendered norms and practices. A central position of this book is that such a view risks marshaling a naïve understanding of feminist movement practices. As I demonstrate, long before the so-called linguistic turn and Eve Ensler's talk of vaginas, feminist movements had both productively challenged and amplified sex in their attempt to change women's lives. Were these challenges, in some obscure way, positing sex as unstable and contingent? Were these practices also questions of sex?

My purpose in this book is to explore to what extent feminism—as a movement and a constellation of ideas—has engaged the *matters of sex* as *questions of sex.* In challenging the notion that feminism has a historically consistent investment in female sexed specificity *as we know it,* I am not uncovering early proto-poststructural theories of sex/gender in feminist advocacy, nor is it my aim to shame early feminists for not "getting it right" about sex/gender all along. Rather, I rethink the terms through which we understand feminist movements and history and emphasize feminism's engagement with sex (not just gender) as a *rhetorical* endeavor—an endeavor, in other words, that is shaped by the instrumental demands of the movement, the exigent situations that called for feminists to respond, and the political traditions that feminist discourse both amplified and resisted. This rhetorical orientation toward the study of feminism and sex offers the chance to examine how "sex" operates not as a platform from which feminism speaks (e.g., speaking for women), but as a cultural milieu within which feminist advocacy participates. When the questionability of sex is sustained, we learn that although the oft-proclaimed subject of feminism is "woman," feminism remains caught in historically varied traditions of identification and difference. Rather than a constant, in other words, "woman" and "female" function as changing prisms through which feminists articulate those differences that matter among a populace, and those that do not. In this book I examine the rhetorical gestures of this commitment and consider the stakes of asserting the questionability of sex for how we understand feminism.

The gestures of feminism's identity commitments are examined through five case studies that position feminist discursive practices within distinct contexts that are indicative of U.S. movements' most defining moments. The assumptions about sex and rhetoric contained in these case studies—in which I look at the circulation of Sojourner Truth's "Ain't I a Woman?" speech in early and contemporary feminist contexts; the public discourse of Elizabeth Cady Stanton and early nineteenth-century ideas about suffrage, sex, and race; the visual rhetorics of the feminist self-help health movement; the conflicts over lesbian sexuality in the 1960s and 1970s; and the discourse that surrounds twenty-first-century SlutWalks—are the focus of the remainder of these introductory remarks. First, the analyses that follow highlight the importance of understanding rhetoric as a *situated practice* with instrumental and constitutive elements. Often understood as a persuasive art, rhetorical discourses clearly embody the aims and goals of their creators—people/movements use rhetoric to do things—but to understand how these rhetorics function, one must also direct attention to the constitutive dynamics in the relationship between a movement's public discourse and the context through which those rhetorics emerge and to which they respond.

Second, my consideration of feminism's rhetorical commitment to sex not only emphasizes the instrumental and constitutive importance of context but also posits an understanding that expands the materiality of sex beyond physiological and anatomical features of the body. This understanding of sex, which is consistent with that of those who build from Foucault's *History of Sexuality,* insists that "sex" emerges within material conditions, broadly conceived, and is not wholly confined to "natural" manifestations of differentiated sexed matter. Sex is contoured by situated practices that produce and maintain it as a fact of human difference.

Finally, these understandings of sex, rhetoric, and context call for an examination of traditions of human differentiation (e.g., sex, race, class, etc.) and the way these traditions and difference itself circulate in feminist advocacy. Although the scholarly revolution seems to have promoted *gender* as a central concept through which to consider the varied attempts of feminism to contour its identity commitments, *sex* is a also of crucial concern, as it reminds critics of the importance of the body for feminist activism. Through a series of what I term *questionable engagements* with feminist practices, this book offers a thickened account of feminism's public advocacies and begins to reimagine feminist history in terms of the very questions of sex, identity, and difference that emerged since the early 1990s.

Situating Feminism, Sex, and Rhetoric

The case studies that follow emphasize the historically contingent ways in which sex functions for many women's movements, demonstrating the importance of a rhetorical perspective for considerations of feminism's relationship to sex and difference. Indeed, a central claim of this book is that feminism's commitment to sex ought to be considered a *rhetorical* one, and that such a claim inevitably conjures a variety of meanings and valences depending on one's understanding of "rhetoric." If one takes the colloquial definition of rhetoric as "mere words" as an apt one, considerations of feminism's commitment to sex as rhetorical might communicate an emptiness to feminist identifications—gestures that lack substance. Those familiar with a number of textbook definitions, by contrast, might understand rhetoric loosely as the "art of persuasion," and offer a more generous interpretation of the claim to emphasize that any feminist commitment to sex is one compelled by feminism's advocacy for women. And for those who have a working understanding of the history of rhetorical theory, a rhetorical commitment to sex might be understood as one that espouses the importance of sex identification and the constitutive force of feminist discourse. Although I would not dispute these two interpretations, in this book I emphasize another aspect of rhetoric to facilitate a better understanding of feminist engagements with sex, namely, the importance of considering rhetoric and public discourse as *situated practices.* Feminism has not simply deployed nor anarchically constructed sex frameworks; it has, however, engaged with, challenged, and amplified sex systems in ways that have borne the burden of the movement's immediate needs and ongoing participation in U.S. political culture. The claim of feminism's rhetorical commitment to sex is a consideration of the way feminism has *engaged* layered sex contexts, necessarily contouring the character of feminism's identity commitment(s) and maybe even "sex" itself.

The emphasis on context is no small matter, as it is a defining aspect of a rhetorical perspective. Arguably, theorists of rhetoric, from its beginning, positioned public discourse as a "situated practice."[17] Aristotle famously defined rhetoric as the "faculty of observing, *in any given case,* the available means of persuasion," and scholars across the field of rhetoric consistently punctuate the importance of contexts, scenes, and situations to their theories and analyses of rhetorical practices (or practices-as-rhetorical).[18] Lloyd Bitzer wrote that "a work is rhetorical because it is a response to a situation of a certain kind."[19] John Poulakos observed that "a rhetorician concerns himself [or herself] with the particular and the pragmatic" and that "his [or her] way is . . . of a relativism of concrete rhetorical situations to which situationally derived truths are the only opportune and appropriate responses."[20] More recently, David Zarefsky characteristically stated the matter plainly and to the point: "Public discourse is situated rhetorical practice. It is the product of a rhetorical transaction in the context of a particular situation."[21] Clearly, these examples are far from exhaustive, as John Muckelbauer notes: "The history of rhetoric itself demonstrates an intimate concern with issues of context [and] situations."[22]

This intimate concern circulates in at least two registers in rhetorical studies:

one that relegates rhetoric to instrumental aims, and another that positions rhetoric in terms of its constitutive force. When one considers rhetoric as an instrumental practice that aims to accomplish a goal (e.g., to persuade an audience to vote for a candidate, or acquit a defendant, or garner support for a policy), then the context in which one speaks is of crucial and strategic importance. For example, questions that emerge in this understanding of rhetoric and context would include: What characteristics are associated with the speaker/writer? Who is the audience? What are their biases? What is the relationship between the speaker/author and the audience? What other rhetorics compete with or, conversely, support the message? What obstacles and opportunities arise from the particular occasion and/or medium of address? As much as these questions position the situational factors as central concerns for those attempting to understand how rhetorical texts are constructed and how they circulate and work within communities, these questions also clearly distinguish those texts from contexts. A skilled rhetor, in other words, develops appropriate strategies to meet the demands of a particular situation. From this perspective, the context becomes the container of public discourse, and in order to understand the potential force of rhetorical performances, one must attend to the situations in which those performances are bound, including the idiosyncrasies and cultural norms of the audiences to which those acts are directed.

Another view of rhetoric takes a slightly more nuanced approach and attends to the instrumentality of rhetoric while also emphasizing the constitutive dynamics of rhetorical texts and contexts. Audiences as extra-rhetorical entities that stand outside rhetorical performances have long been considered problematic, as such a view does not account for the way these rhetorical acts shape individuals as interlocutors and participants in public narratives. Maurice Charland, for example, used Kenneth Burke's idea that rhetoric works through identification and Louis Althusser's notion of interpellation to challenge the view of rhetoric as simply an instrumental art of persuasion. He argues that "theories of rhetoric as persuasion cannot account for the audiences that rhetoric addresses. If it is easier to praise Athens before Athenians than before Laecedemonians, we should ask how those in Athens come to experience themselves as Athenians."[23] Rhetoric, in this view, constitutes individuals as political subjects apt to accept the ideological terms of the rhetorical act. Rather than extra-rhetorical receivers of discourse, audiences are indelible subjects of constitutive rhetorical discourse. In Charland's words, "the position one embodies as a subject is a rhetorical effect."[24]

Rhetoric as both an instrumental and a constitutive art has grounded much of our understanding of the way feminist movement discourse functions in broad cultural contexts. The most enduring rhetorical obstacles for early feminist activists, for example, were sexed/gendered norms that posited womanhood as an identity that by definition was confined to the private sphere. This was a problem for those women committed to a number of reform movements for at least two related reasons. First, as Karlyn Kohrs Campbell explains, "women encountered profound resistance to their efforts for moral reform because rhetorical action of any sort was . . . a masculine activity."[25] As a result, women rhetors were largely discredited and were forced to demonstrate not only that they had the capacity to participate competently in public reform, but also that they should do so. Second, the credibility problems faced by individual speakers translated into distinct audience barriers when women sought to provoke other women to join their efforts. After all, for many female audience members, engagements in political reform movements were also actions that defied one's self and one's public identity as *woman*. And therein lay the problem: in order to effectively persuade audiences to engage in and or accept the claims of the various movements, women rhetors had to constitute womanhood differently. If "true womanhood" confined women exclusively to the private sphere, womanhood needed to be reconfigured in order to allow for public action. And that is precisely what early reformers did.[26]

Campbell's work on feminist rhetoric demonstrates quite clearly how early reformers enacted women's political capacities and rhetorical acumen and helped change the relationship between womanhood and the public sphere.[27] And not only did these rhetorics begin to shape "woman" as a public and political subject, but also there is evidence that the identities of those who participated in reform movements shifted from *woman* as domesticated subject to a private and public recognition of *women*, including themselves, as political subjects and citizens. Such a recognition is no small matter, as Susan Zaeske explains, for by "defining themselves as members of the national polity," women moved closer "to seeing themselves as national citizens entitled to the rights accorded by national citizenship," including the right to vote.[28] The constitutive rhetorical attempts of early movements to contour "woman" and interpellate female audiences as public citizens, in other words, were concomitant with, and necessary antecedents to, the goals of early feminist movements.

The efficacy and validity of feminism's instrumental rhetoric often demand these kinds of concerted constitutive efforts. Though no longer as forceful as it was in the nineteenth century, the idea that women's proper role is to be in service to others in private domestic settings continues to emerge as one of feminism's most persistent rhetorical problems. I am consistently reminded of this through interactions with students in a number of my introductory and advanced gender courses as the views that women are naturally nurturing and are inherently the most appropriate caretaker of the home (and those in it) continue to surface in class discussions. These seemingly gendered claims about women's roles often accompany arguments that link gender roles directly to understandings of differentiated sexed matter. According to these students, since a woman's sexed anatomy has the capacity to carry a fetus, women are naturally better caretakers. What appears to be a situation overdetermined by gender is in fact a context wherein both sex and gender are pinioned to reproduction. When feminists address these views, they are not simply debating opposing views of gender with no claim in sex; rather, they are constitutively engaging matters of sexed differentiation.

This example not only serves as a reminder of the importance of sex but also tells us that the consideration of rhetoric as a situated practice with both instrumental and constitutive elements goes beyond an understanding of the interpellation of individuals as subjects and includes more abstract norms, values, and idioms that circulate in social contexts. James Jasinski urges rhetorical critics to understand a more expansive notion of context in a way that breaks from a simple, instrumental portrait of a rhetorical scene.[29] As indicated earlier, an instrumental idea of a rhetorical situation posits that rhetorical acts respond to a distinct set of variables. Within this scene, there is often an immediate exigency as well as obstacles to which the rhetor is directly called upon to respond. For Jasinski, a rhetorical context is not merely an aggregate of immediate variables (e.g., audience, rhetor, medium, topic obstacles, setting, etc.), nor is it exclusively the producer of pressing exigencies.[30] Rather, context saturates public discourse, comprising both itself and rhetorical acts as amalgamations and orchestrations of various traditions. These traditions are more enduring than any immediate political scene, and they in turn comprise and are constituted by a multitude of rhetorical acts. As John M. Murphy writes, "A multiplicity of traditions infuse the social world; speakers orchestrate the resources of traditions in acts of rhetorical invention aimed at extending, transforming, or adapting rhetorical possibilities to specific circumstances."[31]

It is important, however, to consider political and rhetorical traditions as performative in that they manifest the various idioms, figurative and argumentative devices, and textual practices that they appear simply to describe.[32] Jasinski directs a critic's attention to a more expansive rhetorical scene, in other words, wherein the relationship between a rhetorical performance and its context is not so discrete. Likewise, for many theorists who constitute the scholarly sex revolution, the discursive practices of, for, and about sex ought to be considered as sex (con)texts wherein no clear boundary lies between talk about sex, the cultural context of that talk, and "sex" itself.[33] As a constitutive force in feminist discursive practices, in other words, performative traditions of sex difference animate feminist advocacy as well as the immediate and enduring contexts with which movements must directly engage. A look at these practices as *rhetorical* ones emphasizes both the performative nature and constitutive aspects of political and discursive traditions, as well as the movement's practical goals and concerns. Feminists encountered layered contexts and responded in ways that were not entirely contained by or distinct from the sexist contexts that provoked their response; feminism's articulation of sex was always already inextricable from, yet irreducible to, these hegemonic systems of sex identification and difference. As a result, one might consider a rhetorical perspective on feminism's encounter with sex as one that emphasizes participation and engagement. That is, feminist movements necessarily responded strategically to and were enabled by idioms, systems, and traditions of (sex) difference that they worked to constitute differently.

Assuredly, abstract traditions and idioms of difference were not the only things feminists were responding to. Women are murdered, raped, assaulted, abused, mocked, ridiculed, and undermined every day. These problems— what some might term material traditions of oppression—also constitute rhetorical scenes, and to ignore them entirely would fail to account for what motivates feminist rhetorical action. In my emphasis on discursive practices, I risk communicating a certain dismissal of the importance of materiality for feminism. As Martha Nussbaum famously articulated in her critique of Butler and "Butlerian feminists," many of those in the scholarly sex revolution focus too much on the relationship between discourse and sex/gender. Feminism should amplify its legacy of material politics, not diverge into "hip quietism" or "manipulative" and "disrespect[ful]" practices of "sophistry and rhetoric."[34] Far from being divorced from materiality, the rhetorical focus in this book on movement practices as those practices engaged "sex" in layered cultural contexts animates feminism as both responsive to and entangled in the material conditions through which feminist movements emerge and resist.

In short, context *matters*, and a rhetorical perspective posits feminist methods of change as situated practices in ways that do not distract from or ignore feminism's legacy of material politics; it highlights and gives nuance to an understanding of feminism's various and situationally responsive attempts to change people's lives.

Sex, Rhetoric, and Materiality

Despite the importance of understanding feminist movement practices as situated ones, questions concerning the *materiality of sex* itself might appear to be quite antithetical to this book's rhetorical perspective. "Materiality" has a lengthy and varied conceptual history, traversing intellectual planes as distinct as the philosophies of Marx and the hypotheses of theoretical physicists. And although rhetorical studies has its contemporary roots in Marxist traditions of historical materialism,[35] the question of matter that pervades the "hard" sciences has yet to find a substantial footing in contemporary rhetorical scholarship. The question of the relationship between the materiality of sex and rhetoric, then, might properly begin with the question of which "materiality" is important to the study of sex. Are we talking about the ideological structures of history—the ways in which sex gains meaning socially and culturally? Is the materiality of sex aptly described in terms of genealogy—a history of bodies? Or are we discussing the substance and force of human anatomy? Indeed, like the concept of "materiality" itself, the *substantive matters* of sex traverse a wide terrain.

Perhaps this is the predicament that Judith Butler faced after the 1990 publication of *Gender Trouble*. In that book, Butler famously critiqued the sex-gender split, wherein sex was understood as a simple biological fact, and gender was the product of social construction. Rather than seeing them as radically distinct, Butler argued that it is only through mechanisms of gender that the facticity of sex emerges. In her words, "gender must . . . designate the very apparatus of production whereby the sexes themselves are established. As a result, gender is not to culture as sex is to nature; gender is also the discursive/cultural means by which 'sexed nature' or a 'natural sex' is produced and established."[36] And since gender was the product of stylized and tenuous repetitions of acts over time, a *performative accomplishment,* it constituted the very sex identity that it was assumed to be expressing. From her idea that sex "was always already gender,"[37] a considerable anxiety surfaced about the supposed absence of the body's materiality from Butler's theory of gender performativity. The sexed body, critics feared, was stripped of substance and significance in Butler's tome; it did not (and had no) matter in her view. Samuel A. Chambers aptly describes critics as pointedly posing the question: "How can [Butler] understand sex as a product of the discourse of gender *without* simply ignoring the body?"[38] In sum, while we might say that Butler was discussing sex in terms of a materialism tied to genealogy *à la* Nietzsche and Foucault, some of her critics were concerned not with the role of the matters of history but with the material substance of the body. The question of the materiality of sex was being articulated in many ways.

Indeed, Foucault had anticipated the question of sex and the body decades earlier in *The History of Sexuality* when he wrote:

> Does this analysis of sexuality necessarily imply the elision of the body, anatomy, the biological, the functional? To this question, I think we can reply in the negative. In any case, the purpose of this present study is in fact to show how deployments of power are directly connected to the body—to bodies, functions, physiological processes, sensations, and pleasures; far from the body having to be effaced, what is needed is to make visible through an analysis in which the biological and the historical are not consecutive to one another . . . but are bound together in an increasingly complex fashion in accordance with the development of the modern technologies of power that take life as their objective.[39]

In this view, the materiality of sex is not confined to a governing historical episteme, nor is it entirely composed of or blind to bodily anatomy—a position that Butler develops with her own twist in her book-length response to her critics, *Bodies That Matter.* Claiming that she shares with Foucault the view that sex is a "regulatory ideal" that is not a "simple fact or static condition of the body" but rather the normative materialization of a governing norm, Butler attends to the body in a way that resists both linguistic monism and biological determinism. For her, the question of materiality and sex is tied to how we might understand matter as the productive effect of processes of materialization that work through exclusion. There is, she concedes, a materiality to the sign of "sex," but this materiality is not to be construed as a prediscursive "surface." Bodies as *sexed* bodies are marked and formed by discursive practices. Such a claim does not maintain that discourse determines, originates, or "exhaustively composes" the body; rather, it insists that "the relation between the body and discourse . . . is one in which discourse cannot fully 'capture' the body, and the body cannot fully elude discourse."[40]

Arguments like these posit that "sex" is not a simple fact of nature, but has been naturalized and materialized as a description of human (and nonhuman) difference. "The more we look for a simple physical basis for 'sex,'" writes Fausto-Sterling, "the more it becomes clear that 'sex' is not a pure physical category."[41] "Sex," to a certain extent, mediates the boundary between biology and identity; it becomes a mechanism through which particular corporeal features and processes are marked as significant, enduring, and natural. As Butler famously puts it: "*Bodies that matter* is not an idle pun, for to be material means to materialize, where the principle of materialization is precisely what 'matters' about the body, its very intelligibility. In this sense, to know the significance of something is to know how and why it matters, where 'to matter' means at once 'to materialize' and 'to mean.'"[42] We might say that "sex" is not so much a (static) condition as an organizing principle of a number of practices that circumscribe (aspects of) bodies and import their significance into the larger cultural contexts. Simply put, sex communicates what matters about the body; it does not simply represent the body-as-matter.

Questioning Sex

When we consider sex as a communicative mechanism for the ways in which the body (and what about the body) does or does not matter in U.S. political culture, it is somewhat surprising that those who study feminist rhetoric most typically articulate their analyses in terms of feminism's relationship with gender, not sex.[43] Although these studies of feminist public address do not ignore sex altogether, "sex" itself is often represented as a blank slate on which the struggle over gender meaning occurs. The importance of gender is reaffirmed through the articulation of a well-founded anxiety among some feminists in rhetorical studies about those practices that reiterate (corporeal-ized) sexed certainties with respect to human subjects. As a result, sex itself becomes marked as suspect among those who champion the social construction of gender and identity fluidity.[44] In a strange turn from those who insist on the fact of sex as the grounds from which feminism must work, the problem in rhetorical studies may be one in which intellectual commitments to gender have turned a discipline's focus away from the way "sex" is at play in feminist advocacy.

There are several possible reasons why this may be the case. First, conventions of rhetoric as an academic discipline oftentimes direct attention to words and their use by more or less disembodied actors.[45] Rhetoricians like myself have been trained to study public discourse, not bodies per se, and there is a rich history of understanding gender in terms of discursive practices. An analysis of sex may appear to require a consideration of the body that is perhaps unfamiliar to those of us who study rhetoric. Additionally, the popularity of theorists like Butler may have promoted increased attention to gender since, in her words, "sex is already gendered."[46] Shannon Holland, for example, aptly characterizes Butler's argument as one that posits *gender* as both "performative and regulatory," and "designed to naturalized sex differences."[47] In this way, we might say that Butler's theory, especially as articulated in *Gender Trouble,* reverses the presumed causality between sex and gender: "Rather than sex causing gender, gender causes sex."[48] This account of the relationship between sex and gender, Chambers warns, risks moving feminists "to the full-scale abandonment of sex and gender to the political realm. And if *both* sex and gender remain fully politicized, utterly contingent (and how could they not be if gender causes sex), then we really have no reason to worry about sex at all."[49] As I discussed in the opening pages of this introduction, the scholarly revolution surrounding "sex" might be better described as a sex/gender one, wherein critics are constantly reminded that any claim about sex is always already circumscribed by gender. In that way *gender,* not *sex,* functions as the crucial concept for feminist analysis—rhetorical or otherwise.

The nearly exclusive emphasis on gender, however, risks an inadvertent assertion that the sexed body is a *passive* object of gendered discursive *action.* Such a move potentially reasserts an ontological distinction between sex and gender, matter and discourse, that not only reaffirms the very dynamics under critique in Butler's and others' theories of sex/gender but also compels a certain silence about sex and feminism that my analysis adamantly resists. As Karen Barad's work reminds us, it is important to consider not just how language, discourse, and culture matter, but also how actual *matter* matters.[50] Barad's revision of Butlerian performativity presents a "relational ontology" developed from the epistemological framework advanced in Bohr's theory of quantum physics. In this ontology, matter (corporeal and otherwise) too is an *active* agent in the process of materialization. The relationship between discursive practices and materiality is an *intra-active* one wherein each is not irreducible to the other, but also not wholly distinct. As a result, according to Barad, "the point is not merely that there are important material factors in addition to discursive ones; rather, the issue is the conjoined material-discursive nature of constraints, conditions, and practices."[51] Barad's notion of performativity has many implications for theories of materiality, discourse, and the body—implications that go well beyond the purview of this book's look at sex and feminism. For my purposes, however, Barad's ideas direct attention to the role of a materiality at work in the contexts and rhetorics of feminist activists.

One cannot, in other words, simply evaluate feminist rhetorics in terms of their adherence to a more liberatory ideal of a particular sex-gender relationship, nor should we understand feminist discourse only in terms of observable effects on the body. Sexed bodies are a multitude of doings—physiological processes, habitual movements, "objects" of violence, potentialities of their own reproduction—that are quite *active* in the rhetorical scene with which feminist movements are forced to engage. Whether pregnancy, physical assault, partner violence, or sexual intimacy, practices of bodies are often the matters that provoke feminist action. Reflecting what Barad might describe as the *intra-activity* between materiality and discursive practice, we can say that it is a number of anatomical doings conjoining with traditions of (sex) differentiation that make up the rhetorical topography of feminist movements. Feminists are not simply responding to a discursive sexing of bodies, nor are they exclusively engaging questions of gender; they are responsive to bodies-as-activities. In this view, sexed bodies are significant and active, and "sex" itself serves as a central concept/matter for any understanding of feminist advocacies over time. We ought not assume, in other words, that the social nature of sex equates it with gender to such an extent that "gender" replaces "sex" as a crucial concept for how we understand feminism. As Chambers reminds us, "one must hold on to a conceptualization of *sex,* so that one does not lose sight/site of the body."[52]

In the chapters that follow, I position the question of sex as a central one for developing a nuanced view of feminism's fundamental commitments. Focusing on how feminist movements have strategically engaged the matters of difference and identification with decidedly mixed results, I attend carefully to various contexts and traditions that helped shape feminist advocacy—the material conditions through which any view of sex gains traction and force, as well as the matters that provoked feminists to act. This rhetorical approach enables a consideration of the relationship between sex and feminism that highlights the ideal and the material, the conceptual and the corporeal, the abstract and the lived as constitutive components of the ways in which feminist movements respond to and amplify traditions of "sex." In so doing, I directly engage the propositions of the sex/gender scholarly revolution that assert the inherent questionability of sex and assess the consequences and contours of various feminist strategic interactions with the traditions and idioms of human differentiation.

When one begins to consider how feminism questions sex, a number of examples come to mind. In the late eighteenth century, Mary Wollstonecraft insisted that women were not naturally the weaker sex, but were only made so by lack of education.[53] Radical/cultural feminists of the 1970s and 1980s rearticulated female sex difference as culturally superior to hegemonic masculinity, and sex-positivity continues to be heralded by the self-proclaimed "third wave" as a characteristic that distinguishes contemporary feminists from those of earlier generations.[54] Clearly, feminism's questionings of sex span from late eighteenth-century liberal political contexts to twenty-first-century new media environments, and it would be difficult, if not impossible, to think of a moment in feminism's history when sex, sexed norms, and the relationship between sex and gender were not being critiqued in some manner. To catalogue exhaustively the ways in which feminism has questioned sex is not the goal of this book. And in fact, the five cases examined in the chapters that follow cannot account for the various ways feminist activists have or have not questioned "sex." These case studies are, however, indicative of three of the most central and divisive features of historical narratives of feminism's development: race/racism and the movement, health and reproduction politics, and sexuality and liberation. As such, they not only allow for a reconsideration of feminist rhetoric in terms of contemporary critiques of sex, but also position feminism's rhetorically managed attempt to question sex-as-we-know-it as a vital concern for feminist activism. These cases do not confine, in other words, questions of sex to abstract debates in feminist philosophical registers; these questions lie at the heart of women's movements' most defining struggles.

Chapter 1 begins this process by demonstrating what I envision as a questionable engagement with feminism and sex. Starting with a provocation—what possibilities emerge when feminism's compulsion to identify sex is itself put into question?—I examine Sojourner Truth's famous "Ain't I a Woman?" speech. Exposed in the early 1990s as an inauthentic account of Truth's words at an 1851 woman's rights convention, "Ain't I a Woman?" nevertheless continues to be a celebrated statement of feminist advocacy. This celebration, however, is riddled with controversy as feminists debate, on multiple grounds, what Truth's question should reveal about feminist commitments to women and its deeply troubled racial past (and present). This controversy is indicative of the rise of multiculturalism in the late 1980s and early 1990s, which set as its aim a commitment to the recognition of feminism's various and excluded others—for example, black women, poor women, third-world women, etc. While such a goal is laudable on its face, the impulse to identify and recognize the other / an other inevitably ends in failure—in what Butler terms an "embarrassed" and "exacerbated 'etc.'"[55] Truth's inauthentic transcript and the discourse that surrounds it in contemporary feminist scholarship offer a unique opportunity to consider these multicultural impulses to identify and recognize sex specifically. Rather than answering Truth's question, rather than *sexing* Truth as either a woman or not, I ask readers to suspend Truth's question as one without a clear answer. To do so, I argue, would be to engage the relationship between Truth and sex as questionable, sustaining the historicity and contingency of sexed distinctions and remembering that many black bodies experienced *sex* in radically different ways from those of white reformers. This kind of questionable engagement with Truth works in the spirit of feminist commitments to alterity without subjecting the so-called other to the recognizable (sexed and raced) terms of the status quo.

In many ways, chapter 1 reminds us that a look at sex difference is always imbricated in various traditions of human differentiation. In chapter 2 I examine the tradition of biological foundationalism that undergirds much of our contemporary understanding of sex difference as that foundationalism animated antebellum discussions of sex, race, and citizenship. I do so by taking a close look at the early rhetorics of Elizabeth Cady Stanton. Like other nineteenth-century woman's rights advocates, Cady Stanton has been criticized, and rightly so, for her consistent attempts to mobilize racist sentiments in order to advance the cause of woman suffrage. Many consider her racist rhetorics symptomatic of nineteenth-century attitudes about race; others consider her advocacy indicative of her opportunistic impulse to marshal support for woman suffrage by appealing to racist sentiments. A closer reflection on these rhetorics as responses to the immediate and enduring demands of American liberal political culture, however, enables an understanding of them as intimately connected to traditions and idioms of difference that circumscribed sexual and racial matters from the start. These liberal rhetorical traditions promoted universal and natural rights among the nation's citizenry while simultaneously and consistently identifying differences that mattered to the distribution of political rights. In particular, as identities among political subjects became increasingly corporealized after the Enlightenment, woman's rights activists faced a rhetorical scene in which women's subjection was justified by and grounded within supposedly "natural" and biological sex difference. I posit that, rather than constituting race purely opportunistically to advance the cause of the female sex, Cady Stanton promoted an extracorporeal view of both race and sex difference which challenged those ideas that used biological understandings of the body to justify the differentiated distribution of rights. Arguing specifically that women, as humans (rational animals), were inherently capable of participating in public life, Cady Stanton used the circumstantial characteristics of immigrant and African American populations as evidence for her claim of their inferior status in the polis, Cady Stanton managed to articulate a liberal feminist vision in which sex did not matter, but race clearly did. This problematic negotiation of a layered rhetorical scene is emblematic of a feminist engagement with sex that eschewed sex (and race) as simply biological, giving evidence that feminists have not always grounded their rhetoric in the sexed specificity of the female body-as-we-know-it.

Chapter 3 turns to a moment when feminists directed attention to, not away from, physiological attributes of sex difference. The women's health movements that emerged in the late 1960s and early 1970s concentrated their efforts on fostering new relationships between women and mainstream health care systems. Taking as their target everything from capitalist health care models to Freudianism to American gynecological practices, women's health movements surfaced within a psycho-medical context that promoted visual encounters with (female) sexed anatomy. These visual encounters were extraordinarily problematic, feminists argued, as the psycho-medical gaze often objectified, pathologized, and standardized women's bodies. In response, feminists offered images and narratives of the healthy variations of female-sexed anatomy, directions for self-examination, and models for women-centered health care practices. One branch of the movement, the Federation of Feminist Women's Health Centers (FFWHC), emphasized the importance of *seeing* sexed anatomy, and it used a number of visual strategies in its public campaign. I examine these strategies and how they responded to, critiqued, and amplified those traditions of sex differentiation premised on seeing sexed anatomy. I find that the FFWHC's visual rhetoric amplified sexed-female anatomy in ways that emphasized women as active sexual and health participants, not passive objects. In so doing, the federation advanced a nuanced perspective on the materiality of sex: *how* one, literally and figuratively, *sees* sex is just as constitutive of the material conditions of sex and/or the so-called matter of which sex is thought to be composed. These visual rhetorics offer the chance to consider the terms through which we evaluate feminism's engagement with systems of sex difference. More specifically, how ought we to evaluate those rhetorics that seem to rely closely on the very systems and mechanisms under critique—in this case, images of the sexed and sexualized female body? Are these questions or reiterations of sex?

In chapter 4 I consider one of the most divisive conflicts in feminist movement history, the gay-straight split that emerged clearly by 1970. The role of sexuality in feminist advocacy of the "second wave" was centrally important to many movements' articulations of sex difference. "Lesbian," in particular, emerged as an articulated figure through which anxieties about sex identity—both public and personal—surfaced. Identified as "menaces" by some and truly "liberated" women by others, lesbians occupied a unique rhetorical space where the truth of feminism's articulated commitment to women was conditioned by the proclaimed sexual practices of feminist women. The conflicts surrounding feminist sexual practices were played out most notably in mainstream news media and the feminist alternative press in the sixties and seventies. In mainstream venues, for example, feminists such as Betty Friedan described lesbians as the movement's "lavender menace," provoking a number of challenges to her motives and leadership. Such conflicts were fodder for journalists looking for good copy. In the alternative press, by contrast, feminists promoted lesbian identity as the true expression of authentic womanhood. Such views not only responded directly to Friedan and others but also worked appropriately within the conventions of the radical alternative press to project lesbians and the feminist press as movement vanguards. Arguing that mainstream and alternative media conventions were precipitating factors in the movement's gay-straight split, I examine more closely the role of sexed identifications in radical and liberal feminist advocacy. I find that media practices worked with movements' concerns about public and private identifications in ways that confined feminists to the exclusionary dogmatism of various and often opposing commitments to political efficacy and radical authenticity. Put simply, the very strategies that aimed to liberate women domesticated feminism through persistent attempts to secure an identification of "woman" that would align with the movements' goals.

In the final chapter I return my focus to an explicit articulation of the importance of *questionable engagements* with past, present, and future feminist practice. At best, feminism has a deeply paradoxical relationship with sex difference—one wherein sex is consistently engaged as questionable while also identified and recognized as a fact of human difference. In chapter 5 I consider this relationship and explore what has been celebrated as the most successful feminist action of the early twenty-first century, SlutWalking. The first SlutWalk, held in Toronto in April 2011, was originally conceived of as a local protest against a comment made by a Toronto police officer that to avoid being raped, women should also avoid "dressing like sluts." The media attention that these protesters received precipitated a global wave of similar marches. Because some participants explicitly attempt to reclaim the term "slut" for liberatory purposes, and to do so, in part, by wearing "slutty" clothing during the protests, SlutWalks have also sparked much feminist praise and criticism. A close look at the discourse from and about various SlutWalk marches reveals quite clearly that in this contemporary "postfeminist" context, feminist activists navigate a rhetorical scene in which questions of sex and difference are inextricably intertwined with what is remembered about feminism's historic relationship to sex and difference. In short, SlutWalks highlight the ways in which perceptions of feminism's past operate in public evaluations and judgments of current feminist practice. In this case, the compulsion to ground feminism in the sexed specificity of the female body-as-we-know-it eclipses the way SlutWalks attempt to subvert such grounding. Like Sojourner Truth's question, in other words, those who debate the value of SlutWalks forget to attend to the questions of sex that feminist rhetoric is consistently provoking. As the conclusion of this book, the chapter interrupts the often repeated terms of the current debate, reiterating the importance of treating feminism's relationship to sex as a rhetorical one. In so doing, it demonstrates the value of questioning sex, and the importance of context for understanding any feminist practices and their relationship to (sex) difference. Such a move concretizes the stakes of questionable engagements of and with feminism's continued relationship to sex as well as its participation in traditions that aim to distinguish which human differences matter and which do not.

1

Recognizing Sex

SOJOURNER TRUTH AND MULTICULTURAL ANXIETY

M OST ARE FAMILIAR with the dramatic historical narrative of Sojourner Truth's delivery of the famous speech, "Ar'n't/A'n't/Ain't I a Woman?" (hereafter A——'t I a Woman") at the 1851 woman's rights convention in Akron, Ohio. The oft-repeated narrative is told in various histories of feminism that describe Truth's delivery as a performance that mesmerized woman's rights activists and subdued the convention's hecklers.[1] Beyond the details of this drama, Truth's pivotal rhetorical question, "A——'t I a woman?" circulates widely among feminists, making it, according to Angela Davis, "one of the most frequently quoted slogans of the nineteenth-century [woman's] movement."[2]

Indeed, Truth's question epitomizes black feminism's critique of white feminist myopia and continues to resonate for many feminists as a powerful symbol of difference, and quite possibly the difference that *difference* should make. For example, in a 2007 issue of the *Journal of Women's History*, Stephanie M. H. Camp writes:

> Among women of color waging the struggle for their womanhood, no symbol was so powerful as the image of the ex-slave, feminist, and abolitionist Sojourner Truth. Truth's powerful rhetorical question—wasn't she a woman . . . ?—was a crucial instrument in highlighting the convergence of social categories that women of color have embodied in the history of the New World. For women of color and especially black women, Truth's insistence on her womanhood . . . was ahead of its time. Truth spoke to the frustrations of those who, when they attempted to engage with white feminism, found there a stubborn insistence that only the forms of oppression faced by white middle-class women mattered.[3]

Camp's assertion of Truth's importance echoes multicultural sentiments that began to surface in the late 1970s, but arose most profoundly in mainstream feminist thought in the 1980s and early 1990s. From the 1981 publication of bell hook's appropriately titled *Ain't I a Woman?* to third wave "manifestas" like *Listen Up* and *To Be Real* published in the mid-1990s, a new generation of feminists cried out louder than ever that "woman" was not a seamless, unified, largely undifferentiated category. Differences of race, class, sexuality, etc., came to matter in feminist rhetoric in a way that was relatively unprecedented. And no better symbol could be imagined for such defiance to the status quo and white feminist politics than Sojourner Truth and her famous rhetorical question.

Or so it seemed.

Truth, her question, and the deployment of both as symbolic of black and/or multicultural feminism are riddled with further questions. Although Truth's exclamatory "A——'t I a woman?" has penetrated our social consciousness, historical and rhetorical scholars have questioned the authenticity of Truth's speech and the mythic narrative of its delivery.[4] In these critiques, scholars have suggested that the once widely accepted transcript of the speech, the one offered by the convention's presiding officer, Frances Dana Gage, in 1863 (twelve years after the speech), is inaccurate and reflective of a Southern slave caricature, not of the "real" Sojourner Truth. In fact, the most inaccurate portion of the speech is believed to be the question by which it is so readily remembered today. Marius Robinson's transcript was arguably the most accurate account, and it was published shortly after the convention in the *Anti-Slavery Bugle*. His account of Truth's speech does not contain anything resembling a refrain-like repetition of "A——'t I a woman?" Rather, according to Robinson, Truth said, "I am a woman's rights," and she said that only once. Karlyn Kohrs Campbell has argued that Truth's question in Gage's transcript "echoes a recurring theme of women's antislavery discourse in which female slaves were given voice through the question, 'Am I not a woman and a sister?'" making Gage's invention of the famous rhetorical question, arguably, traceable to other rhetorics of the time.[5] Similarly, both Teresa C. Zackodnik and Nell Irvin Painter point to Gage's own work as an advocate for working-class women as an inventional clue for her transcript's emphasis on the intersection of womanhood and work.[6] Clearly, not only is there evidence that Gage's transcript is inaccurate, but also there are noteworthy efforts explaining *why* Gage crafted the oft-quoted transcript.[7] It is therefore difficult, if not impossible, to find anyone who can convincingly defend Gage's account as the most accurate transcript of the speech given in Akron that day.

The inquiries concerning Truth's question, however, do not end with searches for accurate historical narratives. Despite the widely accepted academic belief that Gage's transcript is more fiction than fact, Truth as emblematized by "A——'t I a Woman?" continues to circulate as a powerful feminist symbol, demanding that attention be paid to the "other" (and "her" concerns) in feminist discourse and actions. In 1994, Painter identifies Truth as an "invented great" like Betsy Ross and Chief Seattle and argues that Truth is "consumed as a signifier and beloved for *what we need her to have said.*"[8] Despite this recognition of the significance of the circulation of Gage's text, by 1996 Painter is bewildered that although her own efforts to render Gage's portrayal of Truth as fictitious were well publicized, students and well-versed historians alike continued to cling to Gage's construction. Why does Gage's Truth prevail over more accurate accounts? According to Painter, "the symbol we require in public life still triumphs over scholarship."[9] The rhetorical force of the emblematic Sojourner Truth, in other words, far exceeds any effects of understanding the historical inaccuracies associated with the construction of her in public discourse, and maybe for good reason. After all, white feminism has a long history of ignoring matters of race and class, and the perseverance of Truth's rhetorical question reminds us of these past and present transgressions, projecting the importance of multiculturalism for feminism's future.

Deployments of Truth's fictional question, however, are not always so generously received. Zackodnik, for example, persuasively argues that the perseverance of Gage's version of Truth is not benign. She takes issue with the tendency to promote Truth as an uncomplicated advocate for the woman's rights movement. Calling attention to the ways that "A——'t I a woman?" works, according to some, to tear "down claims that female weakness was incompatible with suffrage," defeating "men's 'weaker sex' argument,"[10] Zackodnik suggests that "Truth became a proxy" through which white woman's rights advocates "were able to speak their political desires without risking their social position."[11] For contemporary white feminists, she insists, Truth still functions as a proxy, allowing "for a deferred or deflected acknowledgement of just how far [racial] oppression reaches and exactly who bears responsibility for it."[12] By ignoring the more complex and rich history of Truth and her message, white feminists can continue to engage in strategies of "elision, deferral, and disavowal" of black women and black feminism.[13] In other words, Truth becomes a way for white women to pay superficial attention to black women's oppression without having to articulate their own role and participation in racial hierarchies. Moreover, the mere recognition of the harsh realities faced by black women may supplant any sustained effort to address racism writ large. Zackodnik pointedly asks, "Are white feminists interested in a form of 'difference,' then, that challenges feminist inquiry to make little difference at all?"[14] As Zackodnik's critique (and her own rhetorical question) begins to reveal, even when stripped of "A——'t I a Woman?" Sojourner Truth is firmly enmeshed in the matters of sexual and racial difference, and, more precisely, the difference that particular differences can and should make.

In this chapter I engage in yet another questioning of the relationships that emerge between feminism, sex, and difference in the instance of Sojourner Truth. Like those before me, I am interested in the questions of difference that surface and circulate in discussions about Truth. Where I depart most clearly from these feminists, however, is precisely on the role of the question and its relationship to difference in the case of Truth specifically and sex more broadly. Taking Truth's rhetorical question seriously offers a unique opportunity to consider the questionability of sex (and) difference as well as the various ways such questionability is compulsively answered and closed through strategies of identification. While the compulsion to answer Truth's question is understandable, familiar, and justifiable, in this chapter I ask feminists to sustain the question and stay suspended in the anxiety and discomfort that such questioning can engender. In what follows, then, I return to "A——'t I a Woman?" proper, as well as its circulation in feminist discourse, to discuss the legacies of sex and difference in that discourse from the nineteenth century onward. Anxieties about difference and feminism surface in these rhetorics as compulsions to find/name others, and desires to make right the disparity between white and black women's feminist commitment often grounds the way feminists encounter Truth and her famous question. The differences between "woman" and "Sojourner Truth" that are at once recognized and effaced by the rhetorical question, I argue, may also be recognized and effaced through (authentic and symbolic) reiterations of her in contemporary feminist discourse. In my engagement with Gage's transcript and various articulations of Sojourner Truth, however, I seek to do something different in order to forward a seemingly simple yet, I hope, uncomfortable argument: there are historical, textual, and conceptual reasons to resist answering the question "A——'t t I a woman?" By taking these reasons to heart and resisting strong compulsions to identify Truth, we might provoke a questionable encounter with Truth, sex, and difference—an encounter that is, like the question itself, undoubtedly tainted and impure, yet imbued with possibility.

Reiterating Truth

The making of Sojourner Truth began in the nineteenth century through a variety of narratives by and about her: *Narrative of Sojourner Truth,* penned by Olive Gilbert and first published in 1851; "Sojourner Truth: The Libyan Sibyl" by Harriet Beecher Stowe, published in 1863 in the *Atlantic Monthly;* and Francis Dana Gage's account of the 1851 Akron convention speech, printed also in 1863 in New York's *Independent.*[15] Notably, all of these texts were combined by 1875, when Frances Titus reprinted Gilbert's *Narrative,* adding a scrapbook-like grouping of a number of texts, titled "Book of Life," including Gage's account and Stowe's story.[16] These accounts of Truth transformed her life story, variously depicting her as ex-slave, passionate reformer, religious crusader, and comic caricature.[17] As pivotal texts in what Roseann M. Mandziuk and Suzanne Pullon Fitch term the "rhetorical construction of Sojourner Truth," these texts contain telling historical inaccuracies and/ or editorial commentary, revealing not only the goals of their authors but also important aspects of the immediate rhetorical scene from which they emerged.[18]

For example, although Gilbert's *Narrative of Sojourner Truth* was marketed as a popular ex-slave narrative, it violates a number of generic components of such narratives.[19] These generic discrepancies clearly highlight a mediation of Truth by and for her contemporaries. Gilbert's *Narrative,* for example, tells the story of slavery in New York, not the plantations of the South, and the reader, expecting a tale of slavery's horrors, may be puzzled to read about Truth's religious revelations and pursuits.[20] Moreover, whereas other ex-slave narratives were written in the first person, Gilbert separates her own words from the alleged words of Truth, writing in the third person and intermittently disagreeing with Truth's assessment of her own life experiences.[21] Although Gilbert's additions of her own "voice" can be read as problematic, Naomi Greyser convincingly argues that such moves are efforts by Gilbert to acknowledge her bias, "not obfuscating her role in the *Narrative*'s production."[22] Importantly for Greyser, as well as Mandziuk and Fitch, these moments in the *Narrative* may reveal that "while Truth focuses on the particulars of her tale rather than its symbolism for a cause," Gilbert, a Garrisonian abolitionist, attends to Truth's story in terms of its ability to preach the evils of slavery.[23] Gilbert, it seems, had specific rhetorical goals in mind; so when Truth's narrative departed from conventional abolitionist understandings of slavery, Gilbert inserted qualifications and explanations. By the time Truth's *Narrative* is retold in contemporary young-adult biographies and historical scholarship, the details that do not conform to common understandings of slavery are omitted or ignored.[24] As a result, Truth, according to Mandziuk and Fitch, "becomes synecdochally figured as the representation of slavery at the cost of diminishing her full prominence and the distinctiveness of her experiences."[25] Truth's story, in other words, is forced to fit a predetermined narrative about slavery. The point here is not that Truth's understanding of slavery is more accurate than others, but that uses and interpretations of her *Narrative* are overdetermined by *what we already know* of slavery, its particular ills and horrors as manifested in a version of the institution as practiced in the South.

Gilbert was not alone in promoting Truth to meet specific rhetorical goals. And since Gilbert's *Narrative* ends before the Akron convention, it is not responsible for the emblematic portrait of Sojourner Truth that has captivated so many contemporary feminists. This more familiar Truth began to emerge most clearly as the result of two publishing events in 1863, each bearing a different rhetorical aim. In 1863 Harriet Beecher Stowe published a peculiar account of Sojourner Truth as "The Libyan Sybil" in the *Atlantic Monthly*. Stowe's tale depicts Truth as a "quaint and innocent exotic who disdained feminism," a character who speaks in "southern negro" dialect and seems to be a source of amusement and entertainment for white audiences.[26] Stowe's version of Truth may be traceable to the success (and wealth) she enjoyed after the publication of *Uncle Tom's Cabin*, as the similarities between Truth and the black characters in *Uncle Tom's Cabin* evidence Stowe's keen sense of marketability. Regardless of Stowe's intent, the quaint exotic Truth of Stowe's imagination did not sit well with more reform-minded women like Frances Dana Gage.[27] Possibly spurred by Stowe's depiction, Gage, an Ohio radical and woman's rights advocate, wrote and published the account of Truth's delivery of "A——'t I a Woman?" in the *Independent* less than one month after Stowe's story appeared in the *Atlantic Monthly*.[28] Gage's Truth, unlike the Truth in Gilbert's *Narrative* and Stowe's "Sibyl," is, like Gage, a committed reformer. In 1875 Truth's *Narrative* was published along with Gage's letter and Stowe's article, but it is the inclusion of Gage's version in the 1881 *History of Woman's Suffrage* that solidified it as a central text in the making of the iconic Sojourner Truth.[29] "Practically by default," according to Painter, "the feminists and abolitionists, who published copiously, fashioned the historic Sojourner Truth in their own image, the one created by the feminist Frances Dana Gage."[30]

Gage's Truth has proved to be particularly enduring for feminists, functioning as a conduit for contemporary feminist goals as well as expressions of cultural anxieties about race and/or gender. More specifically, there seem to be at least two interpretations of Gage's text that have predominated in feminist studies. Each interpretation positions Truth's question as a rhetorical one, whose answer is signaled in the speech itself. The first, and arguably "all too common," interpretation reads the question as one that posits Truth as proof of woman's equality to man.[31] Such a reading assumes that racial differences matter only inasmuch as those differences have resulted in (regrettable) circumstances whereby a woman has been forced to prove her capacity to be equal to a man. In Zackodnik's terms, such a reading ignores the complexity of Truth's rhetoric, fashioning it instead as an "unproblematic advocacy of woman's rights."[32] Moreover, such a view, clearly promoted in the *History of Woman Suffrage* and consequently heavily implied in Flexner and Fitzpatrick's *Century of Struggle,* risks an exploitation of Truth—rendering her a "victim for the white woman to claim agency as liberator."[33]

The second predominant reading argues that Truth's question is directed not only toward opponents of woman's rights but also toward white feminism itself. In such readings Truth becomes an emblematic black feminist who emphasizes the importance of the intersection of race and gender and white feminism's own exclusion of black women. Some examples of such readings can be found in the work of contemporary black feminists, like bell hooks, for which Truth functions as a vehicle for depicting "exclusion[s] from white feminists' definitions of 'woman.' "[34] Zackodnik, however, has concerns about this contemporary deployment of Gage's text. She argues that both black and white feminists have interpreted the text as a powerful statement against exclusion and racism; but when white feminists depict Truth in this way, they don't so much capture black feminism's strident critique as they replicate nineteenth-century deployments of Truth. For white feminists today, as in the nineteenth century, Truth is a convenient symbol of "the material conditions that they argue must be overcome without acknowledging that these conditions are not only very different from their own but, in fact, sustain their own racialized class and gender identities."[35]

Though not mentioned by Zackodnik, the feminist alternative press may provide a good illustration of her argument. Published during the feminist alternative press boom of the 1970s, Iowa City's *Ain't I a Woman?* and Seattle's *And Ain't a Woman?* were not self-identified as "black feminist" publications, but each made an explicit effort throughout its publishing run to attend to the issues faced by a broad spectrum of women. On the one hand, this attention ostensibly speaks to a consideration of women that goes beyond the white heterosexual middle-class feminist experience. On the other hand, such a rhetorical tactic also indirectly posits Truth as a figure of feminist unity.[36] Take, for instance, the inaugural issue of *Ain't I a Woman?* Its cover displays a hand-drawn Truth, with a disproportionately large and appropriately raised arm, declaiming in a dialogue box her famous speech; yet one needs only to read the opening editorial to realize that for the feminists of Iowa City, the question of Truth and womanhood, *if it is a guiding question at all,* was one that reiterated a demand for attention to difference and unity, not to the uniqueness of a black woman's experience or the complicity of white women in racist systems.[37] In the editorial, a call to expand their kind of collectivity to "*all* sisters in the mid-west," the organizers of the Iowa City Women's Liberation Front (WLF) wrote: "Unlike our sisters in Chicago or Detroit, who have large brown and black populations and proportionately large working class populations, most of us [in Iowa City] tend to work in groups that are campus based rather than community based. We find ourselves dealing with middle-class, university privilege and bourgeois mentality and find it difficult to gear our actions toward meeting the needs of the last first even though we are committed to do this."[38] Not surprisingly, the editorial makes no mention of Truth, and it appears that the Iowa City WLF is a fitting example of the same strategic deferral and distancing of black women from feminism that, according to Zackodnik, circulates within white feminist uses of Truth and her Akron speech. To be blunt, the cover highlights a black woman's experiences in a way that clearly makes little to no difference for actual living black women. While the Iowa City WLF desires to organize and act for the community (read: other, non–white middle-class populations), they find it "difficult" to do so, and they remain unreflective about their own role in racist hierarchies. If this is the kind of rhetorical tactic Zackodnik is referring to, then it is no surprise that she would argue that "many white feminists have yet to really hear what Truth or her modern-day counterparts have to say."[39]

But what does Truth *really* have to say? For Zackodnik, the answer to that question lies in the particulars: we must continue to historicize Truth and authenticate texts in order to hear aspects of her "double-voiced" critique. Once we do so, Truth will become a "less convenient symbol" for white feminists to continue their "well-worn strategies of elision, deferral, and disavowal" of black feminists, black women, and their concerns.[40] The irony of Zackodnik's concluding call is that she has prefigured the effects of what further study of Truth would offer. This conclusion is particularly telling in that it points to a dynamic at work in Zackodnik's critique as well as in contemporary reiterations of Truth. Truth is figured *in advance* in terms of sexual and racial difference, the role these differences play in feminist politics, and, most important, what we need her to represent. As in the reiterations of Truth in Gilbert's *Narrative,* Stowe's "Libyan Sibyl," and more recent biographies, when feminists answer Truth's famous question, they do so in a way that positions Truth as one who symbolically resolves contemporary anxieties about race and gender and speaks for particular causes. Perhaps, then, Zackodnik's reiteration of Truth is, like others, also overdetermined, this time not by what we already know about slavery but by what we know of the problems of exclusion and its hold on white feminist politics. To return to Stephanie Camp:

> Despite the fact that Truth was enslaved in the North, she came to represent enslaved women in the South. In turn, enslaved women came to embody the radical difference between white women and black women most dramatically. Freedom to work? Freedom from chivalry? "Please," Truth seemed to say. The students and teachers who read about Truth in the women's studies, women's history, and black history classes in the 1980s reveled in the message. That Truth did not actually say those words, as we now know, does not change the fact that the message articulated beautifully one of the main lessons learned by U.S. feminists in the 1970s and 1980s.[41]

If the nineteenth-century writers were apt to figure Truth as a symbol for abolition and/or woman's rights, perhaps more recent reiterations are equally apt to position her as a symbol that registers contemporary concerns related to multiculturalism. Or to be even more precise, perhaps reiterations of Truth are responsive to and necessitated by anxieties about representing *all* women—black, white, gay, straight, etc.—in feminist politics.[42]

Describing what I think might be a driving force in the various reiterations of Truth and readings of Gage's text, Jeffrey Nealon writes, "These days, it seems everybody loves 'the other.' "[43] From corporate diversity training to the critiques of the racism and heterosexism of feminism's first wave, Nealon vividly portrays multiculturalism and its attentiveness to difference as devolving into "a flurry of anxious criticisms," each pointing to yet another *other* that is ignored or dismissed.[44] The result in feminist studies, as elsewhere, might

be viewed as compulsory identification—a perpetual identificatory acknowledgment of *others* in such a way as to signal adherence to an ethos of authentic and expansive inclusion. As Butler noted in *Gender Trouble,* however, the
various ways feminists elaborate women's identity with "predicates of color,
sexuality, ethnicity, class, and able-bodiness invariably close with an embarrassed 'etc.' "[45] The "etc."—a mark of the yet-to-be-identified other—which
signals one's commitment to the inclusion of all others is also a "sign of ex-
haustion," signifying an inevitable failure to fulfill this obligation. In the case
of Truth, as with other identified black women, the problem of continual
misrepresentation is intensified by the history of feminism itself. After all,
part of Zackodnik's criticism of white uses of Truth is that these are emblematic of a pattern of deferral and dismissal of black women. Although this
history is important, and anxiety about exclusion, I believe, can be productive, if we take Butler and Nealon seriously, we may also begin to resist this
compulsive, anxiety-ridden impulse to name, find, and recognize the other.
If we do so, another kind of engagement with Truth and her question can
emerge—an engagement that keeps in its sight a reflection of the way Truth
is perpetually articulated in terms of the rhetorical aims of various authors,
as well as the way these articulations foreclose who Truth is from the start.

Indeed, my concern with Truth's various reiterations, which I see as a result of the kind of multiculturalism Nealon and Butler describe, is that they
figure in advance not just the grounds on which Truth emerges as woman but
the prisms through which Truth can emerge at all. Whether it is an emphasis
on her womanhood, black womanhood, black slave womanhood, etc., each
articulation is marked by the paradox facing any project of inclusion predi-
cated on identity and recognition: facilitating the inclusion of those previously excluded through practices and policies of inclusion depends upon,
and thus simultaneously sanctions and reinforces, the "naturalness" of predetermined categories of identity that contribute significantly to the social
dynamics of exclusion. No particular reiteration of Truth is more politically
pure, correct, authentic, or accurate than any other, and each reiteration assuredly remains enmeshed within regimes of identification and recognition
that in some sense may be unavoidable. Identification and recognition, however, ought not to be the only ways we encounter Truth; disagreeing about
how Truth does or does not embody black, slave, woman, feminist, etc. can
get us only so far. Perhaps we might learn to engage the questions of and
about Truth via a critical suspension of identification and recognition itself,
responding to her question in a radically different way.

More specifically, I want to respond to Truth (constructed or otherwise) in a way that engages the very categories through which she is identifiable, and thus includable—womanhood, blackness, etc.—as themselves questions, not exclusive answers to "A——'t I a woman?" My response strives to resist the multicultural obligation of recognized inclusion and attempts to circumvent the pervasive cultural imperatives to understand race and sex as natural givens, seeking to enact questionable practices vis-à-vis processes of differentiation, identification, and recognition. In the engagement that follows, then, I endeavor to diminish the force of the imperative to recognize and identify, failing to answer "A——'t I a woman?" in any way in order to sustain the question of difference.

Historical and Textual Questions of Truth's Sex

For most of feminism's history, few have sustained Truth's question as a question. A clear case in point is Angela Davis's reading of "A——'t I a woman?" in her germinal *Race, Class, and Sex*. Davis's reading is emblematic of the two common interpretations of Gage's text, both of which assume that Truth's question is rhetorical in that the answer is implied by the text itself. Davis begins her discussion of Gage's text by contending that it was a powerful counterpoint to the then common assertion that women were the "weaker" sex. She adds that the idea that Truth's question argues primarily for gender equality misses the "deeper implications" of the speech. "When this Black woman did rise to speak," Davis writes, "her answer to the male supremacists also contained a profound lesson for the white women. In repeating her question . . . no less than four times, she exposed the class-bias and racism of the new women's movement. All women were not white and all women did not enjoy the material comfort of the middle class. . . . Sojourner Truth herself was Black . . . but she was no less a woman than any of her white sisters at the convention.[46] Clearly, for Davis, Gage's text is a powerful critique of gender, class, and racial hierarchies, and though different, Truth emerges as *woman* precisely through the implied answer to the speech's refrain. Indeed, Davis answers Gage's question as if it is a perlocutionary command, identifying Truth and grammatically positioning her in a way that Gage's text does not: "She was . . . a woman." Such recognition is important for a book that broke new ground in exposing the race and class bias of feminism's "first wave." Truth's question is answered in terms of certain clues in Gage's text and also in terms of larger rhetorical aims of Davis's text. Simply put, Truth says what Davis needs her to say, even when Truth didn't say it at all, but not because Davis quotes an inaccurate transcript. Rather, Davis posits Truth grammatically as a woman in a way that even Gage's transcript does not, and doing so allows Davis to underscore her arguments about black womanhood in the nineteenth century. Even Gage's Truth did not say "I am a woman," but Davis's use of Truth compels this grammatical identification.

The grammar of sex-making, according to Butler, is of no small concern, and there are conceptual reasons for my uneasiness with Davis's and others' compulsory response to Truth's question—ones that I discuss more fully later on. For now, however, I want to consider how such answers neglect to take into account aspects of race-sex intersections of the nineteenth century. Rhetorical and historical scholars often cite Barbara Welter's notion of the "cult of true womanhood" as a guiding heuristic for the politics of identification of this time. According to Welter, "true women" were morally and sexually pure, pious, submissive, and domestic. This notion of womanhood was decidedly tied to the experiences of white, middle- to upper-class women, making black women, according to Davis, "hardly 'women' in the accepted sense."[47] As historical scholars have noted, the exclusion of black women from "true womanhood," so-termed, came about in part because slave women were not seen as mothers and protectors of the home but were instead viewed as breeders, whose value was calculated in terms of their ability to reproduce units of labor.[48] Donna Haraway explains that black women were raped and sexually abused like women but were forced to work like men; in this way, black women were "marked female . . . but not as woman."[49]

One should be careful, however, not to read Haraway's comment as evidence of a fully marked distinction between a gendered notion of womanhood and a sexed conception of femaleness. Butler's work shows that "sex" was never a blank slate on which gender painted meaning; rather, the production of sex has always worked through the mechanisms of what we now term *gender*. Moreover, it is difficult, if not impossible, to separate the cult of true womanhood from biological notions of sexual difference. As I will discuss in more detail later, ideas of two distinct biological sexes worked hand in hand with the same nineteenth-century separate sphere arguments in which the cult of true womanhood was enmeshed. The emphasis on purity, submissiveness, and domesticity was directly tied to the anatomy of reproduction, for example, grounding gendered womanhood in biologically sexed distinctions. What is important to distinguish, however, are the ways biology, roles, and capacities were linked differently when articulated in terms of the black body. Perhaps to take the historical scene seriously, one should consider not how black women, like Truth, were excluded from gendered womanhood while being included in sexual distinction, but how black women were figured outside a particular biological foundationalism in which (white) women's bodies prefigured certain private domestic roles in a liberal republic. Yes, in a very real sense black women were not women, but such a view also meant that their anatomy was interpreted and mobilized in radically different ways than the anatomy of white women.

While my point seems to be minor, it has profound implications when we consider the emergence of Truth via Gage's text. To answer Truth's question, to posit her grammatically as a woman, one must read her question as a rhetorical one, in that the answer is implied. Gage's Truth repeats her famous refrain four times after pointing to supposed contradiction between her experiences and assumptions about women. The first three question-example couplings all refer to Truth's experiences that diverge from typical female roles and behaviors. Gage's text reads:

> [1] Dat man ober dar say dat womin needs to be helped into carriages, and lifted ober ditches, and to hab de best place everywhar. Nobody eber helps me into carriages, or ober mud-puddles, or gibs me any best place! And raising herself to her full height, and her voice to a pitch like rolling thunder, she asked "And a'n't I a woman?
>
> [2] Look at me! Look at my arm! (and she bared her right arm to the shoulder, showing her tremendous muscular power). I have ploughed, and planted, and gathered into barns, and no man could head me! And a'n't I a woman?
>
> [3] I could work as much and eat as much as a man—when I could get it—and bear de lash as well! And a'n't I a woman?[50]

Reading these three couplings, one gets the sense that women are both weak and respected, incapable of working like men or performing simple tasks like getting into a carriage. Except for these qualities, we are not to know what makes a woman a woman from these first lines alone. If one answers Truth's question, then, other assumptions about womanhood must be read into the interpretation of Gage's text. Those assumptions most likely are that Truth was physiologically female—she had breasts, two XX chromosomes, a vagina, a uterus, etc. Indeed, part of the mythology that surrounds Truth is that at one speaking event she had to bare her breasts to prove that she was a woman because her height, muscular structure, and voice, as Gage's text itself suggests, were not compatible with female characteristics. In a sense, to answer Truth's question in Gage's text is to reenact this undressing. That is, in positing Truth as woman, critics and historians must bare Truth's breasts for her. How else are we to know she is a woman?

Perhaps such symbolic disrobing is not off the mark. Gage's Truth does end her refrain with a fourth question-experience coupling that, at the very least, alludes to biological sex characteristics: "I have borne thirteen children, and seen 'em mos' all sold off to slavery, and when I cried out with my mother's grief, none but Jesus heard me! And a'n't I a woman?"[51] This coupling, more than any other, underscores the fact that black women were reproductively female yet denied the social status of white women's role in reproduction: motherhood. On the one hand, this is where we find evidence that assumptions about Truth's body as sexed female are not all that unfounded; in fact, Gage's Truth does point to having biological characteristics that work consistently with notions of the female and reproduction. On the other hand, this last coupling also reminds us that the biological foundationalism that seemed to govern the exclusion of white women from certain roles in a republic simply did not apply to black women. In short, Truth's capacity to give birth did not dictate her differentiation from men in terms of workload or types of punishment and did not dictate honor, respect, or even acknowledgment of her role as a mother. What this last coupling accentuates, then, is that matters of sex difference varied greatly among political subjects. In answering Truth's question, one risks not only normalizing biologically based womanhood but also undermining the profound differences in the configuration of sex, gender, and race. Recognizing Truth as a woman reduces difference to presumed anatomy, while also ignoring the severity of the conditions that could have enabled the question from the start.[52] These conditions posited black bodies, male or female, as other than human, compartmentalizing black differences on an entirely different plane of political identification. It is quite possible, then, that when one answers Truth's question, one transports Gage's text onto a more contemporary plane of identification, one also riddled with assumptions about the body, race, sex, and identity, and perhaps conveniently blind to the historical contingency of such assumptions. As Haraway argues, Truth as a black female or black woman is "not a coherent substance with two or more attributes, but an oxymoronic singularity."[53]

The historical question of sex is thus eclipsed when feminists unhesitatingly answer Truth's question, grammatically and unproblematically positing Truth as a woman. Yet one could easily argue that although Truth's immediate rhetorical scene rendered a quick articulation of her as "woman" untenable, that does not mean contemporary feminists should feel trapped in such an obviously problematic and white hegemonic context. Indeed, articulating Truth as a woman is in some way a "speaking back" to hegemonic identifications of black womanhood; arguably these two moves, making Truth a woman and reflecting on race and sex in the nineteenth century, are not mutually exclusive. While I find both of these arguments compelling, I want to reflect on this compulsion to answer Truth's question by considering further the question of sexual identification and recognition. One of the predominant trends in feminist engagements with Truth seems perpetually to provide answers, and to identify Truth in particular, and usually sexed, ways. Although these engagements have produced significant critiques of feminist and hegemonic exclusion and significant recognitions of various black women and their histories, they neglect to consider seriously the question of recognition and identification and the legacies of sexual and racial identification. They neglect, in other words, to question the necessity of the very terms (i.e., woman, black, slave) through which Truth is understood at all.

Indeed, while I argue that to give a quick affirmative answer to the question in Gage's text is in some way to turn a blind eye to the historical scene of racial and sexual difference from which it arose, simple recourse to the matters of history (in general) and Truth's historical biography (in particular) may also fail to sustain further questioning of the very schemas (systems of sex and race difference) through which Truth is forced to emerge. Can we engage with Sojourner Truth while also engaging with the apparatus of (sexual and racial) identification itself? Haraway, I believe, makes the most significant gesture in this direction. It is to her essay and the conceptual question of Truth's identification and recognition that I now turn.

Recognizing Truth

In her essay "Ecce Homo, Ain't (Ar'n't) I a Woman, and Inappropriate/d Others," Haraway theorizes the possibility of a "feminist humanity" with a different face. She makes clear the stakes of this kind of humanity in her opening paragraph:

> Humanity has a generic face, a universal shape. Humanity's face has been the face of man. Feminist humanity must have another shape, other gestures; but, I believe, we must have feminist figures of humanity. They cannot be man or woman. . . . Feminist figures cannot, finally, have a name; they cannot be native. Feminist humanity must, somehow, both resist representation, resist literal figuration, and still erupt in powerful new tropes, new figures of speech, new turns of historical possibility. . . . This essay tells a history of such a speaker [Sojourner Truth] who might figure the self-contradictory and necessary condition of a nongeneric humanity.[54]

As a figure of "nongeneric humanity," or, as Haraway later articulates, a *specific* figure of critical subjectivity forged "not in the sacred image of the same, but in the self-critical practice of 'difference,'" Truth offers Haraway an opportunity to consider difference and identification (naming).[55] And while Truth for Haraway, as for the others I have already discussed, is fully enmeshed in the matters of difference, this time difference is not wholly confined on a plane of familiar sex identification; feminist figures of humanity "cannot be man or woman."[56] Yet for Haraway, difference does not have to part with identity altogether. We need to "resist representation" and "erupt in powerful new tropes."[57] We need to name, but not within the terms inherited from the status quo.

Such a formulation, from the outset, seems difficult if not impossible to sustain. The relationship between identity and difference is a paradoxical one wherein identity and sameness at once require and circumscribe difference. Take, for instance, a reading of Gage's text which suggests that "A——'t I a Woman?" calls attention to ways in which black women were treated differently from white women. Truth's womanhood, black womanhood, as well as white womanhood, become identifiable precisely through a movement that differentiates one from the other. As Nealon so aptly describes the work of linguists and multiculturalists, "Identity is structured like a language: we can only recognize . . . a particular identity insofar as it differentiates itself."[58] For rhetoricians, like myself, the idea of identity requiring difference is often associated with Kenneth Burke and his argument that we know what *is* only through recourse to what it *is not*—a movement perhaps more commonly associated with Hegel's dialectical negation. Moreover, while identity, whether it be white womanhood, black womanhood, or other, does *require* difference to maintain itself as recognizable, intelligible, and, yes, identifiable, it is also true that such a dependence lends itself to a circumscription of that requisite difference. In the case of Truth, one might say that an understanding of black womanhood is *confined* to its relationship to (white) womanhood. Such a move keeps white womanhood an invisible hermeneutic and normalized center from which all else is differentiated—women versus women of color, for instance. It is this second problem, wherein difference is circumscribed by sameness, that Haraway seems particularly concerned about. In her terms, she wants to tackle the problem of figuring a feminist humanity outside the familiar narratives of humanism. How, then, does Haraway theorize this critical subject—one whose difference shakes the system up, as it were, without being domesticated by that very system?

Haraway's answer seems to rest on a somewhat opaque articulation of this figure as traveling (Sojourner) in a liminal space between identifications. For example, she makes explicit the problem with thinking of Truth as simply a different kind of woman. Such a view not only reduces her difference to her anatomy but also remains blind to the "racist/sexist logic that made the very flesh of the black person in the New World indecipherable, doubtful, out of place, confounding."[59] Challenging the categories of possible identifications, Haraway insists, again, on specificity: "Each condition of oppression requires specific analysis that both refuses the separations and insists on the nonidentities of race, sex, sexuality, and class."[60] As a result, it seems as if Haraway is attempting to affirm Truth's difference, singularity, and specificity, but not her identity (read: sex, race, etc.). Nevertheless, while resisting particular regimes of identification, Haraway insists on other specific identifications of Truth. She writes:

> One nineteenth century, friendly reporter decided he could not put Truth's words into writing at all: "She spoke but a few minutes. To report her words would have been impossible. As well attempt to report the seven apocalyptic thunders." . . . Perhaps what most needs cleaning up here is an inability to hear Sojourner Truth's language, to face her specificity, to acknowledge her, but *not* as the voice of the seven apocalyptic thunders. Instead, perhaps we need to see her as the Afro-Dutch-English New World itinerant preacher whose disruptive and risk-taking practice led her "to leave the house of bondage," to leave the subject-making (and humanist) dynamics of master and slave, and seek new names in a dangerous world. . . . She is one of Gloria Anzaldúa's *mestizas,* speaking the unrecognized hyphenated languages, living in the borderlands of history and consciousness where crossings are never safe and names never original.[61]

As "unwomanly" and "mestiza," "inappropriate/d" and "itinerant preacher," Haraway's Truth is figured as both "nongeneric" and "nonoriginal." Indeed, for Haraway, Truth is so magnificent precisely because her name condenses the very *movement* within truth that Haraway sees as the potential for a feminist humanity—"displacement as the ground of connection."[62]

Interestingly, Haraway's radical reconfiguration of Truth-as-*mestiza* is remarkably similar to Zackodnik's call for feminists to hear Truth's "double-voiced" critique. More specifically, Zackodnik worries that Truth is often (re)configured as an advocate for (white) women's advancement. For example, at an 1867 American Equal Rights Association (AERA) convention, Truth reportedly argued: "I have a right to have just as much as a man. . . . You see, the colored man has got his rights, but has the colored woman? . . . The colored man has got his rights, but nobody makes [cries] about de colored woman's rights. Why, de colored man will be massa ober de woman, an it will be jus as bad as before."[63] As Zackodnik points out, these words from Truth are often used by feminists to mark Truth as different from other nineteenth-century black feminists, like Frances Harper, who chose to stand with their race over their sex. What these feminists miss, however, is the powerful double-voiced critique used both to advocate woman's rights and to critique the white myopia of the movement. As Zackodnik explains, "Truth made answering for both an art, crafting addresses that were taken up as advocating the very cause she was questioning and pushing her fellow reformers to consider the issues they were eliding."[64] Truth speaks against and stands as witness to particular sexual and racial (in)equalities.

Keeping Truth's defiance and "double-edged song" in mind, let's turn to Haraway's reference to Gloria Anzaldúa and her discussion of *la mestiza*. From Anzaldúa, we learn that *mestiza* is an Aztec word meaning "torn between two ways."[65] *Mestizas* move in the borderlands: "Cradled in one culture, sandwiched between two cultures, straddling all three cultures and their value systems, *la mestiza* undergoes a struggle of flesh, a struggle of borders, an inner war."[66] When *la mestiza* speaks, she speaks against cultural domination and sexual domination; indeed, her message is defiant and doubly directed:

> Though we "understand" the root causes of male hatred and fear, and the subsequent wounding of women, we do no excuse, we do not condone, and we will no longer put up with it. . . . As long as woman is put down, the Indian and the Black in all of us is put down. The struggle of the *mestiza* is above all a feminist one. . . . We need to say to white society: We need you to accept the fact that Chicanos are different, to acknowledge your rejection and negation of us. We need you to own the fact that you looked upon us as less than human, that you stole our lands, our personhood, our self-respect. . . . To say that you are afraid of us, that to put distance between us, you wear the mask of contempt. Admit that Mexico is your double, that exists in the shadow of this country, that we are irrevocably tied to her. Gringo, accept the doppelganger in your psyche.[67]

While arguably much more direct and explicit than some of Truth's speeches, *la mestiza*'s message may also be described as double-voiced, making Zackodnik's and Haraway's articulations remarkably similar.

I highlight this similarity because Haraway gets surprisingly little attention in Zackodnik's far-reaching critique of feminist uses and interpretations of Truth. In fact, Haraway is never discussed in the essay proper and is merely cited as an example of uses of Truth as "strategic negotiations of identification . . . in attempts to ground abstract arguments or theories."[68] In other words, Haraway, for Zackodnik, is yet another example of someone who appropriates Truth in problematic ways. Zackodnik's superficial critique of Haraway is even more surprising when one considers that like Zackodnik, Haraway calls out feminists who blindly deploy Gage's text and Truth's "southern-negro" dialect. She writes, "The undifferentiated black slave could figure for a humanist abolitionist discourse, and its descendants on the walls of women's studies offices, an ideal type, a victim (hero), . . . a special human, not one that could bind up the whole people through her unremitting figuring of critical difference—that is, not an unruly agent preaching her own unique gospel of displacement as the ground of connection."[69] What is it about Haraway that Zackodnik finds so problematic? Do Haraway's sometimes opaque theoretical investments eclipse her historical accounts and political advocacy? Or perhaps a better question to ask would be: Since both projects are committed to some version of multiculturalism, albeit differently defined, what do the similarities between Zackodnik and Haraway tell us about identification and difference when their similar positions are read together? After all, whatever Truth is—*mestiza*, a (not *the*) black feminist, woman, etc.—"she" is a recognizable something, and it is precisely through Truth's unique historical narrative that Haraway, like Zackodnik and others, authorizes that alterity. We are duly assured, by pretty much everyone, that Truth is different. She is grammatically made so in a number of ways.

Although Haraway's and Zackodnik's specific identifications of Truth are alike, a more fundamental similarity between the two (as well as among other feminist readings) is the movement of identification itself. Recalling the anxiety imbued in the embarrassed "etc.," we find that there seems to be an investment not only in identification but also in the specific content of any identity. We must know in advance whom we are to fight for, consider, and include in the drive toward multiculturalism. The problem with this compulsion, *if there is one*, is that all encounters with difference, truth, alterity, and others are confined by a project that keeps recognition on the horizon and authentic inclusion as a realizable possibility. Perhaps for Zackodnik "double-voiced" is more accurate than "*mestiza*," and for Haraway "*mestiza*" is more apt than simply "black woman." Regardless, while both feminists seek to question the particulars of identifications and Truth, each is reluctant to engage Truth in any way other than an identificatory move. As a result, they, like those who came before them, articulate Truth in more or less appropriative ways to calm anxieties left by the other/others in an implicit rhetorical effort to name a better kind of humanity.

Questionable Engagements

In *Giving an Account of Oneself,* Butler discusses Foucault's comments about the difficulties of giving an account that honors and does not efface. Butler argues, rightly I think, that for Foucault, one's intelligibility and recognizability as a subject is firmly enmeshed in particular regimes of truth, and that any account of oneself or of others that does not acknowledge the questionability of practices of truth-telling is not without its costs. Telling Truth's truth, for example, or recognizing her as woman, as black woman, as *mestiza,* as "etc.," comes at a price, and that price, to echo Butler (and Foucault), is the "suspension of a critical relation to the truth regime in which we live."[70] It seems to me that there is a certain productivity, which it must be acknowledged is not without its own risks, to maintaining the question of sex, the question of race, the question of difference as questions—to maintain a critical relationship not only to systems of racism, sexism, etc. but also to those regimes of identification and recognition that so often close off the possibilities of questioning from the start. Of course, there are often times when political identifications are needed and, undoubtedly, absolutely necessary. I am not arguing for a "feminism without women." What possibilities emerge, however, when we resist relating to and accounting for Truth exclusively through identification? What opportunities are missed when we engage Truth, sex, and difference with recognition on the horizon? As Butler writes in *Undoing Gender:* "How might we encounter the difference that calls our grids of intelligibility into question . . . ? What might it mean to learn to live in the anxiety of that challenge, to feel the surety of one's epistemological and ontological anchor go . . . ? [This response] lives with its unknowingness. . . . [S]ustaining the bond that the question opens is finally more valuable than knowing in advance what holds us in common, as if we already have all the resources we need to know what defines the human, what its future life might be."[71] Perhaps, then, providing the best account, most accurate identification, and politically pure recognition of Truth and her accomplishments can be productively supplemented by an engagement with identification and recognition itself.

Such an encounter is undoubtedly risky.[72] I should make it clear that I am in no way positing a necessarily better or less appropriative engagement with Truth. Nor am I suggesting that we can/should escape identification and recognition altogether. What I do want to suggest is a supplementary engagement, one that fails to keep recognition on the horizon while also removing non-appropriation as a realizable possibility in any encounter. What I am suggesting is a questionable engagement with Truth and with feminism itself. Such encounters are both unsettled and impure. They begin with the assumption of the contingency of sex and neglect to promote the knowability of sex. These engagements do not offer certainty, nor can they ensure radical subversion, but they can begin to provide productive and expansively varied reflections on the ways sex has functioned and can function in feminist advocacy over time. Indeed, what I find remarkable about possible engagements with Gage's text in the twenty-first century is that such an encounter would be obviously tainted from the start as the invocation of the question "A——'t I a woman?" is imbued with rhetorical aims, reiterated in a myriad of ways, and articulated in a form that quite possibly demands a particular response; the question in Gage's text shreds any hope of writing an authentic, politically pure, nonviolent response to or account of Truth. It eschews multicultural authentic inclusion as the possibility, allowing for an encounter that is not pigeonholed by recognition and intelligibility. It engages womanhood, race, and sex as utterly and perpetually questionable, and thus assuredly unresolved.

Perhaps questionable engagements with feminist history may lie at heart of the struggle in feminist communities over the role of sex's scholarly revolution for how we consider feminist movements and activism. At a 2009 conference on rhetorical theory, Erik Doxtader reminded participants that "questions are not innocents. They can be leading and loaded. And, they can be fired. . . . That we hear 'no question' in a question may signal a forgetting of contingency or a recollection of what cannot be asked or answered."[73] Arguably, the circulation of Truth's question and its various answers in feminist communities is a synecdoche for the way the question of sex is not "heard" and/or is resisted as feminists debate the matters of sex for feminist activism. Indeed, the explicit and implied insistence that feminism requires female sex specificity is in many ways a proposition that sex is inherently unquestionable; arguments, in other words, that position inquiries concerning feminism's relationship to sex are ones that should not be asked or answered. The case of Truth, as well as the analyses that follow, suggest otherwise.

2

Matters of Sex and Race

ELIZABETH CADY STANTON,
BIOLOGICAL FOUNDATIONALISM,
AND NINETEENTH-CENTURY LIBERALISM

I N A LETTER to the editor of the *National Anti-Slavery Standard* dated December 26, 1865, Elizabeth Cady Stanton made the now infamously racist remark: "The representative women of the nation have done their uttermost for the last thirty years to secure freedom for the negro, and so long as he was lowest in the scale of being we were willing to press *his* claims; but now, as the celestial gate to civil rights is slowly moving on its hinges, it becomes a serious question whether we had better stand aside and see 'Sambo' walk into the kingdom first."[1] Cady Stanton's commentary in this passage—equating black male suffrage with "Sambo's" walk through the "celestial gate of civil rights"—is just one example of her response to the promotion of black male suffrage over universal suffrage at the conclusion of the Civil War. Many woman suffrage advocates, like Cady Stanton, thought that their work during the Civil War would be rewarded because they had voluntarily suspended their efforts to gain rights for women in order to commit fully to the Union.[2] Cady Stanton and others "believed in all sincerity" that the black and woman suffrage causes could help, not harm, each other and they urged adoption of universal suffrage as part of the Civil War constitutional amendments.[3] Despite the sacrifices of many woman's rights advocates and Cady Stanton's and others' efforts to promote universal, not manhood, suffrage, many who they'd hoped would be allies of woman suffrage argued that attention needed to be paid exclusively to the enfranchisement of black men. It was "the Negro's hour," they insisted, and therefore it was not politically prudent or expedient to pursue a constitutional amendment that would enfranchise women.[4]

Cady Stanton's letter, however, is not simply a benign reflection of her commitment to universal suffrage; it indicates how she, like many other white abolitionists, was apt to promote racism if it served the interests of privileged white women. In fact, Angela Davis opens her chapter "Racism in the Woman Suffrage Movement" in *Women, Race, and Class* with Cady Stanton's letter and describes her remarks as "opportunistic and unfortunately racist." She argues that Cady Stanton "was determined . . . to prevent further progress of Black people—for 'Sambo' no less—if it meant that white women might not enjoy the immediate benefits of that progress."[5] Clearly, it would be difficult to dismiss Cady Stanton's letter as mere words that should not overshadow her larger commitment to sex and racial equality. It is also, however, problematic simply to characterize Cady Stanton as a no-holds-barred advocate of woman's rights before the rights of any others. Although this latter characterization appears to be a fair assessment of her commitment to women's struggles, it also may be an oversimplification of the political ideologies and strategies that grounded her efforts to win the ballot.

More specifically, Cady Stanton's advocacy about race and suffrage was inextricable from her commitment to woman, and she was not alone. Racist sentiments like Cady Stanton's emerged throughout white woman's rights movements in the nineteenth century, punctuating the white middle-class and upper-class myopia of many of the activists credited with being at the heart of what has been termed feminism's "first wave."[6] Although no single explanation can suffice for the various forms in which racism emerged in woman suffrage advocacy, including Cady Stanton's, most explanations set these racist remarks and actions within the context of competing commitments to equal rights and political expediency. As the historian Suzanne M. Marilley puts it, "Although elite white leaders *succumbed* to racist and nativist sentiments, such sentiments never fully eclipsed their egalitarian aims."[7] In fact, a rhetorical understanding informs accounts of racism in feminism's "first wave" as these actions and remarks are described as *responses* to immediate rhetorical contexts. The kinds of contexts that seem to have invited racist rhetoric include the successful promotion of "manhood suffrage" over universal suffrage after the Civil War, the influx of immigrants in the 1890s, and the perceived need to recruit and retain Southern support for woman's suffrage at the turn of the century.[8] It stands to reason that in the minds of some nineteenth-century advocates, these contexts pitted sex against race, and those who advocated for woman attempted to ensure that white womanhood would win in the end.

Such an explanation is not entirely off the mark. In the case of Cady Stanton, although racist sentiments run through her rhetoric before the Civil War, the kind of vitriol that characterizes the letter quoted at the beginning of this chapter did not emerge until the debates over the Fifteenth Amendment. Understanding Cady Stanton's rhetoric of this time as purely opportunistic, however, ignores how race functioned in her rhetoric before the Civil War and neglects to account for her participation in the politics of difference in nineteenth-century liberal political culture—a context wherein appeals to universal human rights were consistently positioned alongside pointed claims of difference among the nation's populace. More specifically, Cady Stanton was not only a central organizer of and primary advocate for early woman's rights activism but also one of the movement's principal theorists. Described as the "leading philosopher" of early U.S. feminism, she is considered to be the nineteenth-century equivalent to Mary Wollstonecraft in the eighteenth century and Simone de Beauvoir in the twentieth.[9] Marilley goes so far as to say that in the early years of the woman suffrage movement, Cady Stanton was its "most consistent and daring liberal thinker."[10] She articulated her liberal philosophy through movement speeches, letters, and essays, and her theories and/or rhetorics were firmly enmeshed with the concerns of a social movement of which she considered herself a part as well as the intellectual and political traditions of liberalism more broadly.[11] Therefore, exclusive attention to Cady Stanton's immediate rhetorical context risks overshadowing her broader commitment (and response) to liberalism and an understanding of difference, sexual and racial, pegged to this commitment. Within the political culture of nineteenth-century reform politics, there was a paradoxical need to recognize race and sex as differences that mattered within a discursive field that championed universal "natural rights." Thus we might come to understand Cady Stanton's rhetoric as one that responded to immediate exigencies while also bearing the burden of negotiating an enduring tension between universality and difference in liberal humanist traditions.

In this chapter I examine Cady Stanton's public discourse, transcribed by Ann D. Gordon in *The Selected Papers of Elizabeth Cady Stanton and Susan B. Anthony,* from the official beginning of the woman's rights movement in 1848 through the ratification of the Fifteenth Amendment in 1870.[12] My goal is to attend carefully to the immediate exigencies produced as a result of her dual commitment to abolition and woman's rights, which, in her view, had come into conflict with each other at the conclusion of the Civil War. At the same time, I consider her discourse in terms of a liberal Enlightenment *idiom of difference.* This idiom maintained an enduring tension in liberal rhetorical cultural of the time, in which ideas of universal natural rights among political subjects ran alongside persistent identifications of corporeal differences among those same subjects as differences that mattered. The confluence of these contexts, I argue, animated Cady Stanton's rhetoric so as to deemphasize the importance of a corporeal-based identity in a humanistic vision of liberal feminism and citizenship. Promoting an extracorporeal view of sex and race identity, Cady Stanton's rhetoric delineates why certain differences matter and why others do not. Such a move deftly usurps liberal political culture's disenfranchisement of women while also amplifying a liberal proclivity toward differentiation in racist and elitist ways.

Although the perception that her racist rhetoric was opportunistic dominates current scholarship, the question of sex in Cady Stanton's philosophy appears to be more perplexing. Readings of some of her earliest work suggest that for Cady Stanton, "the differences between men and women were rooted purely in social custom."[13] Even her later work, most notably her speech "The Solitude of Self," emphasized not difference but commonalities between the sexes.[14] As Karlyn Kohrs Campbell points out, it "was a speech for woman's rights broadly conceived; more properly, it was a speech for human rights."[15] Other scholars, however, highlight aspects of Cady Stanton's rhetoric that emphasize profound differences between men and women. William Leach argues that she "developed an unwavering belief in the basic 'human' differences between the sexes."[16] Leach's claim rests on his analysis of the ways in which Auguste Comte's positivism often privileged the morality of a "feminine element" over the "masculine element," and thus influenced Cady Stanton's rhetoric and/or feminist philosophy. As Kathi Kern asserts, in Comte, Cady Stanton found a "theorist who explicitly privileged women's role in the world order."[17] Arguably, the issue of sex difference for Cady Stanton remains undecided, in part because previous examinations of her discourse focus exclusively on questions of male and female sameness or difference. Such an approach falls short, for it asks the question of sex difference and sameness without considering the traditions and idioms of human differentiation. The analysis that follows makes clear that when considerations of sex and race in Cady Stanton's discourse are read alongside each other, we begin to see a richer and more complex sense of difference operating in her public advocacy. Such an analysis helps to account for the bases on which both sex and race are grounded, the avenues through which they are advanced, and the ways sex and race work together as a response to and a reinvigoration of the liberal identity politics of the early nineteenth century.

Liberals Make Sex

In his historical examination of the making of sex, Thomas Laqueur points out that "sex as we know it" was not invented until the eighteenth century.[18] Up until that time, male and female bodies were rendered as "hierarchically, vertically, ordered versions of one-sex," as opposed to the more familiar and contemporary two-sex model of difference.[19] Scientific accounts, like that of Galen in the second century CE, claimed that female bodies were essentially male bodies that lacked the vital heat necessary for internal (phallic) structures to become externally visible. The use of the same term to refer to female ovaries and male testes (Galen's *orcheis* and Herophilus's *didymoi*), as well as the once prevailing gynecological belief that the inside of the vagina was "one giant foreskin of the female interior penis," evidence an understanding of the body that established "man" as the hermeneutic center.[20] Add to these beliefs views such as those found in Aristotle which simultaneously insisted on the differences between men and women while conflating male and female sexual organs, and it is not hard to see how hierarchical conceptions of "male" and "female" differences took on an extracorporeal nature. According to Laqueur, within this one-sex model of difference, anatomy mattered less than the supposed metaphysical hierarchies that sexed organs represented: "resonant throughout the cosmos," differences in reproductive organs were "paradigmatic sites for displaying hierarchy."[21] To turn around a contemporary phrase, it was not so much that anatomy was one's destiny, as that one's destiny had already been determined by a cosmologically framed interpretation of one's anatomy.

This last point is crucial; as Laqueur points out, although differences of the body are embedded in the language of science, the nature of sex difference is "logically independent of biological facts."[22] Scientific discovery in and of itself did not bring about a shift to a two-sex model; rather, as a result of the Enlightenment, rhetorical exigencies emerged that necessitated a change in the way corporeal differences were interpreted and mobilized in power struggles. Simply put, biological sex needed to do the cultural work of women's subordination, not appeals to a belief in a transcendent order. Laqueur explains:

> Aristotle did not need the facts of sexual difference to support the claim that woman was a lesser being than man. . . . Of course males and females were in daily life identified by their corporeal characteristics, but the assertion that in generation the male was the efficient and the female the material cause was, in principle, not physically demonstrable; it was itself a restatement of what

it *meant* to be male or female. The specific nature of the ovaries or the uterus was thus only incidental to defining sexual difference. By the eighteenth century, this was no longer the case. The womb, which had been a sort of negative phallus, became the uterus—an organ whose fibers, nerves, and vasculature provided a naturalistic explanation and justification for the social status of women.[23]

Some may think of the shift to a two-sex understanding of difference as a clear result of better science: through the appropriate methods, scientists *discovered* the truth that there are actually two sexes, not one. Laqueur complicates this assumption, however, and demonstrates that the Enlightenment did not lead scientists to figure out the more accurate facts of sex. Rather, it precipitated an epistemological shift that emphasized the importance of what could be observable in the *natural* world as the proper grounds for understanding difference. Sex became a product not of *what* we knew but of *how* we knew, and arguments about difference (and hierarchy) needed to be grounded in nature, biology, and physical facts, not in an allusion to a transcendent cosmological order.

One need only look at anti–woman suffrage rhetoric of the time to see how biological differences served as justifications and foundations for differences in rights. Catherine Palczewski, for example, in looking at anti-suffrage postcards, found that women's lack of physical strength to enforce their vote served as a reason for denying the franchise to women.[24] Linda Nicholson provides further evidence for Laqueur's point and contrasts older "theological views" of the self with the one that emerged in the seventeenth and eighteenth centuries, an idea of the self that was firmly grounded in the body as a *source* of knowledge.[25] Moreover, it's not as if the shift to biological foundationalism was tied to sex alone. As both Nicholson and Laqueur point out, "race" as a distinction founded in the body is also a post-Enlightenment formulation.[26] According to Laqueur, post-Enlightenment claims that "negroes have stronger, coarser nerves than Europeans because they have smaller brains, and that these facts explain the inferiority of their culture, are parallel to those which held that the uterus naturally disposes women toward domesticity."[27]

Not surprisingly, liberal political philosophy, which emerged in the immediate wake of the Enlightenment, also points to a shift toward the body and biology as the bases on which to ground differences among political subjects. According to Marilley, the "liberal principle" of this time "held [that] because all persons possess natural rights, all must be guaranteed political

rights and stand as equal citizens."[28] While these theories ostensibly supported human "equality," they also worked within a biological foundationalism
to secure male domination of the public sphere and the subordination of
women. Locke, Hobbes, and Rousseau excluded women from full citizenship
and used newly interpreted biological facts, such as man's superior physical
strength and women's vulnerable reproductive situation, to offer a historical (yet inevitably transhistorical) justification for female subordination.[29] A
"sexual contract" between men and women, according to Carole Pateman,
preceded any "social contract" among men, in part because it was thought
that women, because of their vulnerable role in reproduction, needed the
protection of their physically superior male counterparts.[30] Although all
"men" were created equal, the biological differences between men and wom-
en served as evidence, and as justification for the exclusion of women from
certain rights and roles. As Laqueur aptly writes, bodies in liberal Enlightenment theory "are not the sign of but the foundation for civil society."[31]

This epistemic shift to biological foundationalism supported a pervasive
change in the political landscape on which an increasing number of struggles
over gender and power emerged. In the post-revolutionary world of the early
nineteenth century, the popularity of liberal Enlightenment theories espous-
ing natural rights precipitated efforts on the part of early feminists to expand
women's role in the public sphere as well as attempts by antifeminists to distinguish between natural and political equality, denying women the latter.[32]
To varying degrees, historians have recognized the opportunities offered by
and the obstacles buttressed by liberal Enlightenment political philosophy
for early woman's rights activists. On the one hand, these theories and their
popularity offered advocates an appealing foundation on which to build their
arguments concerning political equality. Described by Aileen S. Kraditor as
"arguments from justice," liberal Enlightenment theories that wed the political rights of a citizenry to the natural, inalienable rights of all humans offered
activists the opportunity to advance arguments establishing the rights and
privileges of women as citizens (petitioning, and eventually suffrage).[33] Although liberal Enlightenment theory provided a solid basis for these natural
rights arguments, early activists also had to work against an explicit identification of a woman's sphere separated from the male public order. Perhaps
it is within the context of a meeting of natural rights philosophies (i.e., articulating the inalienable rights of *humanity* and privileges of a citizenry)
with the prevailing two-sex model of sexual difference (i.e., identifying in-
commensurably sexed bodies as foundational aspects of civil society) that

gendered notions of civic duty and political rights emerge. These notions, which often articulated female citizenship in terms of a politicized domesticity or limited women's civic rights and duties to certain activities in narrowly defined venues, created a formidable barrier for anyone claiming women's political equality.[34] The rhetorical situation for woman's rights activists, then, was riddled with seemingly contradictory ideas of *universal* human equality, liberty, and distinct biological sexual *difference,* dictating profoundly varied views about citizenship and rights.

Historians and rhetoricians have consistently categorized feminist responses to this situation as positing the sexes either as essentially the same or as fundamentally different. Employing categories identified by Kraditor, Campbell succinctly explains that the "*argument from justice* was drawn from natural rights philosophy and affirmed the personhood of women in their right to all the civil and political privileges of citizenship. It was a demand for rights affirming that, at least in law and politics, there were no differences between the sexes. By contrast, the *argument from expediency* presumed that women and men were fundamentally different, so that it would be beneficial, that is, desirable and prudent, to give women rights because of the effect on society."[35] Similarly, Marilley contrasts Cady Stanton's and Susan B. Anthony's "feminism of equality," which "insisted that women's natural rights be recognized as no less sacred than men's," with Francis Willard's arguments "showing women how they could fashion meaningful forms of political participation without relinquishing their distinctive identities."[36] In Sara M. Evans's terms, "the former emphasized similarities; the latter, differences."[37] Similarities, differences, distinct and indistinct identities all point to various ideas about "man" and "woman" among woman's rights advocates. At stake in the *biological* bifurcation of sex, however, is something beyond various articulations of sameness and difference. A perspective that does not take a two-sex model of sexual difference as a natural consequence of biology and/or scientific discovery directs an examination of feminist discourse that underscores how the body, biology, and/or nature came to bear on its own mobilization of sex difference. To what extent did "first wave" feminists participate in the production of sex as natural and/or biological? How much, if at all, does the body figure in the way these feminists (re)configured difference?

These are the questions that bring me back to Laqueur and his distinction between a one-sex and a two-sex understanding of difference. Laqueur's analysis is remarkable in part because it demonstrates an examination of sex that does not take two-biological sexes as a given. Falling outside the interpretive trappings of biological foundationalism, in other words, his analysis offers a model of difference with much heuristic potential. Laqueur's description of a pre-Enlightenment understanding of difference, in particular, highlights a one-sex paradigm as both a hierarchical and an extracorporeal view of human subjects. Because of its dual investment in hierarchy and extracorporeality, the one-sex model is a fitting heuristic for understanding how Cady Stanton's rhetoric manages the problem of biological foundationalism and liberalism in the nineteenth century. It is quite clear that she was firmly committed to and influenced by liberal Enlightenment ideas of natural rights and equal privileges of the citizenry. In fact, Josephine Donovan describes "The Declaration of Sentiments," drafted primarily by Cady Stanton, as "the most dramatic early attempt to apply the basic natural rights doctrine to women."[38] Unlike other liberal Enlightenment theorists, Cady Stanton deemphasized any perceived natural and biological differences between men and women in a way that positioned the latter as equal inheritors of citizens' rights and privileges. Her views of certain inalienable rights for citizens, expressed profoundly in her support of universal suffrage after the Civil War, came into conflict, however, with the ways in which she seems to have viewed her immediate rhetorical scene. In this context, wherein male immigrants were naturalized and expeditiously granted the right to vote, and the enfranchisement of black men was seen as more politically feasible than universal suffrage, Cady Stanton's advocacy shifted from universal ideas of citizenship to a model of difference that assumed an aggregate of hierarchically ordered citizens with extracorporeal identities. Such a shift gained rhetorical traction because it marshaled and challenged liberal Enlightenment performative traditions composed in part by an idiom that corporealized difference so as to account for sexual and racial exceptions to universal natural rights claims. Her rhetoric, in other words, orchestrated these traditions in a manner that responded to specific political exigencies that emerged after the Civil War, as well as the enduring tension between universality and difference that persisted in liberal political thought.

Elizabeth Cady Stanton's Enlightened Racism

In her 1848 address on woman's rights, Cady Stanton remarked: "Men bless their innocence are fond of representing themselves as beings of reason—of intellect—while women are mere creatures of the affections. There is self-conceit that makes the possessor infinitely happy and one would dislike to dispel the illusion, if it were possible to endure it."[39] The separation of woman from the public realm of "reason" was a persistent cultural obstacle for woman's rights advocates. Josephine Donovan explains, "Inherent in the vaunting of human (male) reason is the idea that rational beings are the lords of creation and have the right to impose their 'reason' on all who lack it—women, non-human creatures, and the earth itself." For Locke specifically, the "primary qualification for citizenship [and] the right to participate in public affairs [was] rationality."[40]

Rather than question the central status of rationality, Cady Stanton, like many of her contemporaries, "dispel[led] the illusion" of male intellectual superiority by explicitly challenging it through refutation as well as by enacting woman's rational and argumentative prowess. In the same 1848 speech, she employed ample evidence within a refutational structure addressing the issue of sex difference and hierarchy in a direct and assertive manner:

> There is a class of men who believe in the natural inborn, inbred superiority of both in body and mind and their full complete Heaven descended right to lord it over the fish of the sea, the fowl of the air, the beast of the field and last tho' not least the immortal being called woman. I would recommend this class to the attentive perusal of their Bibles—to historical research, to foreign travel—to a closer observation of the manifestations of mind about them and to an humble comparison of themselves to women such as Catherine of Russia, [and] Elizabeth of England distinguished for their statesman-like qualities, Harriet Martineau and Madame de Stael for their literary attainments, or Caroline Herschel and Mary Summerville for their scientific researches, or for the physical equality to that whole nation of famous women the Amazons. We seldom find this class of objectors among liberally educated persons . . . but barbarians tho' they be in entertaining such an opinion—they must be met and fairly vanquished.[41]

Calling attention to the ways women are grouped with those who lack the status of human and to numerous examples that refute any notion of male superiority, Cady Stanton articulated the bases for woman's rights through the precepts of natural rights philosophy. Deemphasizing differences of sex and race, she reiterated this philosophy by framing woman's rights in terms of the rights of the "governed," "the people," "citizens," and "persons."[42] As she put it in 1866, the Constitution "recognizes as persons all citizens who obey the laws and support the State, and if the Constitutions of the several States were brought into harmony with the broad principles of the Federal Constitution, the women of the nation would no longer be taxed without representation, or governed without their consent."[43]

Beyond examples and enactments of woman's rationality, one finds a metaphysical dimension to Cady Stanton's theory. In "The Solitude of Self" (1892), she argued for woman's rights via the importance of human self-sovereignty. Although critics have been quick to point out that the speech does not reiterate "typical speeches and arguments of the nineteenth-century feminists," it is important to note that the central rationale of that speech—that every human has responsibility over one's own life—can be found in her earlier rhetoric.[44] "The individuality of woman," she wrote in 1857, "must be asserted and upheld, and she must ever hold in her own hands the means of self-support and protection."[45] Similarly, in her 1848 address, she stated that "each human being is morally accountable for himself . . . no one can throw upon another his burden of responsibility, that neither Father, Husband, Brother, nor son, however willing they may be, can relieve woman from this weight, can stand in her stead when called into the presence of the searcher of spirits."[46] Later, she reiterated the theme of the importance of self-sovereignty by citing Alexander Hamilton: "Helpless and dependent, woman must ever be the victim of society. 'Give a man right over my subsistence,' says Alexander Hamilton, 'and he has a right over my whole moral being.' "[47] Though in nascent form, comments such as these demonstrate that Cady Stanton's humanistic vision animated even her earliest work. More important, however, is that this liberal humanist vision emphasizes the common condition of self-reliance and moral self-determination for all humans. Amplifying the distinction between animals and humans, Cady Stanton's insistence on self-sovereignty as a defining characteristic of humanity served as a metaphysical justification for certain rights and treatment under the law. As Campbell rightly puts it, such arguments present "the rights of women as a natural and inevitable part of the *human* birthright."[48] Cady Stanton's insistence on a common human birthright did not, however, dismiss difference among humans altogether.

More specifically, not only did Cady Stanton reiterate liberal humanism's commitment to rationality and natural rights, but also she inherited a strategy of differentiation that employed a liberal commitment to education.[49] As this was tied to the values of rationality and reason, the importance of liberal education for Cady Stanton is not all that surprising. Her eighteenth-century philosophical predecessor Wollstonecraft reiterated the importance of reason and education in *A Vindication of the Rights of Woman,* arguing that it is only via the cultivation of reason through education that one (and society) can become virtuous.[50] In Donovan's terms, early liberal feminists not only

viewed individuals as solitary but also believed that all humans were rational entities. As a result of the shared capacity for reason, the importance of
(universal) education (re)surfaced as "the most effective means to effect social change and transform society."[51] However much Cady Stanton's specific
championing of education was grounded in an understanding of universal
human characteristics, education was also the primary means by which she
distinguished political subjects. For her, an ideal citizenry was populated by
those who had cultivated their rational capacities through education.[52] Consequently, certain humans were better equipped, intellectually and morally,
to participate in public life. Campbell remarks on the ways Cady Stanton's
1848 address distinguished educated women from uneducated "barbarians,"
and argues that such instances reveal "the indignation she and others like her
felt at being at a disadvantage to those men whom they saw as their intellectual and moral inferiors."[53]

Indeed, Cady Stanton often used education as a means to distinguish political subjects hierarchically. In an 1854 address to the New York legislature,
she stated:

> [Women] are moral, virtuous and intelligent, and in all respects quite equal
> to the proud white man himself, and yet by your laws [she is] classed with
> idiots, lunatics and negroes; and though we do not feel honored by the place
> assigned us, yet, in fact, our legal position is lower than that of either. . . . Can
> it be that . . . you . . . would willingly build up an aristocracy that places the
> ignorant and vulgar above the educated and refined—the alien and the ditch-
> digger above the authors and poets of the day—an aristocracy that would
> raise the sons above the mothers that bore them?[54]

In comments such as these she clearly revealed her elitism, asserting that rule
by those less educated than white middle-class women should be understood
as a gross violation of the fundamental principles and values of a liberal republic. Echoing the sentiments of Thomas Jefferson's "natural aristocracy,"
she argued, "It is better to be the slave of an educated white man, than of a
degraded, ignorant black one."[55]

As it became increasingly apparent that the Civil War amendments would
not enfranchise both women and black men, Cady Stanton emphasized education in explicitly racist ways as a factor that distinguishes human subjects
from one another. By the 1860s, the more or less implicit comparisons between women and other dispossessed classes became much more explicit as
those classes threatened to become possessors of rights. In an 1868 article in
The Revolution, she wrote:

Just so if woman finds it hard to bear the oppressive laws of a few Saxon Fathers, of the best orders of manhood, what may she not be called to endure when all the lower orders, natives and foreigners, Dutch, Irish, Chinese and African, legislate for her and her daughters? . . . Think of Patrick and Sambo and Hans and Yung Tung who do not know the difference between a Monarchy and Republic, who never read the Declaration of Independence or Webster's spelling book, making laws for Lydia Maria Child, Lucretia Mott, or Fanny Kemble.[56]

This racist and nativist amplification of the importance of education is commonly used by historians as evidence of the ways that immediate exigencies, ranging from the promotion of manhood suffrage to the need for expeditious naturalization and enfranchisement of male immigrants and others, provoked a strategic change from universal suffrage to educated suffrage.[57] Although these immediate factors provoked a substantial shift in Cady Stanton's rhetoric, we miss an important feature of her theory when we allow such exigencies to overdetermine our understanding of the distinctions she was drawing. Perhaps the various iterations of the importance of education, racist and otherwise, when considered alongside her articulations of a common human condition, highlight a strategic identification of human differences, themselves not biologically determined. Rather than view her racist rhetoric as exclusively *opportunistic*, it is useful to consider these moments as *emblematic* of a divergent way of theorizing difference. In contrast to prevailing liberal Enlightenment discourse, which often based its hierarchy of humans in anatomical distinctions, what if such hierarchical difference functioned in Cady Stanton's discourse to make corporeal difference, and differences in biological sex in particular, inconsequential? In her words: "There is only one safe, sure way to build a government, and that is on the equality of all its citizens, male and female, black and white. The aristocratic idea in any form is opposed to the genius of our institutions and the civilization of the age. Of all kinds of aristocracy, that of sex is the most odious and unnatural."[58]

Rather than constituting a simple replication of a liberal Enlightenment double play between universality and difference, or in this case human rights and expedient racism, Cady Stanton's early rhetoric illustrates a fundamental departure from the nineteenth-century liberal republic's identifications of biologically determined exceptions to universal natural rights claims. Arguably, the way Cady Stanton identifies differences between white women and black men, or immigrants vis-à-vis education, suggests an extracorporeal articulation of race that does not use the body as its foundation. While she differentiated the educated human from the uneducated "barbarian," "foreigner," and "Sambo," she did so within a theory of humanity's ontological and metaphysical commonality. Elitist and racist to be sure, Cady Stanton's educated hierarchy premised its racism not on immutable biological characteristics—not, in her terms, on "black and white" bodies—but on the historically contingent social circumstances of human subjects.

It is the combined force of a hierarchically based conceptualization of human subjects and a denial of biological foundationalism that animated Cady Stanton's early liberal feminist theory as a reiteration of a one-sex/flesh understanding of difference. What is at issue in her formulation of race—beyond a response to the Civil War amendments and immigration policy—is the very problem of political differentiation itself. Responding to the immediate exigencies of mid-nineteenth-century identity politics, Cady Stanton engaged liberal Enlightenment traditions, mobilizing and challenging them in ways that accentuated certain racial exceptions to universality while, as the next section demonstrates, mitigating sexual ones.

Cady Stanton (Un)Makes Sex

In his reading of "The Solitude of Self," Nathan Stormer argues that the speech "materializes a body whose naturalness was not determined by sex."[59] For Stormer, Cady Stanton accomplishes this by replacing the sexed body with a "common body" that articulates an "embodied humanism" through an extension of rights to women justified by the doctrine of natural rights principles. Even in the early years, before "The Solitude of Self," when Cady Stanton talked of sex, she made it clear that perceived differences between men and women should not serve as foundations for the exclusion of woman from the public sphere. By proclaiming that "there is no sex in mind," she oftentimes turned the presumption of foundational sex difference on its head:

> All man's laws, his theology, his daily life, go to prove the fixed idea in his mind of the entire difference in the sexes, a difference so broad, that what would be considered cruel and unjust between man and man, is kind and just between man and woman. Having discarded the idea of the oneness of the sexes, how can man judge of the needs and wants of a being so wholly unlike himself? . . . He cannot! . . . But when man shall fully grasp the idea that woman is a being of like feelings, thoughts, and passions with himself, he may be able to legislate for her, as one code would answer for both. But until then, a sense of justice, a wise self-love, impels us to demand a voice in his councils.[60]

Of course, if woman were judged wholly like man, principles of natural rights would also necessitate equal rights under the law. As she would later put it, "In answer to what we demand, it matters not whether women and men are like or unlike, woman has the same right man has to choose her own place."[61] Responding to "manhood suffrage" specifically, she argued, "If the civilization of the age calls for an extension of the suffrage, a government of the most virtuous, educated men and women would better represent the whole humanitarian idea, and more perfectly protect the interests of all, than could a representation of either sex alone."[62] She appeals to the widely held beliefs in fair representation and natural rights, and as a result she describes a liberal republic where sex difference matters only insofar as it justifies an extension of rights to woman, not an exclusion.[63]

Although Stormer offers an astute reading of "The Solitude of Self," his observations do little to describe the complex entanglement of sex, difference, universality, and the body in Cady Stanton's early work. In her early efforts, she often distinguished the sexes by describing the "male element" as "a destructive force; stern, selfish, aggrandizing; loving war, violence, conquest, acquisition; breeding discord, disorder, disease and death," while at the same time equating the feminine with the "diviner elements of human nature."[64] As she noted in 1868: "All late writers on the science of government recognize in woman the great humanizing element of the new era we are now entering, in which moral power is to govern brute force. It is only through the infusion of the mother soul into our legislation, that life will be held sacred, the interests of the many guarded, capital reconciled to labor, the criminal treated like a moral patient, education made practical and attractive, and labor profitable and honorable to all."[65]

Moreover, in an article in *The Revolution* published in the same year, she refuted the claim that "the attribute of sex does not extend to mind," arguing: "We started on Miss Becker's ground twenty years ago, because we thought, from that standpoint, we could draw the strongest arguments for woman's enfranchisement. And there we stood firmly entrenched, until we saw that stronger arguments could be drawn from a difference in sex, in mind as well as in body. But while admitting a difference, we claim that that difference gives man no superiority, no rights over woman that she has not over him."[66] Whether in the promotion of a "mother soul / feminine element," the degradation of the brute "male element," or the explicit reference to the sexed body and mind, Cady Stanton's articulation of fundamental differences between women and men challenges any interpretation of her work as consistently

erasing sex difference. It is important, however, not to understand sex difference as entirely resonant with the body, nor is it wise to read her work within
a logic of difference versus universality. An alternate interpretation of these
passages is warranted when the question of corporeality's relationship to sex
and identity come to bear on their reading.

Consider, for example, that while Cady Stanton identified differences between men and women, she did so amid further substantiations of an extra-
corporeal-based view of the human political subject. She argues:

> We need not prove ourselves equal to Daniel Webster to enjoy [the] privilege
> [to vote,] for the most ignorant Irishman in the ditch has all the civil rights
> he has, we need not prove our muscular power equal to this same Irishman
> to enjoy this privilege for the most tiny, weak, ill shaped, imbecile stripling of
> 21 has all the civil rights of the Irishman. . . . All men in this country have the
> same rights however they differ in mind, body, or estate. The right is ours. . . .
> We should not feel so sorely grieved if no man who had not attained the full
> stature of a Webster, Van Buren, Clay, or Gerrit Smith could claim the right of
> the elective franchise, but to have the rights of drunkards, idiots, . . . ignorant
> foreigners, and silly boys fully recognised, whilst we ourselves are thrust out
> from all the rights that belong to citizens—it is too grossly insulting to the
> dignity of woman to be longer quietly submitted to. . . . The great truth that no
> just government can be formed without the consent of the governed, we shall
> echo and re-echo in the ears of the unjust judge until by continual coming we
> shall weary him.[67]

Forecasting a later turn to "educated suffrage," this passage also highlights
how she acknowledged differences between men and women while simultaneously undermining any idea that sex differences *matter* to the question of
rights. Butler's doubled use of the term "matter" is helpful for understanding
the ways in which anatomy or the materiality of bodies determined what
mattered with regard to the distribution of rights—or, more to the point, why
the female body was not to ma(t)ter(ialize) in the public sphere. For Cady
Stanton, the answer to this dilemma challenged the then dominant liberal
Enlightenment idiom that relied on the sexed body as the ground for distinctions with regard to political rights and status. In her view, the sexed body's
matter did not justify the political exclusions of women, since *bodily matters
did not, or should not, matter at all.*

Perhaps a better understanding of Cady Stanton's position on sex difference depends on our willingness to ignore the differences or similarities
between men and women. To argue that Cady Stanton's humanism placed
sex difference in the background in favor of universal human rights is not

to argue that she failed to identify and/or recognize sex difference per se. To equate recognition of difference with a commitment to the incommensurability of two distinct sexes, however, risks mistaking her articulation of "woman" and "man" as necessarily biological categories. It is quite possible that for Cady Stanton, distinctions of sex, like racial distinctions, were extracorporeal. And while this extracorporeal view of sex is irreducible to the body, it is also not entirely sociological.[68] Just as the question of sex difference for her was not one that can be answered within a framework defined by the biological difference of a man and a woman, neither should the question be understood in terms of nature versus nurture, sex versus gender, or any other traditional binary opposition. A more nuanced reading of her early work suggests that sex difference was constituted by gender performance and signified by the body, but irreducible to neither.

In her 1848 address, for example, she refuted the use of bodily differences between men and women as justifications for woman's exclusion by providing illustrations of the way differences in the body might be better accounted for in social circumstances. After denying that the "power of mind" had any direct relationship to the "strength of body," she argued, "We cannot say what the woman might be physically, if the girl were allowed all the freedom of the boy in romping, climbing, swimming, [and] playing hoop and ball."[69] Using as examples women fighting and hunting in Tartar "tribes" and the agricultural labor of Croatian women, Cady Stanton highlighted the fact that the body does not in and of itself determine abilities or capacities. Similarly, in 1851 she asked, "If a woman has her ribs lapped from tight lacing, her spine crooked from stooping, her feet covered with corns, from tight shoes, why she is as much disabled as a *little man* with gout, inflammatory rheumatism, and a broken leg."[70] In fact, these examples suggest that sociological considerations are more important than biological ones in accounting for many sex differences, making woman's unfair treatment a distortion of natural rights philosophies. "It is not nature," she charged in 1868, "but man's assumptions" that fix woman's political status.[71]

Such a view is remarkably similar to the one taken by Wollstonecraft in *Vindication*. Wollstonecraft, a firm supporter of liberal education, argued that it is not "natural" differences between men and women that make women "foolish and vicious," but it is "from the tyranny of man [that] the greater number of female follies proceed." Accordingly, sex distinctions were "arbitrary," as women's faults were a "natural consequence of their education [or lack thereof] and status."[72] Clearly influenced by such views, Cady Stanton wrote in 1869, "The direct effect of concentrating all woman's thoughts and interest on home life intensifies her selfishness and narrows her ideas in every direction, hence she is arbitrary in her views of government, bigoted in religion and exclusive in society."[73] While the clear link to Wollstonecraft fails to speak explicitly to the role of the body, it does highlight the ways in which social circumstances always already determine assumptions—bodily or otherwise—surrounding sex difference in Cady Stanton's view.

To argue, however, that Cady Stanton circumscribed difference as social distinctions misses the important fact that she did not deny differences between sexed bodies. Certainly, in some cases, she did speak of womanhood as something separate and distinct from the body and/or mind. In 1857 she declared, "To those who in their own bodies and souls have borne the yoke of womanhood, who have groaned under . . . abuses, a *new* revelation is made."[74] Similarly, she separated "womanhood" from the self when she argued that woman "is not happy—her life is objectless—there is no scope or freedom for the acting out of her womanhood."[75] Yet in other cases, the sexed body and womanhood were conjoined. In her discussion of woman's dress, she argued that the "true idea is for the sexes to dress as nearly alike as possible." She continued, "When [women] have a voice in legislation, we shall dress as we please, and if, by concealing our sex, we find that we too, can roam up and down the earth, in safety[,] . . . we shall keep our womanhood a profound secret."[76] If dress conceals "sex" and thus keeps "womanhood" a secret, must it necessarily be the case that sex difference is primarily a biological distinction? Although one could take these moments to support opposing positions—womanhood as product of culture versus womanhood as a product of the body—such oppositions fall prey to an orientation toward difference dictated by the presumed fact of two biological sexes. According to Laqueur, it was in the emergence of two biological sexes concomitant with the Enlightenment that a distinction between biological sex and sociological gender was sharpened. In other words, it was not until sex identity was corporealized that "the framework in which the natural and the social could be clearly distinguished came into being."[77]

If we think about the one-sex model as a guiding interpretive frame, we recall that prior to the Enlightenment, bodies were identified in terms of "male" and "female." These bodies, however, were signs of difference, not biological foundations. Arguably, then, Cady Stanton challenged the mobilization of biological foundationalism by describing materialized gendered elements (e.g., clothing) and the body as *signifiers* of difference while at the same time grounding sex differences in the extracorporeal features of transcendent gendered elements (male versus feminine) and the differing social circumstances (lack of education and physical training) of women and men. That is, Cady Stanton emphasized sex as extracorporeal in a variety of ways, doing little to undermine how bodies signify difference, and simultaneously doing much to undermine a larger system of sexual differentiation that was hurting women in the public sphere. Such a strategic play with difference, however, not only challenged the idiom of corporealized difference symptomatic of the liberal Enlightenment, but also reinvigorated that tradition's embattled relationship between universality and difference through its supplementary claim of an educated hierarchy.

Feminism and Difference

Caught between ideals of universal and natural rights and recognitions of difference among human subjects, then, Cady Stanton's rhetorical practices were characteristically liberal in many ways: she regularly advanced the case for woman's rights through arguments from justice, asserting that woman, as citizen, is imbued with natural inalienable rights; her ideas echoed a variety of liberal Enlightenment thinkers, including Mary Wollstonecraft, John Stuart Mill, Alexander Hamilton, and Thomas Jefferson; and she was firmly committed to the importance of education, an often cited defining characteristic of liberal political thought. She clearly participated in the liberal rhetorical culture of the nineteenth century as she articulated her case for woman's rights within and against the performative traditions of that culture, claiming universality as well as delineating differences that mattered.

Perhaps what must be reiterated most clearly is that Cady Stanton was not simply responding to the fact that women were excluded from the public sphere. Her rhetoric engaged a specific idiom of difference that constituted biologically founded notions of sex and race. This idiom of difference worked productively with larger liberal Enlightenment performative traditions—including the privileging and identification of an educated citizenry and the use of bodily difference to justify universal natural rights claims—in the disenfranchisement of women. Indeed, if Laqueur and others are correct, this nineteenth-century liberal Enlightenment idiom of difference was a constellation of arguments and rhetorical forms that rendered the body as the grounds on which difference and exceptions to the universal rights claims *must* be articulated. Nineteenth-century liberal political culture, quite simply, wed difference to the body, constituting sex and race as corporeal and politically significant identifications of human "citizens."

As a result, when we consider Cady Stanton's early rhetoric, we must take into account not just the *fact* that sex-based differences became relevant in nineteenth-century political culture, but also the *ways* those differences came to ma(t)ter(ialize) in liberal political discourse. This is a fine distinction but one that has a substantial impact on how we understand Cady Stanton's engagement with the immediate challenge of woman suffrage after the Civil War as well as her participation in liberal politics. I think it most apropos to describe her engagement as an orchestration of traditions and idioms, a marshaling of certain tropes, arguments, and forms, and a challenging of others. A discourse that is indebted to, but also much greater in force than, the sum of all its influences. A making of sex, race, and difference that is at once a product of and resistant to prevailing liberal political theories of the time.

Any discussion of Cady Stanton's savvy and inventive rhetorical acumen, however, including her portrait of sex and race as extracorporeal, must walk a fine line between censure and celebration as it also acknowledges the racism, nativism, and elitism that ran through her discourse. I think there is good reason to walk this line as we think further about the relationship between sex, race, and feminism in the early nineteenth century. In Cady Stanton's case, the potential conflict between her ideas about natural rights and her anti-aristocratic advocacy with her explicit privileging of the claim of white educated women to the franchise over other, less educated (and oftentimes black) groups is often glossed over by scholars. Some will point to her racism, nativism, and elitism as an opportunistic response to rhetorical exigencies produced during Reconstruction. Such a response, as I have already noted, understands her rhetoric almost exclusively as instrumental and responsive to an immediate rhetorical scene. Other responses to Cady Stanton's racist rhetoric may unwittingly downplay the elitism and racism by stressing that she was a product of her time, but committed to equality nonetheless. Each of these responses fails to reflect on a more expansive rhetorical context in the nineteenth century, one in which egalitarianism, as well as sexisms and racisms, were both enabled and constrained by an idiom of corporealized difference. Efforts, then, to dismiss Cady Stanton's arguments about race as insignificant in general, or inconsistent with her idea of sex, fail to consider the multitude of ways in which these arguments participated in liberal Enlightenment rhetorical culture, reifying and transgressing the mode of identity politics endemic to that culture. Once carefully contextualized, Cady Stanton's discourse emerges as a rhetoric that both challenged public vocabularies of corporealized sexual and racial differences and revital-

ized racism and nativism on the familiar grounds of an (enlightening) education, all the while making the likely experience of race matter more than the
bodily matters of sex.

E. Michele Ramsey has noted that "an overarching theme of much scholarship concerning historical women's public address has been the tendency
to focus on the rhetorical strategies of first wave and other movement leaders in response to immediate context issues." Ramsey asks critics to consider broader cultural contexts and public vocabularies of womanhood when
thinking about women's public address.[78] Cady Stanton's case demonstrates
the importance of Ramsey's call as well as the one set out by the "sex/gender
revolution" in contemporary rhetorical studies. Propelling Ramsey's argument further, I would say that Cady Stanton's intervention in nineteenth-
century sex politics reminds us that any question of womanhood is always
already enmeshed within various performative traditions and an idiom of
difference itself. As a participant in a certain production of sex and race,
Cady Stanton both reified and resisted prevailing trends in the differentiation of human political subjects. And while her case might not appear to be
as subversive as contemporary efforts at gender-bending, her early rhetoric
calls attention to the need for feminist scholars to attend to feminism's varied
historical attempts to transgress, subvert, reify, and amplify not just woman
but *sex, race,* and *difference* in extraordinary ways.

3

Visions of Sex

FREUD, GYNECOLOGY, AND THE FEDERATION OF FEMINIST WOMEN'S HEALTH CENTERS

O N APRIL 7, 1971, six women organized and hosted a meeting in Los Angeles to discuss and devise strategies that would challenge the criminalization of abortion. At that meeting, co-organizer Carol Downer famously pushed everything off a desk, took off her underwear, pulled up her skirt, inserted a plastic speculum into her vagina, and using a flashlight and a mirror demonstrated cervical self-examination.[1] In an interview with feminist historian Michelle Murphy, Lorraine Rothman recalled: "We were all standing there all around her absolutely, totally amazed at what she was able to do. And the fact that this particular area of the body that has been inaccessible to us is now *visualized*. . . . It was revolutionary! Just the simple act of putting a speculum in the vagina ourselves and bringing up that part of our body and being able to see it in the same commonsense way we look at our face every morning."[2] Revolutionary indeed, Downer's demonstration of cervical self-examination was celebrated by many. As feminists Lolly Hirsch and Jeanne Hirsch remarked in 1972, "April 7, 1971 should be declared a holy day, a momentous holiday in the lives of all modern women."[3]

It would be difficult to overstate the importance of Downer's act for the emerging women's health movement of the time. The act, alongside the subsequent expressions of its importance for women's liberation, precipitated what would soon become a substantial component of this movement: the Federation of Feminist Women's Health Centers/Clinics (FFWHC). The FFWHC reiterated what was enacted in Downer's demonstration—a rhetoric of "self-help" that eschewed the epistemic authority of the male medical establishment. Women could *know* their own bodies in radically new ways and use such knowledge to take control of their own health care. Within a year of that meeting the attendees opened the first Feminist Women's Health Clinic in Los Angeles, and Downer and Rothman embarked on a twenty-three-city tour to demonstrate and teach cervical self-examination and menstrual extraction techniques.[4] Over two thousand women attended these meetings.[5] "Everywhere, women bought their own plastic speculums, and new self-help groups sprang up," writes Sandra Morgen. "The idea spread like wildfire."[6] By 1976 there were an estimated fifty feminist women's health clinics across the United States, each promoting the benefits of self-help, self-examination, and women-controlled / woman-centered health care. Downer's act became legendary, and "like all legends," says Morgen, "it was repeated over and over again."[7]

The founding narrative of the FFWHC is enmeshed in both personal and political matters. Mention of Downer's examination of her own cervix was often punctuated with the biographical fact that despite having given birth to six children, she knew little about her own body. Downer's story functioned as an emblem of the material manifestations of gender hierarchies, whereby male-defined interests mediated, among other things, women's sexuality and health care. Clearly the "second wave" radical feminist rallying call, "the personal is political," is central to understanding the rhetorical force of Downer's act and its circulated narrative. For the women involved in Feminist Women's Health Centers, practices of self-help and self-examination were more than the foundations of *personal* liberation; they were imbued with, and necessary performances of, political analysis. Women's health movement activist-historian Michelle Murphy explains that "self-examination, despite its name, was not an exercise in individual self-reflection. Alone, it was easy for someone to perceive her genitalia as strange. Through comparative analysis women translated the experience of looking at their cervix into information about 'women' as a class. Group acts interpellated women as part of a movement. . . . And like consciousness raising, the first lesson one learned in a self-help meeting was that of commonality."[8] As another mode of consciousness-raising, self-help and self-examination enabled women, like Downer, to see themselves within a larger network of associations and identifications, which in turn laid the groundwork for liberation. "The plastic speculum," according to Susan E. Bell and Susan M. Reverby, "became the transparent symbol of the new power, in which the physician's tool was used by women . . . to *see for themselves.*"[9] And with this newfound vision, a particular woman's—and, concomitantly, women's—liberation also came into view.

Using vaginal and cervical self-examination as a mode of feminist consciousness-raising, however, was not without risks. Ruth Rosen notes that the women's health movement helped "feminists rediscover their 'difference,'" using such biological difference as the basis to celebrate "women's distinct experiences."[10] Downer's story quite explicitly reiterates a "discovery" of women's differences through the visual examination of vaginas and cervixes. As the constitutive link between "woman" and anatomy gets amplified via the clitoris, uterus, ovaries, and breasts in the FFWHC's and other radical feminists' discourse of the time, the importance of recognizing women's supposed biological reproductive differences as sexed differences is readily apparent. Although such recognition has benefits that cannot be easily dismissed, this identification also risks reinforcing a connection between "woman" and organs of the body that have justified women's subordination in a variety of ways. Indeed much has been written and debated about feminist uses of biological difference and whether the emphasis on so-called natural, sometimes reproductive difference eclipses simultaneous claims of equality.[11] While these critiques are important, in the case of the FFWHC, similarly minded critiques risk dismissing a highly multifaceted intervention in women's health care and reproductive politics as "theoretically naïve or methodologically flawed."[12]

Perhaps Downer's story functions in another way to remind us of the importance of visual encounters in the constitution of sex difference. The self-help movement emerged in a layered psycho-medical context in which the materiality of female anatomy was visually marked in such a way as to reinforce sex hierarchies. Whether through Freudian or gynecological practices, as I show in this chapter, the sight of differentiated sexed anatomy surfaced in the 1960s (and beyond) in ways that reinforced and conferred male dominance. And it is clear that the women of the FFWHC were far from naïve about the visual politics of sex-making as they consistently told of the importance of self-help health care via visual technologies (e.g., the speculum and mirror), circulated a number of images of sexed anatomy in their publications, and quite explicitly discussed the shift in consciousness that occurs subsequent to "seeing" one's vagina, cervix, clitoris, etc.[13] Downer's story and self-help feminist discourse, in other words, demand that one pay attention to not only the importance of reproductive anatomy and corporeality in the making of sex difference, but also the centrality of the *visual* as a constitutive component in sex differentiation. What is at stake for feminists in *seeing* anatomy that is sexed female? How do feminist uses of images speak to the visual politics of sex in the 1970s and beyond?

In what follows, I consider these questions and explore the visual encounters in women's health movements. Feminist publications of the 1960s and 1970s often image female anatomy. The FFWHC, however, privileged seeing in a way that accentuates a number of visual strategies. Focusing on two widely distributed publications—*A New View of a Woman's Body* and *How to Stay Out of the Gynecologist's Office,* I find that feminists of the FFWHC used visual cues as constitutive tropes in the construction of women as *subjects* and their anatomy as *present,* and I highlight imaging as a crucial strategy of feminist interventions in psycho-medical sex-making contexts. In other words, images were not incidental to the movement's sex interventions; they were defining aspects of feminist critiques. By redefining the female sex through a variety of visual encounters, feminists taught readers *what* and *how* to see, reiterating once again the importance of *seeing sex* from the start.

Visual Politics of Sex

In the opening pages of *New View,* feminists of the FFWHC argue that "society is full of negative images of women's bodies."[14] From "scantily clad women" on billboards and in magazines, to the lack of self-examination instruction in mainstream women's health care practices, women, they claim, "are given a very clear message: be sexually available, but do not look at, touch, or understand your bodies."[15] By now, the fact that feminists have criticized the way the female body is often presented as an object of a sexualizing gaze is common knowledge. It is crucial to emphasize, however, that the critiques of FFWHC feminists were not confined to, nor did they specifically target, the spectacular objectifying gaze promoted in mainstream popular culture. They were focused on the gaze promoted and described in both psychoanalytic and medical discourses, as well as the practices that laid claim to understanding women's bodies in a neutral and objective way. And indeed, a closer look at the visual politics of Freudianism and gynecology reveals that feminists had a lot to be concerned about.

Freud's Vision of Sex

In her book *Sexual Politics,* Kate Millett argues that the influence of Freud in American sexual politics is "almost incalculable," as his work has been taken up to "rationalize the invidious relationship between the sexes, to ratify traditional roles, and to validate temperamental differences."[16] Freud and his theories were hot topics in the 1960s and early 1970s, as Freudian psychoanalysis and its understanding of female sexuality came under considerable scrutiny.

Two reports in particular challenged Freud's view of female sexuality: Alfred Kinsey's *Sexual Behavior in the Human Female* (1953) and William Masters and Virginia Johnson's *Human Sexual Response* (1966). Taken together, these publications reported substantial sociological and physiological data which undermined Freud's idea that sexuality is rooted in unconscious desires and that well-adjusted women have only vaginal, not clitoral, orgasms. The emergence of these texts, according to Jane Gerhard, provided women of the 1960s "an intellectual bridge out of Freudianism and into feminism."[17]

More specifically, by the 1970s, the critiques of Freud found in feminist tomes such as Betty Friedan's *Feminine Mystique,* Shulamith Firestone's *Dialectic of Sex,* Kate Millett's *Sexual Politics,* and Germaine Greer's *Female Eunuch* were buttressed by essays such as Anne Koedt's "Myth of the Vaginal Discourse" and the work of feminist groups such as C.L.I.T., the Boston Women's Health Collective, and the FFWHC advocates. Many of these activists turned their attention directly to the clitoris—its repression by male-dominated interests, its central role in women's liberation, and its undervalued status in Freudian psychoanalysis. As Gerhard notes, "Feminists used the sexological remapping of the female body, with its attention to the clitoris, to overturn the Freudian emphasis on the vagina."[18] One need take only a quick glance at "second wave" literature to find evidence of Gerhard's claim that these feminist actions were *explicit* attacks on Freudianism. Koedt, for example, begins by arguing that many so-called experts have pathologized the clitoral orgasm because women have been defined sexually "in terms of what pleases men": the vagina.[19] Although at this point in the essay Koedt does not explicitly name the pathologizing experts to whom she is referring, it soon becomes clear that her target is Freud and the ripple effect of his theories. In her words, Sigmund Freud is a "father of the vaginal orgasm," and thus the father of women's sexual repression.[20]

Josephine Donovan goes so far as to claim that "a central component of second-wave feminist theory [was] its rejection of Freudianism."[21] Many "second wave" feminists did in fact see themselves as responding directly to Freudianism, and the women of the FFWHC were no exception, as they explicitly tied their discussion of female sexual response and the clitoris to a repudiation of Freud.[22] The question surfaces, then: To what exactly in Freud's theories were feminists responding? In general, they took issue with (1) Freud's biologically determined view of psychosexual development, (2) the role of male bias in his theories, and most specifically (3) the material consequences of Freud's privileging of the vagina over the clitoris in normalizing women's sexuality (i.e., by pathologizing women who do not follow predefined scripts of femininity).[23] It is not too surprising that feminists would critique a theorist who articulated human psychosexual development in terms of, among other things, "penis envy" and "castration anxiety."

Important, and sometimes overlooked in our understanding of these feminist interventions into Freudianism, however, is the role that the visual plays in Freud's discussions of psychosexual development. Luce Irigaray discusses the "predominance of the visual" in Freudianism, emphasizing his idea that it is a *visual* encounter with another's genitalia that precipitates the differing psychosexual development of boys and girls. She writes that it is the "*sight* of the penis . . . [that] shows the girl to what extent her clitoris is unworthy of comparison to the boy's sex organ. . . . *She recognizes, or ought to recognize* that compared to the boy she has no sex, or least *what she thought was a valuable sex organ is only a truncated penis.*"[24] Terri Kapsalis claims that for Freud, the "single most traumatic experience for the male child is *viewing* female genitalia, out of which arises a lifelong condition known as castration anxiety and an aptitude for engaging in fetishism."[25] Although contemporary Lacanian psychoanalysts may emphasize that the child does not necessarily need to have a visual encounter with an other's sex in order for "penis envy," "castration anxiety," or similar processes to become governing components in libidinal development, such arguments depend on a well-reasoned yet less literal interpretation of Freud's work.

Consider, for example, Freud's lecture "Some Psychical Consequences of the Anatomical Distinctions between the Sexes," in which he argues that "when a little boy first catches *sight* of a girl's genital region, he begins by showing irresolution and lack of interest; he *sees* nothing or disavows what he has *seen*."[26] By contrast, he remarks in the same lecture, "[Girls] notice the penis of a brother or playmate, *strikingly visible* and of large proportions, at once recognize it as the superior counterpart of their own small inconspicuous organ, and from that time forward fall victim to envy for the penis."[27] As Millett would write later, "Much of Freudian theory rests upon th[ese] moment[s] of discovery."[28]

I am not concerned here with the predominance of the visual in Freud because I want to counter other, less literal translations of his theory. Instead, I am interested in the way this particular literal rendering of the importance of sight and vision in Freud's theory illuminates the importance of images in sex-making discourse for some feminists. In one of the most substantial "second wave" feminist critiques of Freud, *Sexual Politics,* for example, Kate

Millett emphasizes the role of the visual in Freud's theory by quoting directly moments in Freud when the synonyms "sight," "vision," "images," and "seeing" are invoked (including the exact moment of striking *visibility* which I have just quoted). Similarly, Germaine Greer in *The Female Eunuch* alludes to the problem of invisibility and evaluation of what is visible when she opens her chapter "Sex" by stating: "Women's sexual organs are shrouded in mystery. It is assumed that most of them are internal and hidden, but even the ones that are external are relatively shady."[29] Moreover, as we begin to consider the FFWHC's uses of images, emphasis on self-examination, and use of the speculum as a rhetorical and literal tool for women's liberation, we should take seriously the fact that the visual encounter with sexed-female anatomy was not an idle concern. The importance of actually *seeing* clitorises, vaginas, and cervixes, within new networks of association and exposition, was crucial to any discursive argument about their actual function and centrality in healthy women's lives.

Gynecology's Visual Pathologies

"No one looks forward to going to the gynecologist," argues the FFWHC in the first lines of *Stay Out*. "Even a routine examination and pap smear are expensive, time consuming, and for most women, unpleasant if not humiliating."[30] From physicians' lack of knowledge about women's bodies and lives, to (male) gynecologists' consistently positioning women as passive and ignorant, the FFWHC identified mainstream gynecological practices as mechanisms through which women's subordination was reinforced in medical contexts. Such criticism is not surprising, as there is much evidence to suggest that gynecology, during this time (and maybe even beyond), greatly contributed to the sexing of female bodies in ways that remained antithetical to (radical) feminist commitments.

Many feminist critiques of gynecology, for example, were part of a larger feminist analysis of the male-physician-dominated health care system more broadly. They pointed to the physician-patient relationship in which the patient was ideally passive and deferential to the physician's authority.[31] They were concerned that most physicians were white men and that medical schools, at the time, restricted female admissions.[32] They challenged the overmedicalization of routine health care, especially the procedures that pertained to women's reproductive health.[33] Finally, they attacked capitalist interests and class, race, and/or sexual hierarchies for dominating health care access and delivery systems in the United States.[34]

Unfortunately, gynecological practices punctuated these general concerns over the U.S. health care system in very noticeable ways. As a practice, modern American gynecology dates back to the work of a native South Carolinian, Dr. Marion Sims. Dr. Sims has been hailed by some as the "Father of American Gynecology" and the "Architect of the Vagina"—an accolade earned through his experimentation on female slaves in Montgomery, Alabama.[35] On these women Sims performed painful surgeries without anesthetic, tested various proto-speculum devices, and tried out a number of procedures to overcome the "[mis]management" of childbirth by "ignorant" midwives.[36] Sims's work was just the beginning of systematic attacks on women-controlled health care.[37] By 1859 the relatively young American Medical Association also took as its target the allegedly "ignorant" midwives when it began its arduous campaign for the criminalization of abortion.[38] Unable to compete with the abortion services provided by women healers, the AMA successfully campaigned to make abortion illegal—a campaign that dramatically decreased women's access to *safe* abortions for over a century. With the successful subversion of midwifery, it is not surprising that by the mid-1970s, an estimated 94 percent of gynecologists were male.[39]

The problem with mainstream gynecology, however, cannot be boiled down to a sordid history and the exclusion of women. Gynecological practices and training were also troublesome. During this time, for example, the male-dominated profession pushed pharmaceutical remedies (e.g., the Pill and IUDs) and medical procedures (e.g., "preparing" the vagina for sexual intercourse, removal of ovaries, tubal ligations without informed consent, etc.) that were harming, sterilizing, and killing women.[40] Additionally, gynecologists were trained on "model patients" that, curiously, could not feel (e.g., anaesthetized women, cadavers, and plastic dolls), training protocols that constituted women as ideally passive objects of the medical gaze and procedures.[41] From the draping during pelvic exams to the explicit pressure to "relax" and "cooperate" with the physician's probing, mainstream gynecological practices, according to feminists, diminished and infantilized women while also reinscribing a "veil of secrecy" surrounding women's bodies.[42] In Kapsalis's terms, such practices should be viewed as gynecological performances wherein prescriptions and definitions of *proper female performance* are embedded and emboldened.[43]

These proper female performances are inextricably linked to visual encounters with sex. Indeed, as Kapsalis argues, a number of gynecology's practices and products—from pelvic exams to medical textbooks—place female anatomy and performance within a politics of vision and visibility.[44] The visual politics of gynecology date to the beginning of its practice as a medical specialty, when Sims bent the handle of a pewter spoon and made a proto-speculum. He and his aides then inserted the speculum into the vagina of a slave named Lucy, who was staying in Sims's backyard hospital. In his words, "I saw everything, as no man had ever seen before."[45] The fact that the first use of a speculum to view the vagina was carried out on a slave woman is not merely coincidence. As Kapsalis explains, "The position of Sims's patients as slaves made them more fitting objects for speculum penetration and the physician's gaze while, at the same time, their status as slaves was reiterated by the physician's probing gaze and penetrating speculum as tools of the medical discipline."[46] As the object of the probing gaze, slave women, and eventually all women, became passive participants in a visual encounter with female-sexed anatomy—an anatomy that itself was encumbered with mystery, passivity, and disdain.

The concept of female-sexed anatomy as passive and pathologized is not wholly produced, however, by the speculum and its historical development. A number of visual strategies deployed in medical textbooks function to shroud female anatomy in both passivity and pathology. According to Kapsalis, gynecological textbooks rarely (if ever) include photographic images of healthy female genitalia. Viewers of the books see images of "healthy-appearing" yet diseased cervixes, labia, vulvas, etc., but "normal" visual variations are not included. The absence of healthy female genitalia is particularly pronounced in contrast to the lack of photographic images of pathologized penises in a popular urology text.[47] Making this comparison, Kapsalis observes that "while written about, the pathologized penis is not represented visually, nor is the penis fixed as pathological in the same way that the vulva is. . . . Drawings of the penis serve to normalize and generalize it in its *healthy* state. While female genitalia are also drawn in order to generalize and normalize them, there is such a profusion of photographs of diseased cervixes and vulvas that this abundance of images may serve to 'fix' the female as *pathological*."[48] Moreover, the rare depictions of female health occur through standardizing photos of objectified bodies. In the popular text *Danforth's Obstetrics and Gynecology* (first published in 1966), for example, there are no images of healthy female genitalia; there are, however, two image sequences that contain photos of white women's bodies, documenting healthy breasts and pubic hair development.[49] These images, Kapsalis astutely argues, by ignoring the immense variations among women's bodies, function insidiously to "disregard the 'originality' and multiformity of that which is normal by replacing it with an arbitrary, limiting, and racially specific average."[50]

The ways in which the medical profession pathologized and standardized female anatomy and fixed women as passive—both in body and in mind—were not lost on feminists of the FFWHC. Writing in *New View,* they argued that through group discussions and self-examination, they had come to realize that their own negative self-image was a direct result of their experiences in the mainstream health care system.[51] Foretelling what the images in *New View* and *Stay Out* also accomplish, such an admission can be read as emphasizing the importance of women's own actions and health, as opposed to the passivity and pathology associated with ideal female patients and their anatomy.

Before I discuss the visual strategies of the FFWHC, however, it is important to highlight a certain paradox that persisted in the confluence of Freudianism and gynecology in female sex-making. Although both disciplines are embedded in visualization, one, Freudianism, characterizes female anatomy as lacking and mutilated, a frightful sight to be sure. The other, gynecology, continually marks female anatomy as invisible and often pathologized. While the Freudian subject recoils at the sight of female anatomy, the gynecological (male) medical practitioner demands that female anatomy be the object of its probing gaze. Female-sexed anatomy thus becomes both the proper yet horrifying object of a male-dominated psycho-medical system's gaze. The task for feminists, then, was to navigate a complex rhetorical terrain where viewings of female anatomy were celebrated and demanded, even though the object (female genitalia) of such viewing was consistently identified as mutilated, pathological, and lacking. When feminists sought to intervene in a way that would radically alter women's health care practices—both psychological and physiological—they faced the arduous undertaking of making female anatomy visible in a manner that acknowledged the visual practices of sex-making that placed women in constricted roles rather than liberated ones. Far from being theoretically naïve, feminists of the FFWHC, it seems, were well aware that propositions—that is, discursive arguments—would not suffice. The problematic assertions of Freudianism and constructions of ideal femininity in gynecological practice were intertwined within the same visual encounters that Freud and gynecology described and promoted. Quite literally, feminists of the FFWHC needed to offer a *re*vision of women's sex.

FFWHC's New Vision

(Re)visioning sex, it seems, was a popular tactic in "second wave" feminist discourse. Throughout the 1970s (and beyond), the two longest-standing feminist periodicals, *Ms.* and *off our backs,* offered readers a look at vaginas, clitorises, labia, uteruses, etc. through literal renderings of them and through more symbolic imagery, including the now all-too-familiar signifier of vulva and vagina, the opening flower.[52] A common feature among these images is that they often broaden the viewer's line of sight. Readers do not see trimmed, hairless, neatly tucked-away labia with clitorises hidden; labia are spread and open, revealing moisture and a variety of layers, textures, and other organs. Take, for example, Barbara Seaman's 1972 article in *Ms.* titled "The Liberated Orgasm." The article opens with a full-page image of a flower. The shape of the flower is more oval than circular, mimicking the shape of a capital *O.* This allusion to "orgasm" is made complete with the exploding, bursting nature of the petal arrangement. Resembling wavy labia, the petals are dripping wet, offering a view of an open and fully blooming flower. Images such as this one begin to amplify female anatomy in a way that constitutes it, as well as the woman it stands in for, as anything but lacking, hidden, or passive: readers *see* woman and her anatomy, and both are replete with complexity, substance, and desire.

While images and imagery of vulvas appeared regularly in *Ms.* and *off our backs,* the two books published by the FFWHC, *A New View of a Woman's Body* and *How to Stay Out of the Gynecologist's Office,* offer a more developed visual strategy of sex-making and identification. Both *New View* and *Stay Out* were originally published in 1981, by Simon and Schuster and Peace Press, respectively.[53] As abridged versions of the FFWHC's larger work *Women's Health in Women's Hands,* the books were conceived of as complementary volumes, each of which discusses the value of self-help clinics and self-examination, emphasizing the importance of visual encounters with sex.[54] The cover of *Stay Out,* for example, features a woman's hand holding a plastic speculum in a manner that is conducive to cervical self-examination—bills of the speculum at the bottom, handles extending upward.[55] Likewise, *New View,* considered the "picture book" of the volumes, uses its opening pages and chapters to make clear that *seeing* and *visual examination* are fundamental aspects of the authors' "view" of a woman's body. They write: "We organized a meeting held in Los Angeles on April 1, 1971, to devise strategies to change the abortion laws which prohibited us from controlling our own reproduction and, thus, our own lives. With other women who joined us, we spent the first half of the evening doing self-examination on a desk in an alcove. . . . Together, we discovered how much our image of our bodies, particularly our genitals, improved after self-examination."[56] Marking the importance of the visual in two different ways—through the act of seeing as well as the resulting image—*New View* and *Stay Out* announce from the beginning that *seeing* is a central practice and performance of the FFWHC's unique perspective.

Reinforcing the importance of *seeing* both visually and textually, the opening chapters of both books tell women how they can take the "master's tools" to create a new liberatory consciousness. "A light, a mirror and plastic vaginal speculum are the basic tools of self-examination," the authors write in *New View,* and these are the tools that will allow women "to acquire knowledge about their bodies and health that has, for years, been solely in the possession of physicians."[57] *Stay Out* describes self-examination on its opening page, declaring: "The distinctive sounds of the Self-Help Clinic are the clicking of speculums, the buzzing of several conversations and intermittent choruses of laughter. An air of discovery and adventure exhilarate most women in the Self-Help Clinic."[58] As the books proceed, readers are instructed how to perform self-examination through written texts and illustrations.

In line with their emphasis on *seeing,* neither *New View* nor *Stay Out* opens with images of the clitoris—the organ that dominates many radical feminist responses to the psycho-medical context of the time.[59] Instead they visually introduce readers to the speculum and the cervix. In *New View,* for example, one sees an illustrated image of slightly bent knees with a hand inserting a speculum into a vagina; then, in an adjacent image, the hand has opened the speculum to allow for a clear view of the cervix. These images are supplemented by step-by-step instructions for vaginal and cervical self-examination.[60] The viewer's attention is directed to the hands, speculum, labia, and cervix by their placement in the central portion of the image. The outer edges contain little detail, while an exceptional amount of visual texture, detail, and shading added to the hands, speculum, labia, and cervix draw the viewer's gaze to the center of the image. Although, in the case of the first image, the self-examining woman would not be able to see her cervix (the speculum is closed), the cervix is visible to the reader of the book, reminding us that its image is the visual goal of the exam. The importance of seeing the cervix is reiterated in the third image of the text, which contains probably one of the most literal manifestations of a "new view"—an illustration of a cervix as seen through a mirror. In this image, an ambiguously (un)attached arm reaches from the bottom of the page and holds a mirror close to the open speculum. This image interpellates the viewer as the self-examiner (or, at the very least, invites readers to view the cervix from the perspective of a self-examiner). When the three opening images of *New View* are read together, then, the importance of seeing the *cervix* via *self-examination* becomes clear.[61]

This last point is crucial, as it highlights the kind of critique and advocacy deployed by the FFWHC. Initiating a look at one of the most difficult to access, yet viewable, of women's sexed organs, the FFWHC not only makes present what is seemingly hidden but also does so in a way that is meant to aid in the production of knowledge of women's bodies from a woman's perspective. Certainly, self-examination was important for the women's health movement more broadly. For example, the extremely popular *Our Bodies, Ourselves,* by the Boston Women's Health Book Collective, images self-examination without a speculum, in which a woman uses a mirror to examine her vulva. It is important to note, however, that the FFWHC consistently uses the speculum (a tool of the medical establishment), not the hand mirror, as an emblem for its claims. This is evidenced not only in the books from the FFWHC, but also in an often reprinted 1973 image from an L.A. group of Wonder Woman wielding a speculum and exclaiming: "With my speculum, I am strong. I can fight."[62] The varying emphases on the speculum and mirror are characteristics that perhaps aptly distinguish the differences between the Boston collective's advocacy and that of the FFWHC, for the latter is much more likely to highlight the crucial importance of cervical and vaginal self-examination for individual women and the movement as a whole, confronting the visual politics of the psycho-medical context more directly.

Indeed, in both books, the FFWHC authors claim that the information being relayed resulted from careful scrutiny of medical texts and scholarship as well as from their work in self-help clinics and self-examination. Like other radical feminist groups of the time and New Left groups more broadly, the FFWHC implies that practice precedes consciousness. In order to gain a level of knowledge that is necessary for women's liberation, women must engage in certain practices, in this case self-examination. Without self-examination, a "new view" of women's bodies and women's health care cannot be attained. So although the reclamation of the clitoris took center stage in many feminist critiques, any reclamation of sexed-female anatomy for the FFWHC had to be preceded by self-examination. As the authors explain: "We looked at anatomical drawings then looked at our own vulvas and clitorises to check Masters and Johnson's validity. In the process, we surprised ourselves by coming to some new conclusions. . . . We realized while doing this research that we needed to redefine the clitoris."[63] For self-help practitioners, *seeing* sex was necessary to set women on a new path to understanding their own bodies. And indeed, that is precisely what both *New View* and *Stay Out* offer their readers—a novel visual encounter with female-sexed anatomy. This visual encounter, composed of a myriad of pencil-drawn illustrations and photographic images, highlights what had been learned through self-examination and feminist principles of self-help. Countering ideas that women's sexual anatomy is lacking, hidden, and/or pathological, these texts enable readers to see women's sexed anatomy as varied, complex, and visible. They also present women as active subjects of desire and participants in their own and others' health care, countering the gendered attribute of hidden genitalia—feminine passivity.

Women's Bodies Amplified

Readers of *New View* and *Stay Out* will find it difficult, if not impossible, to avoid images of sexed-female anatomy. Of the eighty images in *Stay Out,* for example, forty-nine feature sexed-female anatomy. In *New View* the visual presentation is even more intense, with 210 images, 182 of which feature sexed-female anatomy and/or physiology. This preponderance of images evidences the importance of sight in these texts. And, more specifically, the fact that the large majority of images highlight sexed-female anatomy and physiology suggests that these texts offer and even promote an extensive and sustained visual engagement with the sexed body. Perhaps when one considers feminist concerns that female anatomy is often hidden and/or "shrouded in mystery," this onslaught of sexed-female anatomy can be described as a strategic use of *amplification.*

Amplification, generally described as a linguistic device that serves to "emphasize . . . a particular point," in this case is one that magnifies, proliferates, expands, and enumerates an object visually and discursively.[64] In so doing, amplification in these texts renders female anatomy as *present,* offering a literally expansive view of female anatomy. In fact, there are at least three strategies of amplification observable in these texts. The first, as I have just described it, is one of proliferation, exposing the viewer to many images of female-sexed anatomy and physiological products (e.g., fertile mucus). By imaging anatomy and physiological products, the FFWHC visually bombards readers, attempting to remove both a material and an ideological veil that cover sexed-female bodies.

The second strategy of amplification is one of enumeration, whereby structures of female anatomy are listed and expanded, making such anatomy seem much more complex than had been previously thought. Titled "The Clitoris: A Feminist Perspective," the third chapter of *New View*, for example, announces that it will challenge some common assumptions about the clitoris. Opening with a brief discussion of Masters and Johnson's research, this chapter discusses the problems with earlier illustrations of the clitoris, the myth of the vaginal orgasm, and the process by which the authors attained a new perspective: "As feminists we wanted to remedy the neglect of women's sexuality and the misdirection of the interests of physicians and sex researchers. As part of a study with this purpose, we took off our pants and . . . using self-examination, personal observation and meticulous analysis, we arrived at *a new view of the clitoris.*"[65] Whereas the clitoris had often been viewed as a miniature penis, this *new view* of the clitoris depicts it as a much more complex organ, functioning quite differently from a penis. Images of the clitoris in both books illustrate what is made clear in the adjacent written text: that although the clitoris had been traditionally defined as only the glans and shaft, it is, according to the FFWHC, composed of the "inner lips, hood, glans, and shaft, legs (or crura), muscles, various erectile bodies, including the bulbs, the urethral sponge, the perineal sponge, suspensory ligament, and the hymen."[66]

In *Stay Out,* furthermore, viewers are introduced to the clitoris through images before encountering any textual descriptions. This introduction consists of three frontal views of the clitoris, two of which show cutaway cross-sections. Each image contains labels of structures, including but not limited to hood, frenulum, inner lip, hymen, fourchette, urethra, glans, perineal sponge, etc. The authors use boldfaced type to mark those structures they consider parts of the clitoris. Of the thirty-one different structures identified, twenty-five are marked as clitoral.[67] Similarly, *New View* emphasizes the complexity of women's reproductive systems with its "view of the uterus," labeling "Artery and vein of the ovarian ligament, Internal iliac vein and artery, Ureter, Round ligament, Cardinal ligament of the uterus, Uterine vein and artery, Pudendal vein and artery of the clitoris, Clitoral opening to the vagina, Vaginal canal, Vaginal walls, Cervix, Uterosacral ligament of the uterus, Fundus of the uterus, [and] Uterus."[68] By enumerating and sometimes multiplying the number of structures and components of sexed-female anatomy, these texts offer a distinctly and uniquely expanded view of female-sexed anatomical structures—an amplification in both sheer number and quality.

In marked contrast to its amplification of female anatomy, the FFWHC illustrates sexed-male anatomy in a comparatively simplistic, almost muted way. *Stay Out* does not image the penis at all. *New View,* however, does image the penis three different times, presumably going against reader expectations for a book committed to imaging women's bodies. In two of the three illustrations the penis appears in sharp contrast with the illustrated female anatomy. Lacking the complexity of the book's depiction of female anatomy, two of the images in *New View* do not label even one complementary or essential structure of the penis. In a third image, the viewer is introduced to seven anatomical structures, none of which is labeled "penis." If in Freudianism the visual encounter with the penis signifies male authority and activity and female passivity and envy, here we get quite the opposite. This plethora of images of female anatomy made visible and complex signifies anything but lack—a visual encounter punctuated by the images of an apparently simplified (and lacking) phallus.

The third strategy of amplification in the texts is one that expands through diversification. Not only are women's organs re-imaged over and over again and in ways that mark their complexity, but also they are imaged as ones that (1) change over the course of a woman's life, (2) change throughout a woman's monthly cycle, and (3) normally vary among women. In the chapter on the clitoris in *New View,* for example, readers see a series of pencil-drawn images of the clitoris, illustrating the visible changes in the glans during sexual arousal. Additionally, throughout *Stay Out,* readers are introduced to a number of photographs and pencil-drawn images of cervixes that highlight typical physiological variations. Such variations include "cervix with fertile mucus," "cervix during menstruation," "cervix with white secretion," "irritation on the cervix from an IUD string," and "cervical cysts."[69] The most sustained example of diversification, however, appears in an eight-page section of color photographs of healthy vulvas, clitorises, and cervixes in *New View.*[70] In the authors' terms, the photographic images represent an impressively wide cross-section of female genitalia, and in doing so they depict "the incredible variety of healthy women's genitals."[71] Here readers see a diversity of textures, colors, sizes, and shapes of labia, urethras, clitorises, and cervixes, and learn that these variations may be due to a number of experiences, including childbirth, abortion, infection, surgeries, and menstrual cycles. For instance, in one of the twenty-four images of cervixes, the authors write: "This woman, age 29, is on day 17 of her cycle. She has one child and has had one abortion. She uses the diaphragm for birth control and has not had sex recently. She thinks that the whitish, bubbly secretion on and around her cervix is possibly from a slight bacterial infection."[72]

These eight pages amplify female anatomy and physiology in a way that highlights experience and personal history, but without directly tying any experience to particular viewable variations. Indeed, although the authors attach a brief notation to each image containing information with some kind of "bearing on [the] woman's condition," particular variations within the image are rarely connected to the "relevant" information in any explicit way.[73] Below one of the first images, for example, the authors write: "This 29-year-old woman's lips are a rosy pink color and flare out widely. Her glans is clearly visible at the top and the clitoral opening to the vagina opens slightly. She has had one birth and one abortion."[74] This brief yet detailed description of the photograph leaves ambiguous the connection of the described features to the experiences of the woman. Is there a correlation, for instance, between rosy coloration and age? Or between childbirth and the flaring out of the "lips"? In another image, the label highlights that a particular nearly hairless vulva is that of an "Asian woman" who is "32 years old and has had two children." While the description also directs the viewer's attention to the "slightly grainy texture" of the vulva, readers are not told how to relate the biographical information to the emphasized visual variation.[75] By offering "relevant" biographical information that does not directly explain differences, the authors challenge the idea that women are all the same by focusing on diversification, not explanation. The visual and discursive encounter works, then, to celebrate difference, not to establish causality.

The effect of this diversification goes beyond amplification for the sake of magnification, expansion, and/or proliferation, as it seems to counter and resist attempts to standardize women's bodies. In fact, while the authors of New View emphasize the remarkable scope they are able to provide in the full-color images, they also note that it would be impossible to depict *fully* the healthy variations of female genitalia.[76] Moreover, in the text accompanying images of the clitoris, they argue that "self-help research has shown that many women's clitorises do not look a great deal like standard anatomy-book illustrations."[77] This kind of amplification strategy—one that highlights variation seemingly for the sake of diversity—does not offer readers a one-size-fits-all template of health or pathology. Instead, these images with accompanying text amplify variation without defined boundaries, infinitely widening the scope of what is considered "healthy" and "normal." And since both texts present images of health that far surpass in number and quality those of pathology, the images in these texts contingently fix women in terms of health and variation, not pathology and standardization.

When taken together, these three visual amplifications—(1) a proliferation of sexed-female anatomy, (2) an expansion of structures associated with sexed-female genitalia, and (3) a diversification of healthy vulvas, clitorises, and cervixes—counter dominant views of female anatomy as hidden, lacking, and pathological. Indeed, *Stay Out* and *New View,* far from being catalogues of pathology and lack, proliferate images of female bodies that are healthy, complex, and visible without the intervention of medical practitioners. By making female anatomy visually *present* as well as normally unique, feminists intervene in psycho-medical contexts in a way that does not challenge the predominance of the visual so much as it supplants the problematic imagery with a vision that literally made observable a new view of sex.

A fine line seems to separate this feminist visual amplification from what some may perceive as a visual assault of female anatomy which occurs in both popular mass-mediated and psycho-medical contexts. But while readers of these texts are offered visions of sexed-female anatomy in a new context, one could also argue that visual bombardment with vulvas and breasts is more indicative of the status quo than radically resistant to it. Although I think this question is important, and indeed maybe even central to an evaluative critique of the FFWHC's public discourse, I also find it important to consider fully the variation and nuance of the images promoted by the FFWHC and the ways it proactively resists visually reducing women to sexual and sexed objects. It did so by instructing readers not merely *what* to see but *how* to see.

Sexed Subjects

As a radical feminist method of personal health care, political analysis, and liberation, self-examination and self-help are irreducible to any particular individual or self. As previously discussed, the purpose of self-examination was not personal discovery, nor was it exclusively to produce an individual visual encounter with sex. The visual product, though celebrated and even reproduced in the FFWHC's texts, was not the primary goal of self-examination. Rather, self-examination was very much process, not product, oriented so that the act was as important as (if not more so than) any particular image the act produced. Put simply, it was acts of *seeing with* other women that laid the groundwork for a more liberated orientation within the patriarchal status quo more broadly, and the male-dominated health care system specifically. Seeing one's own characteristically distinct cervix was just a bonus.

The written discourse in these texts emphasizes the importance of the act of self-examination in a sustained and consistent way. By reminding readers that the information being offered in each chapter is a result of work in self-help / self-examination groups and also by directing readers to use self-examination as part of their regular health care routine, each text highlights the processual aspects of self-help / self-examination. Typical of these texts, the propositional advocacy of process orientation is buttressed by a sustained visual strategy. Visually emphasizing a *process* can be a tricky endeavor, yet the FFWHC accomplishes as much by (1) using visual cues to frame all images in terms of the process of self-examination, (2) imaging female anatomy and physiology in ways that emphasize collective self-help and Feminist Women's Health Clinic contexts, and (3) depicting participants as active, not static or passive observers, in self-examination scenes.

The most often repeated image in the first pages of both *New View* and *Stay Out* is that of the speculum. As discussed earlier, the only image on the cover of *Stay Out* is that of a hand holding a speculum in a way that a self-examiner, not a gynecologist, would position the device before insertion. Although *New View* offers images of sexed anatomy and physiology on its cover, readers open the text and immediately see the same hand-holding-speculum image that adorns the cover of *Stay Out,* this time encapsulated in the astrological Venus symbol, commonly used as the symbol for "woman" or "female." The speculum is in fact featured in the first eight images in *New View* and the first four in *Stay Out.* The visual repetition of the speculum as used in self-examination works with its placement at the beginning of these texts as a framing strategy for the images that follow. Put simply, through this emphasis on the self-examining speculum, viewers are reminded of a process, even as they are introduced to one of the productive aspects of the self-examination—an image of the cervix.

The repetition of the speculum, however positioned, would not suffice as a cogent strategy of process emphasis. Indeed the FFWHC does not rely on this framing to highlight visually the importance of self-examination. The most sustained strategy of process emphasis is one in which the texts explicitly present images of female anatomy in collective self-examining contexts. This strategy plainly directs the viewer to *look with* not *look at* women. In *Stay Out,* for example, the opening chapter begins with a pencil-drawn image of "a Self-Help Group sharing vaginal self-examination."[78] Later in this text we see a number of photographs of women performing breast exams and cervical self-examinations in well-woman group clinic contexts.[79] *New View* deploys a similar strategy, adding to these views of group self-examination contexts images of groups participating as self-helpers in menstrual extraction and abortion.[80] As a result, viewers are themselves invited to participate in a collective visual engagement of sexed-female anatomy, looking with others, not simply at a sex(ed) object.

Finally, the FFWHC sustains the *looking with* motif by highlighting the participation of the examined person as an active participant in the visual and medical endeavor. In particular, a number of illustrations in these texts depict a woman examining her own cervix, clitoris, and/or vagina,[81] performing a breast self-exam,[82] stretching and massaging herself,[83] inserting a diaphragm,[84] and helping with her own menstrual extraction and/or pap smear.[85] In a series of images unique to *New View*, readers are introduced to pencil-drawn images of the various stages of arousal of the clitoris. In this series of images, a woman's hands are in clear view in each stage and are the only apparent source of arousal—as is made explicit in the textual description of these images.[86] The images, combined with their textual description, invite the viewer to see not just a clitoris but a "woman" who is actively stimulating her clitoris.[87]

The clitoral-arousal image series in *New View* is indicative of a common feature of these texts whereby the FFWHC uses images of hands to remind the viewer of the viewed woman's participation in the visual encounter. This use of hands, as opposed to images of fully embodied women, allows for a focus on the sexed anatomy while also suggesting activity on the part of the image's subject. In many images, for example, a woman's hands pull back and spread skin in order to give the viewer a clearer view of the focal point of the image.[88] In others, hands are used to signify the viewed woman's or multiple women's participation in the visual and health care practice.[89] Rather than positioning the woman as the passive object of a gaze, the book invites us to *look with* an active examining participant. *Stay Out* goes so far as to punctuate comically how *looking with* disrupts the male-dominated health care system. A cartoon that appears late in the book shows a woman lifting up a typical gynecological exam sheet. The male gynecologist at the other end of the exam table jumps back in bewildered surprise, and even chagrin, at the sight of the woman lifting the veiling sheet.[90] "A-Ha," reads the caption, again reiterating the liberatory importance of self-examination.

While the texts do contain a number of images of disembodied sexed anatomy, the repeated emphasis on examinations and procedures conducted in group contexts, combined with the reiteration of the viewed subject's active participation in the visual and medical encounter, works productively to frame all the images in terms of the crucial importance of self-examination, not objectified sex. Rather than being interpellated as unseen voyeurs of sexed-female anatomy, readers of these texts are acknowledged and invited to be participants in the encounter. Such a move positions the viewer and the viewed as active subjects of the observation, not passive objects of a medical gaze. Quite literally we see what the subject of the image *enables* us to see, positioning the self-examiner / self-examined as the primary agent of and within the encounter. When viewers are invited to *look with,* they too are positioned as active participants, liberated from passive acceptance of a male-dominated view and firmly implicated as interlocutors in a visual interaction.

Revisions or Reiterations?

My suggestion that the FFWHC's rhetoric promotes visual interactions, not objectification, may be an overly generous one. Similar visual conventions are apparent in pornographic photos, for example, in which the photo's subject participates in the visual encounter by stimulating her clitoris, spreading her labia, or initiating an inviting look at the viewer. Clearly, however, the various ways pornography constructs its *voyeur* as a heterosexual male contrast sharply with the interpellated *viewer* of/in feminist self-help practices. Nevertheless, the evaluative question of the FFWHC's sex intervention as one that reaffirms the importance of visual encounters with sexed anatomy remains a significant one. Rather than asking the question exclusively in terms of these images' similarity to pornographic visions, we must consider how these rhetorics respond to the psycho-medical context that I discussed in the opening pages of this chapter. More specifically, inasmuch as the visual encounters promoted by the FFWHC privilege activity (over passivity), presence (over lack), and health (over pathology), do they risk also reiterating the dichotomies of a phallic economy? Put another way, does the FFWHC simply phallicize woman, amplifying and inverting the rhetorical conventions through which women as sexed humans are devalued and demeaned?

These questions are ones that have been asked, in different ways, of other feminist interventions into the representational practices of sexed-female anatomy. From the art installations of Judy Chicago and Georgia O'Keeffe to the performances of Annie Sprinkle and Eve Ensler, all of which make (symbols of) female anatomy present in a variety of ways, critics have asked if these so-called revisions are more akin to repetitions of the problem rather than serious challenges to oppressive sex systems. In particular, the work of Annie Sprinkle, who is a self-identified porn star, prostitute rights activist, and performance artist, offers a more recent example of a visual encounter with sex that parallels the conventions of feminist self-help discourse. Sprin-

kle, in her show *Public Cervix Announcement,* inserts a speculum into her vagina and invites audience members to view her self-acclaimed beautiful cervix. In many ways Sprinkle's performance is not so unlike the demonstration
of Carol Downer (and self-help activists) in the 1970s, a point that Kapsalis
emphasizes. What makes Sprinkle's performance unique, however, is that it
explicitly promotes aesthetic, pornographic, and medical visions of the cervix. As a result, Kapsalis asks. "Is Sprinkle hopelessly replicating norms or is
she creating something new by chipping away at pornographic and medical representational structures, while simultaneously adopting them in her
performance of cervical display?"[91] Kapsalis does not answer this evaluative
question, instead leaving open the question of the revolutionary potential of
Sprinkle's act.[92]

Leaving the question of efficacy unanswered is an important move for
many reasons. It reminds us that rhetorical interventions into sex systems
work in a myriad of laudable as well as questionable ways. To discount the
FFWHC movement as a naïve reiteration of the foundational terms of Freudianism, for example, is also to discredit the ways this movement helped influence positive changes in women's health care. Conversely, it seems equally
problematic to allow any celebration of the positive effects of these practices
and rhetorics to overdetermine our understanding of how the FFWHC amplified and resisted modes of sexual differentiation in psycho-medical contexts. Pitting the material effects (better health care) against conceptual ones
(phallic logics), and vice versa, sidesteps any effort to consider how sex and
difference function within feminism. Feminists respond to and amplify various contexts—immediate and enduring, material and ideal. The matters of
sex and difference are always already discursive and material; they are at once
constituted by and irreducible to either bodies or rhetorics. Thus, evaluative
questions of sex and feminism, in this case the FFWHC, must be careful not
to privilege one over the other.

Perhaps the rhetorics of the FFWHC productively obscure questions of
sex difference and feminism in ways that highlight a more expansive view of
the matters of sex. There seems to be an astute awareness of mechanisms and
forms of the materialization of sex that circulates in the FFWHC's discourse.
This discourse intervenes not only in *what* sex has become in the 1960s psycho-medical context (female passivity and pathology, for example) but also
in *how* sex materializes in visual encounters with anatomy and descriptions
thereof. *How* and *what* one sees function in FFWHC rhetoric in constitutive
ways, enabling the matters of sex to exceed the body proper to encompass

the conditions through which that body is experienced, encountered, and visually engaged. According to the FFWHC, in other words, the materiality of sex cannot be wholly reduced to biological, psychological, or physiological attributes, for the matter that is understood as sex is inextricable from the literal and figurative perspective offered by various practices, traditions, and contexts.

This reading of the visual rhetorics of the FFWHC evidences a tradition of questioning sex and articulating an expansive view of its materiality not simply as a philosophical exercise but as a response to the practical concerns of movements. Indeed, just as the rhetoric of Cady Stanton reminds us of the importance of understanding feminist movements' historical participation in abstract epistemic shifts and enduring philosophical questions, the FF-WHC's rhetoric reminds us that readings which highlight the most conceptual of interventions—in this case expanding an understanding of the materiality of sex to include (among other things) visual practices—must keep in mind those movements' immediate practical goals. It is likely, in other words, that the FFWHC's aim of creating a better model of health care for women inspired its conceptual challenge to sex-making practices, not vice versa.

Indeed, it's the FFWHC's primary commitment to women's (reproductive) health care which suggests that with all of its revolutionary potential—conceptual and practical—the FFWHC was firmly committed to the sexed-female subject, albeit differently understood. While we may say, then, that the FFWHC's rhetoric posits an expansive view of the materiality of sex in ways that question the necessary facts of sex difference in the 1960s, and possibly even the fact of sex difference at all, we must also say that these same rhetorics disable questions of sex, too, by insisting on a newly identified sexed-female as the more authentic representation of woman. This is the perplexing paradox hinted at in my introductory remarks: Is there a feminist legacy of identity commitments that insists on sex's questionability and facticity simultaneously? And if so, how ought we to frame the stakes of these commitments for not only how we understand (and evaluate) feminist history but also how we think about feminism's future? Are/were these commitments necessary in order for feminism to address the material forms of oppression that women (however conceived) face every day? Or do/did they hopelessly eclipse feminism's potentially productive obfuscation of sex-as-we-know-it?

4

Sexing Woman

LESBIAN IDENTIFICATIONS, MEDIA, AND "SECOND WAVE" FEMINISM

THE MATTERS OF sex differentiation, according to *Merriam-Webster's Dictionary,* are undoubtedly tied to the characteristics of *two* forms of individuals—female or male—and those characteristics are inextricably intertwined with the act of reproduction:

¹**sex** (\'seks\) *noun*
1: either of the two major forms of individuals that occur in many species and that are distinguished respectively as female or male especially on the basis of their reproductive organs and structures
2: the sum of the structural, functional, and behavioral characteristics of organisms that are involved in reproduction marked by the union of gametes and that distinguish males and females
3 a: sexually motivated phenomena or behavior b: sexual intercourse
4: genitalia

²**sex** *transitive verb*
1: to identify the sex of <*sex* newborn chicks>
2 a: to increase the sexual appeal of—often used with *up* b: to arouse the sexual desires of

Sex, it seems, is never just about one's genitals; what one *does* with one's genitals is of constitutive importance. As succinct as it is clear, the *Merriam-Webster's* definition is indicative of a now familiar critique of heteronormativity and its relationship to systems of sex difference: "the regime of heterosexuality operates to circumscribe and contour the 'materiality' of sex."[1] *Merriam-Webster's,* however, also calls one's attention to sex-as-action. And as a verb, the act of sexing is transitive, most often engaging in identification of another. I cannot sex. I can, however, sex Sally. This identificatory process is normative and productive, a making of identities that are doubly sexed—male-female, man-woman, and *hetero*sexual. Perhaps the transitive verb *sexing* reminds us to consider carefully the stakes of feminism's engagements with sex as ones that act; ones that sex people. While one could look at just about any moment in feminist rhetorical history to examine this kind of sexing, conflicts over sexuality among many feminists in the 1960s and 1970s crystallize dimensions of the various relationships among identity politics, sex, and sexuality more clearly than any other.

In her book *Desiring Revolution,* Jane Gerhard argues that from the late 1960s through the 1970s, sexuality and sexual pleasure mattered to feminism in a way that it hadn't before: "Sex was at the center of women's impending liberation." Thus, "sexuality mattered," according to Gerhard, "because feminists saw it as the raw material out of which standards of womanhood were forged."[2] For these feminists, certain sexual practices reinforced oppressive ideals of "normal" womanhood. Some radical feminists, like those of Cell 16, for example, advocated celibacy. In the group's appropriately titled publication *No More Fun and Games,* Roxanne Dunbar called for women's "liberation from sexuality," proclaiming that for many women, sex meant "brutalization, rape, submission, someone having power over them, [and/or] another baby to care for and support."[3] And although Dunbar's denunciation of sexuality appears to be aimed primarily at heterosexual practices, she and other members of Cell 16 also criticized lesbian sexuality as a merely "personal" solution to the problem of male oppression. "What I want to do is get women out of bed," Dunbar reportedly declared. "Women can love each other but they don't have to sleep together."[4] Even Ti Grace-Atkinson, who would later be credited with the famous axiom "Feminism is the theory, lesbianism the practice," argued in the late 1960s that the problem of lesbian sexuality, like that of heterosexuality, was one of ideology because "sex 'as a social act' [reinforced] male dominance and female subordination."[5] Gerhard describes the discourse of this time best: "Conflicts over sexuality for many women—about what they wanted from sex, about what they had learned about themselves (and men) by learning about sex, about what counted as 'real' sex—lay the groundwork for what would become their feminism."[6] As a result, the experience of being one of the two sexes had everything to do with the sex one was (or was not) having sex with.

Undoubtedly these early discussions of sexuality played a pivotal role in a rhetorical scene in which one of the most divisive conflicts in feminist history erupted: the "gay/straight split." This split, characterized most succinctly by Betty Friedan's infamous identification of lesbians as the movement's "lavender menace" and the group Radicalesbians' articulation of lesbians as the only truly liberated women, was deeply enmeshed in battles over identity—the movement's public identity as well as the identity commitment(s) of the movement itself. As liberal feminism strove for mainstream acceptance of feminists and women, radical feminists became increasingly committed to maintaining a revolutionary alternative to mainstream structures, values, and systems.[7] As a result, lesbianism became a divisive issue, in which liberal groups downplayed any public link between lesbian sexuality and the movement in order to preserve the movement's credibility, while the more radical activists championed lesbian acts as necessary to a gender revolution. Whether perceived as malignant or liberatory, lesbian identity, and thus sex(uality), became a site of constitutive contestation for both liberal and radical feminists—a site where the making of sex was undoubtedly tied to the making of feminism itself.

In the preceding chapters I explored some of the remarkably inventive and reiterative ways feminists engaged layered sex contexts. In each of those cases my aim was more critically descriptive than evaluative, as I focused (though not exclusively so) on how feminists engaged external movement factors. Here I shift to a more evaluative position in order to accentuate the mechanisms and consequences of sex differentiation and identification. By looking at internal movement struggles, as well as the media context through which these struggles emerged, I examine the stakes of feminism's commitment to strategic and sexed identifications. In this chapter, then, I offer a narrative of a feminist conflict over lesbian sexuality as that conflict engaged and was constructed within the mainstream and alternative press. In their attempts to challenge and amplify the *hetero*sexing of women, feminists also contained and domesticated *woman* to a predefined and predetermined locale, an identity "home" that disciplined the very people feminism sought to liberate.

Liberal Feminism and Credible Sex

Originally conceived of as a sort of NAACP for women, the National Organization for Women (NOW) was primarily focused on gaining meaningful political advances in the mainstream public domain.[8] NOW's first actions, for example, were aimed at ensuring the federal enforcement of Title VII, at gaining ratification of the Equal Rights Amendment (ERA), and at securing a woman's right to an abortion.[9] The organization considered mainstream public support necessary in order to achieve these goals. As a result, some members of NOW, like Betty Friedan, expressed a good deal of concern over the impact of lesbian members on the movement's image, a concern directly tied to NOW's strategy regarding mainstream media.[10] Patricia Bradley argues that press attention to the movement "was the penultimate political tactic" for NOW, and most of its actions had a media component.[11] NOW led picketing of newspapers that published sex-segregated help-wanted ads, for example, in ways that garnered attention from local news outlets, and this media attention aided in NOW's successful campaign (and lawsuit) toward a government ban of those advertisements.[12] Although the profoundly influential role of the mass media in the construction of the movement's public identity can hardly be denied, the "media pragmatism" approach of NOW, as Bernadette Barker-Plummer notes, was tied to NOW's anti-lesbian reputation: fearful that the presence of lesbians within the movement would cause "image problems," Friedan and her supporters turned away from the "personal politics" that until then had been "the hallmark of the feminist movement."[13]

Consider, for example, that in 1968 the San Francisco chapter of NOW accepted lesbian couple Del Martin and Phyllis Lyon at the reduced couple rate. Such a move appeared to be consistent with a rejection of heterosexist bias in favor of legitimate partnerships and supportive of lesbian membership.[14] Many events that followed, however, provided substantial evidence of NOW's increasingly anti-lesbian position. In 1969 the Daughters of Bilitis (founded by Martin and Lyon as the first lesbian organization) was omitted from a press release listing sponsors of the First Congress to Unite Women.[15] Following that event, Rita Mae Brown, who, more than anyone else, had been attempting to bring lesbian issues to NOW's attention, was fired as the editor of New York NOW's newsletter.[16] Late in 1969 Friedan spoke of the dangers of lesbian identifications to the movement at a meeting of NOW's executive board. Friedan continued her crusade and in 1970 led efforts to defeat a NOW resolution supporting lesbian rights, arguing that lesbians were a "lavender menace" to the movement.[17] Friedan's warnings resulted in NOW's first lesbian purge, which consisted of three events: Rita Mae Brown, as I mentioned, was fired and left NOW to join the radical feminist group the Redstockings; Ivy Bottini proposed a "sexual privacy" amendment to NOW's bill of rights at an executive board meeting but was forced to withdraw it because the board did not want to go on record either for or against it; and Dolores Alexander was fired from NOW's executive board on the basis of Friedan's fear that she might be a lesbian infiltrator, despite the fact that Alexander, at the time, self-identified as heterosexual.[18] By the end of 1970, Kate Millett, who once had been hailed by the mainstream press as the "Mao Tse-Tung of Women's Liberation," had been outed to the mainstream public by *Time* magazine in an effort to discredit the movement.[19] Millett's anointment as a "leader" by the media and her subsequent outing seemed to confirm Friedan's fear, as Millett literally provided the face for Friedan's dreaded "lavender menace."[20] In her later reflections on this time, Friedan claimed that her disavowal of lesbians was born not from homophobia but from political necessity, and such a claim, in theory, resonates with the understanding of liberal feminism's position on equality and legal reform that I have just described.[21] Put another way, NOW was committed to containing any potential political threat that lesbians posed to the movement's public identity.

NOW's strategy backfired, however, only exacerbating internal movement conflicts. These made for good copy and were covered extensively in the mainstream press. NOW's attempt to define the movement's public identity and contain the threat posed by lesbians to that identity, in other words, not only was largely unsuccessful but also helped realize its own fears. Indeed, a closer look at contemporary press coverage reveals that Friedan, more often than not, authored the "lesbian threat" more consistently than any mainstream commentator. Quite the opposite of containment, Friedan's and others' identification of lesbians as a menace to NOW only amplified in the mainstream press the role and influence that lesbian identity exercised within the movement.

Lavender Herrings and Menaces

Writing in the *New York Times Magazine,* Susan Brownmiller summed up the relationship between lesbian and feminist politics in one notorious phrase: "Each time a man sloughs off the women's movement with the comment, 'They're nothing but a bunch of lesbians and frustrated bitches,' we quiver with collective rage. How can such a charge be answered in rational terms? It cannot be. (The supersensitivity of the movement to the lesbian issue, and the existence of a few militant lesbians within the movement once prompted Friedan herself to grouse about 'the lavender menace' that was threatening to warp the image of women's rights. A lavender *herring,* perhaps, but surely no clear and present danger)."[22] While Brownmiller asserted that lesbians posed "no clear and present danger," others continued to warn of their overwhelmingly threatening influence.[23] Retorting that the movement did not need a "sexual *red herring*" as a diversion, Friedan herself argued that "trying to equate lesbianism with the women's liberation movement is playing into the hands of the enemy."[24]

Although Friedan's comment seems to indicate that some outside force was authoring the feminism = lesbianism equation, it was, more often than not, feminists themselves who unwittingly authorized the idea that lesbians were both present in and disruptive to the movement. The mainstream press seemed almost reluctant to let commentators outside the movement declare a lesbian political influence. In fact, media commentators explicitly "disclaimed" any idea that the movement consisted largely of lesbians.[25] Meanwhile, Friedan blamed the external backlash on the inclusion of sexual politics in radical feminist critiques (such as Kate Millett's *Sexual Politics*).[26] The focus on sexual politics had detracted from the movement's "real goals," according to Friedan. In a letter to the editor of the *New York Times Magazine,* she urged feminists to "join with the men we can now know and love as friends as well as lovers."[27] As if that was not enough, Friedan published an even lengthier assault in the *Times Magazine* on March 4, 1973. This attack, far more scathing than her previous remarks, attributes the Lavender Menace (later to be known as Radicalesbians) "zap action" at the Second Congress to Unite Women to the "man-hating faction" of the movement, and expresses astonishment and disdain that "lesbians were *organizing* to take over NOW."[28] Consistently referring to lesbians as "man-haters" and "disrupters" of the feminist movement, Friedan charged: "The man-haters are given publicity far out of proportion to their numbers in the movement because of the media's hunger for sensationalism. . . . Many women in the movement go through a temporary period of great hostility to men when they first become conscious of their situation, but when they start acting to change their situation, they outgrow what I call the pseudoradical infantilism. But that man-hating rhetoric increasingly disturbs most women in the movement, in addition to the women it keeps out of the movement."[29] Although Friedan accused the mainstream press of capitalizing on the "sensationalism" provided by lesbians within the movement, her own comments were much more insidious than any reports in the print press. As Robin Morgan put it in her response to Friedan, "[her comments make] one wonder who indeed is behind this manufactured news event, first attempted when Friedan attacked [Bella] Abzug and [Gloria] Steinem in (fittingly) McCall's; *in whose interest is it to set well-known figures of the Movement at one another's public throats?*"[30]

In this brief account of Morgan's response, I begin to show how the threat of a lesbian takeover seems to have been the result of both the paranoid rhetoric of some feminists and Friedan's efforts to purge the movement of a lesbian influence. In her *New York Times Magazine* article, Friedan indirectly accuses the CIA of using radical and lesbian women to infiltrate the movement. After labeling Ti-Grace Atkinson one of the radical disrupters, Friedan confesses: "I never told anyone, but very early, Ti-Grace Atkinson took me to lunch in Philadelphia with the wife of a top C.I.A. official, who offered to help us. I told Ti-Grace we didn't want the help from the C.I.A. Sometime in 1968, we heard that 200 women had been trained by the F.B.I. or the C.I.A. to infiltrate the women's movement—as is known was done by the F.B.I. in the student and radical movements."[31] Friedan also pushes readers to interpret the "zap action" at the Second Congress to Unite Women as a conspiracy, writing, "But after the man-hating faction broke up the second Congress to Unite Women with hate talk, and even violence, I heard a young radical say, 'If I were an agent of the C.I.A. and wanted to disrupt this movement, that's just what I would do.'"[32] The construction of lesbian politics as a danger to the movement is taken to a new level in these remarks. Lesbians are seen not just as a growing menace to the movement's public identity but as a damaging conspiratorial influence, one *intentionally* designed to discredit the movement.

Not surprisingly, feminists responded to Friedan's article through a series of letters to the editor. Although in one letter Pauli Murray of the ACLU supported Friedan, claiming that "her fear is realistic," adding, "Women, being one half of the human race, are a broad spectrum of humanity of which those who have preference for one's own sex are only a minority," the rest of the responses attempted to undermine Friedan's position as a feminist spokeswoman.[33] Robin Morgan, for example, argued:

> It is, after all *women* that the Feminist movement is all about: lesbians *and* heterosexuals *and* celibate women, mothers and nuns, welfare clients, housewives, students, factory workers, secretaries, women of all races and classes. . . . We will not be divided by irrelevancies, nor exploited or defamed by any individual woman's pitiable obsession for male acceptance in the U.S. Senate. . . . If the eminent sister would remain at all relevant she should recall these words of Gandhi: "There go my people: I must hurry and catch up with them, for I am their leader."[34]

Morgan's comments were further supported by Ginny Vida and Jean O'Leary's cry that "as lesbians and feminists, we deplore Betty Friedan's article. . . . [Lesbian] voices will not be stilled by the fearful words of a sister whom the 'sex role revolution' has left behind,"[35] and Mim Kelber's call to feminists to "dissociate ourselves from [Friedan's] 'leadership.' "[36]

More prominent and visible feminists like Jill Johnston accused Friedan of "woman-hating" and "dyke-baiting."[37] Similarly, Ti-Grace Atkinson wrote that she was "stunned and outraged by Betty Friedan's smear article,"[38] just as Toni Carabillo insisted that "no group or agency has 'taken over' NOW" and that Friedan's version of the history of the movement was inaccurate.[39] Friedan's response to these attacks?

> I do not find truth in the man-hating rhetoric of sex-class warfare which Ti-Grace Atkinson and Jill Johnston and Robin Morgan continue to promulgate and which I will continue to fight. I believe this anti-man note is a sexual red herring and basically irrelevant and even inimical to our movement. . . . I respect the rights and sexual differences of my lesbian sisters even if their way is not mine and I will fight anyone who attempts to persecute them, but black women and housewives as well as men have been unnecessarily alienated by the man-hating rhetoric.[40]

The significance of this exchange in the *New York Times Magazine* cannot be underestimated, as Betty Friedan had already secured her place as an authoritative figurehead for the movement in the mainstream press. Susan Douglas notes that before the media elevated Gloria Steinem to that position in 1971, Friedan received most of the media's attention. As the author of the germinal book *The Feminine Mystique* and the founder and former president of NOW, Friedan was hardly denied "legitimate authority" by the press, as evidenced by her proclaimed status as the "mother," "high priestess," "spiritual leader," and "founder" of the women's movement.[41] Since Friedan's role as the leader of the women's movement was rarely questioned in the mainstream press, her ability to define her constituency rhetorically, and to deny lesbian feminists any claim to be representatives of *"real"* feminist goals, assuredly worked with a substantial rhetorical force. Moreover, thanks to the responses to Friedan's article in *New York Times Magazine,* which called further attention to lesbians' role in the movement, Friedan's fear of an identification of lesbians with feminism became a self-fulfilling prophecy. That is, goaded into reacting to her homophobic denigration of lesbians in the women's movement, lesbian feminists and their supporters made the importance of lesbian politics to the movement even more visible than it was before. Liberal feminists may have strategized to promote the movement's credibility and mainstream palatability, but such efforts were, at the very least, compromised by their own fear that lesbians were incommensurate with this strategy.

Pragmatic Containments?

I find it useful to consider Friedan's attempt to manage lesbian identifications in the mainstream press as one motivated by the rhetorical possibilities of *containment*. Containment rhetorics often aim to tame a potential threat to hegemonic culture and/or the norms of the status quo. Karin Vasby Anderson offers an interesting consideration of the relationship between containment rhetorics and gender, analyzing the ways "bitch" functions as a tool of sexual containment in mainstream discourse about women.[42] Containment rhetorics, we learn from Anderson, tame the threat of "powerful" women through discipline and confinement, clearly articulating that certain women are outside the dominant values and structures of U.S. culture. Such a normative move has been a persistent mode of expression in U.S. mainstream political discourse.

Strategies of containment, however, are not so much a U.S. rhetorical invention as they are an ongoing hegemonic response to acts of resistance. Although John Murphy does not use the term "containment," his analysis of the 1961 civil rights Freedom Rides teaches us that hegemonic forces often domesticate and accommodate dissent by articulating resistance in terms of dominant systems of meaning.[43] Building from the work of Antonio Gramsci, Murphy argues that hegemonic culture's relationship to social agitation can be described as a dynamic and responsive one, resulting in a negotiation of various identifications and visions. As he remarks, "What is interesting to the rhetorician are the strategies used within the negotiation," and more specifically, "Of prime interest to critics of hegemony . . . are not the strategies used by opponents, but rather the symbolic means to bring recalcitrant rhetors 'into the fold.' "[44] In the case of the Freedom Rides, he finds that the press and the Kennedy administration "domesticated" the dissent by redirecting the agitators' energy into a much more palatable and culture-affirming activity: voter registration. In other words, the potential for the emergence of radical critique was confined in terms of what would reinforce the most fundamental institutions and assumptions of the status quo. Again, while Murphy does not define "domestication" explicitly, the strategy emerges in his essay as one that has a remarkably similar operational goal to that of rhetorics of containment—to strengthen the status quo, minimizing the damage that alternative rhetorics and/or social dissent could inflict on dominant values and meanings. Moreover, both rhetorics of containment and domestication mark aberrant behaviors, ideals, and actions as such, explicitly separating such behaviors, ideals, and actions from the norms of the status quo.

Anderson's and Murphy's analyses shed light on how we might begin to (re)consider Friedan's rhetoric as well as contexts in which containment rhetorics circulate. Put simply, hegemonic mainstream culture may not be exclusively responsible for disciplinary rhetorics of containment. Whether they express the competing claims of other social movements, dissent within the movement, mainstream norms, the status quo, or any other mechanism of hegemonic culture that threatens the movement's goals, social agitators may also have a stake in containing the threat of other rhetorics in order to preserve the rhetorical force and terms of the movement's own critique. Remarkably, such critiques are not directed outward toward the other so much as they are directed inward to mitigate a supposed threat. Arguably, then, Friedan's rhetoric is suggestive of one motivated by a desire to contain a perceived threat. Rather than directing attention to outside forces, Friedan homes in on the perceived "disruptors," "infiltrators," and "menaces" within the movement itself. Simply put, Friedan's containment rhetoric is recursive, turning back on portions of the very constituency ("women" and "feminists") whose interests she claimed to champion.

Interestingly, while turning against others in the movement was problematic in an abstract ethical sense, it was also disruptive to the movement's material goals. As Douglas notes:

> Even if most women *did* want a liberation movement, its success was doomed, according to news accounts, because women were constitutionally incapable of cooperating with one another. Certainly there were real divisions within what was broadly termed the media reinforced stereotype that women were completely incompetent as politicians, tacticians, and organizers and had proved, once again, that they didn't deserve to be active anywhere but in the kitchen, the bedroom, and the nursery. . . . The media representation of feminism reinforced the division between the acceptable and the deviant, between the refined and the grotesque, between deserving ladies and disorderly dogs.[45]

In this respect Friedan was right. Lesbian politics threatened the movement's credibility, but primarily because she and others made lesbian sexuality such a visibly divisive issue. If Douglas's remarks are correct, what Friedan and others did not foresee is that their own attempts to silence and dismiss lesbians within the movement compelled a construction of the movement's public identity that denied the credibility of any woman. In other words, when one considers that the mainstream press's representations of the relationship between lesbian and feminist politics were couched in liberal feminism's public constructions of lesbians as lavender menaces and lavender herrings, what becomes evident is that lesbians themselves did not prove to be the "disruptors" of the movement. Fears of their influence, however, did. The pragmatically motivated strategy of containment functioned as anything but; rather than mitigating the lesbian–equals–feminist movement identification, Friedan's containment strategy only amplified the link between lesbian sexuality and feminism. She was not the only one to use lesbian sexuality as a conduit for disciplinary actions against members of the movement, however. Radical feminists also confined their feminist sisters, this time in terms of taming the threat of mainstream values and the status quo.

Radical Feminism, Liberation, and Sex

The interaction of the mainstream media and women's movements during feminism's "second wave" was a tenuous one at best. Media conventions not only nullified NOW's attempt to control its own image but also undermined radical feminism's dedication to a nonhierarchical social alternative. Radical feminism, or the Women's Liberation Movement / Women's Liberation Front (WLM/WLF), was largely born from a larger radical movement consisting of the New Left, antiwar, and civil rights movements.[46] Radical feminists were not interested in playing by the terms set out by mainstream politics. As a result, they were less concerned with issues of mainstream appeal, were adamantly against having public spokeswomen (in their terms, perceived "leaders"), and feared that the mainstream press itself perpetuated less than ideal social relationships. In fact, radical feminist groups emphasized the importance of breaking away from status quo structures, relationships, and norms in order to offer a more politically pure alternative. To accomplish this goal, many radical feminist groups enforced a number of rules on group members, which ranged from the kinds of relationships one was allowed to have with men (and sometimes women) to the relationship one could have with the mainstream press. Consequently, when certain radical feminists "cooperated" with mainstream media, they were disciplined. Ti-Grace Atkinson, for example, was kicked out of the group she had founded because of her participation in the mainstream press.

Simply put, as "media subversives," radical feminists did not develop strategies to work within mainstream media. Instead, they formed their own alternative media as an answer to the problems of the status quo. As the editorial in the first edition of *Ain't I a Woman?* stated: "There are special reasons . . . why we needed a paper for and by women. . . . We want new structures that do not allow people to fall into leader/follower, boss/worker, power-ful/powerless roles. We don't want to work in any situation in which we are oppressed or in any situation in which we do oppress."[47] With more than 560 radical feminist publications circulating between 1968 and 1973, radical feminists were able to establish crucial links between groups and devise al-ternative media conventions (e.g., collective editing and authorship) to align internal movement structures with their radical vision.[48]

Not surprisingly, lesbian identity and sexual practices, like media protocols, also provided a site for radical feminists to rearticulate their commitments to self-definition and revolution. Unlike those of liberal feminism, however, the commitments of radical feminism had nothing to do with defining the move-ment within the mainstream press. Radical feminists' conceptualization of self-definition was articulated, like their commitment to liberation, against the status quo / mainstream—against male definition / domination / identifi-cation. And while the development of a feminist alternative press was based in these commitments, the importance of self-definition was not confined to radical feminist media politics. Indeed, self-definition became a founda-tional concept for the movement and the identities contained therein.

For example, in a 1970 number of *It Ain't Me Babe,* Barbara Burris argued: "There can be no sexual revolution until there is *first* of all a successful wom-an's revolution in which women free themselves from male definitions and domination in *all* areas of society. . . . [W]omen's liberation can *not* be defined by men. Women have been defined and dehumanized by men for thousands of years. The women's liberation movement is a movement in which *women define themselves.*"[49] As the WLM became more and more committed to no-tions of self-definition, Brown critiqued anti-lesbian sentiment within the movement by equating it with male-definition: "To ignore the issue of women loving other women, to lable [*sic*] it lesbianism and divisive, is to turn around and define me and all my sisters in the same manner in which women are defined by men, by my sexual activity and function."[50] Of course, both radical and liberal feminism placed an importance on self-definition to guide their media and sexual politics. Founded on different needs and goals, however, radical and liberal feminism's desires for self-definition dictated entirely diver-gent relationships when it came to lesbian identification. In the case of radical feminism, lesbian identity, like radical feminism's alternative press, become yet another way to secure a politically pure position outside the status quo. By 1970, radical feminism's term for this pure position or identification was the "woman-identified-woman," and it provoked and grounded some of the most disciplinary modes of containment of feminist movements of the time.

"Woman identification" entered radical/lesbian feminist discourse in May 1970 with the presentation of the position paper "W-I-W" at the Second Congress to Unite Women. The essay was reprinted several times in radical feminist journals, including germinal publications like *RAT, Ain't I a Woman?*, and *Notes from the Third Year*. Some publications accompanied the essay with descriptions of the zap action and personal testaments to the importance of woman identification for the movement.[51] On the one hand, some women were dismissed as being too "man-identified," and bisexual women specifically were criticized by questions such as "How does [a bisexual] become woman-identified?"[52] Certain feminists like Rita Mae Brown, on the other hand, were praised as being "woman-identified," and *Ain't I a Woman?* was commended as being "more woman-identified than any other" publication.[53] "W-I-W" as Helen Tate puts it, "provided a rhetorical site of revolutionary identity, a constitutive rhetoric marked with the telos of liberation from male tyranny," positioning "lesbian feminists at the center of feminist identity."[54]

"W-I-W" articulated this revolutionary identity through juxtaposition and ambiguity. The paper defines the woman-identified woman through a discussion of her oppressed opposite, the male-defined woman, and in so doing adopts a mode of articulation characteristic of Kenneth Burke's notion that the rhetoric of identification requires division and difference. In fact, "W-I-W" never makes explicit that "lesbian" marks true woman identification. The paper, however, worked implicitly toward that end by juxtaposing lesbians' *real* solidarity with the "basic heterosexual structure that binds [women] in one-to-one relationships with [their] oppressors." In the end, it is no surprise to read that "only women can give each other a new sense of self" and that "with that real self . . . [feminists] can begin a revolution to end the imposition of all coercive identifications and to achieve maximum autonomy in human expression."[55] As a founding principle of both the radical/lesbian feminist press and its discourse, woman identification attempted nothing short of constituting a new notion of *woman,* as well as a new space for women to exist—a structural alternative. Its continual reiteration was necessary both to secure it as a grounding standard and to fine-tune its interpellative call.

When the Personal Is Political

In the years that followed the presentation of "W-I-W," radical/lesbian feminists reiterated its original juxtaposition of male identification and woman identification in such a way that the call to become a self-identified *lesbian* was made explicit. Cathy Nelson, in *Lavender Woman*, argued that "straight society sees a woman as a mere extention [*sic*] of the male ego,"[56] and

Charlotte Bunch, in *The Furies,* warned that by making "women define themselves through men," heterosexuality "separates women from each other."[57] As Jill Johnston put it, "Living with men is an act of collaboration and women must withdraw their energies from men and give all their commitment to women. . . . Political philosophy means total commitment, you can't split yourself."[58] And if heterosexuality threatened women's commitment, radical/lesbian feminists charged that lesbian identity was the best way to confront male domination, arguing, for example, that "lesbianism threatens male supremacy at its core," that "to be gay implies imminent defeat of the heterosexual standard controlled by men for their self interest," and that "gay is twice as good as straight."[59]

To *be* gay, to *be* woman-identified, however, became a site of reinterpretation. The emphasis in "W-I-W" on political *consciousness* risked divorcing lesbian sexual acts from those acts' presumed consciousness effects (i.e., authentic existence). According to Tate, woman identification allowed lesbian feminists to expand "the meaning of 'lesbian' to include all women who identify with women as a class, *regardless of sexual orientation.*"[60] As a result, some feminists claimed that they were woman-identified and even "political lesbians" although they continued to have sexual relationships with men. The immediate legacy of woman identification, however, was not so sexually open, as claims of political lesbianism, like claims of bisexuality, were continually marked as suspect. For example, one feminist wrote, "It is not good enough for straight women to say they do love women and then turn to give their ultimate love to their oppressor."[61] Indeed, while bisexual woman was accused of "functioning under her oppressor's definition of herself,"[62] self-proclaimed "political lesbians" were not only stripped of their "lesbian" status but also, in the case of Robin Morgan, indicted for using political lesbianism to secure a leadership position in the movement.[63] Clearly, political lesbianism divorced from lesbian sexual encounters posed a threat to radical visions that from the outset were presented as an authentic alternative to the expulsion and degradation of lesbians in the movement. Again, in an ironic twist, the very discourse that had once responded to the ways liberal feminism and the mainstream press sought to contain the threat posed by lesbians and radical women now itself began to facilitate another mode of containment, confining liberation, women, lesbians, and feminists to a predetermined locale, a distinct identity.

In a move seemingly compelled by the apparent gaps in the ambiguous conceptualization in "W-I-W" of a consciousness not necessarily wedded to particular acts, radical/lesbian feminists now rearticulated woman identification in terms of the importance of political consciousness tied to certain lesbian (sexual) practices.[64] Stating the demands directly, Francis Chapman wrote in *off our backs*: "Radicalesbian demands are: leave men, including your male children, become a lesbian, live with women, preferably in a women's commune, understand that sexism is the root cause of all the world's ills and that the hope of the planet is a woman's revolution, and devote all your energies to women, in an extreme form, to lesbians alone. Radicalesbians hope to persuade 'straight' women to become lesbians and lesbians to a radical political position."[65] As I will further substantiate, lesbian acts, in and of themselves, were the necessary beginnings of a revolutionary consciousness. Radical/lesbian feminists reasserted the importance of a particular identity, which must be inhabited through daily practices, revealed by personal sexual commitments, and imbued with political sensibilities; this identity was the foundation and enactment of women's liberation.

Rita Mae Brown situated the locus of a revolutionary consciousness within a particular identity when she claimed that "before there was WLM there were always a number of women who questioned the system and found it destructive to themselves. Those women became women-identified. I am one of those women. The male culture's world for this kind of woman is Lesbian."[66] Similarly, in *Ain't I a Woman?* a lesbian within the movement wrote about her inherent woman identification: "Every time someone asks me to explain what a woman identified woman is, I can't. And yet it is very clear to me what it means in personal actions and political ones. About this time I realized that I have been woman identified for just about all of my life and so I guess it's not so strange that it would be something that I would know inside and find it hard to explain."[67] Embedded in personal experiences, which are necessarily woman-identified, radical/lesbian feminists wed a lesbian identity, expressed through regular embodied practices, with political consciousness. And when lesbian status was referred to as the only identity able to divorce itself from oppressive male identifications—a woman-identified identity—radical/lesbian feminists tied the very possibility of social change to an authentic being.

The drive toward authenticity can be traced directly back to "W-I-W" proper, where Radicalesbians make explicit the importance of liberation (absolute autonomy) to authenticity. The escape from male identifications was necessary, according to Radicalesbians, because women could never *be* for themselves, *be* woman-identified, in male-defined social structures.

> To be a woman who belongs to no man is to be invisible, pathetic, inauthentic, unreal. . . . As long as we are dependent on male culture for this definition, for

this approval, we cannot be free. The consequence of internalizing this role is an enormous reservoir of self-hate. . . . As the source of self-hate and the lack of real self are rooted in our male-given identity, we must create a new sense of self. As long as we cling to the idea of "being a woman," we will sense some conflict with that incipient self, that sense of I, that sense of a whole person.[68]

Since inauthenticity was a direct result of male identifications, the potential of the real self could be developed only through woman identification. By positing woman identification as a real, authentic self, "W-I-W" presumably suggests that authenticity is possible only when one is "freed" from male domination.

At first glance it seems that notions of authenticity via woman identification relied on an explicit exclusion of heterosexual women. Radical/lesbian feminists, however, formulated a much more fluid conceptualization of sexual identity, arguing that within every woman was a lesbian. Martha Shelley, for example, argued that "straight women fear lesbians because of the lesbian inside of them, because we represent the alternative."[69] Similarly, Brown claimed that any "woman can confront the issue of Lesbianism because she has the potential to be a Lesbian,"[70] and Loretta Ulmschneider argued, "Lesbians represent that part of every woman that male supremacy has destroyed and suppressed."[71] When coupled with arguments suggesting that lesbianism was a political necessity, the conceptualization of all women's inherent lesbianism reveals a clear link between identity and social change: women's authentic self was rooted in their lesbian sexuality, and since that authentic self was the foundation for revolutionary social change, women should identify as lesbians—both in practice and in their own consciousness. *Being* lesbian was not merely an identity necessary to secure a revolutionary force; it was the identity of the revolution's goal—liberation. In this way, political consciousness, invariably tied to a lesbian identity, structured the collapse of the political into the very *being* of the personal.

On one level, this structural collapse can easily be understood in terms of feminism's familiar adage, "the personal is political." Initially developed through consciousness-raising groups, radical feminism used "the personal is political" as a way to theorize the private sphere—the sphere "left untouched by liberal political theory"—as in fact political, public, and "riddled with power relations."[72] This supposed expansion of the political realm into the personal would presumably allow the collective sharing of women's personal experiences to yield directions for political action. Charlotte Bunch, in her own expression of radical/lesbian feminism, evidenced the radical commitment to the expansion of the political when she argued that lesbian feminism "[is] a notion of a consciousness and community which is political, *not just personal.*"[73] Despite Bunch's attempt to suggest otherwise, by collapsing the political into the very *being* of the personal, radical/lesbian feminists inadvertently revised radical feminism's fundamental adage in a way that confined liberation to a particular identity. Since this authentic identity could be achieved only through certain practices imbued with a political consciousness, radical/lesbian feminists constructed their own version of a lifestyle feminism. In a real sense, "feminist politics [became] feminist *identity.*"[74] The "entire success of the revolution," one feminist wrote in an article titled "Lesbian Demands," depended on "woman freeing herself of all crippling male identities and realizing the strength that is found in solidarity with her sisters."[75]

The ironic twist to this collapse of the political into the personal is that it once again contained *lesbian* and *woman* in order to meet the movement's demands. For Friedan, containing the lesbian threat entailed public denunciations of lesbians and their concerns. For radical/lesbian feminists, the threat posed by the status quo, liberal feminism, bisexuals, mainstream media, etc. offered not an opportunity to tame the other but an occasion to discipline the self further. When viewed as overlapping components of a larger rhetorical operation, the circulation of woman identification's reiterations within a stratum of media which itself constructed its own distinct rules of appropriate (read: liberatory) response and action, and the further confinement of women's liberation to personalized political identities, work hand in hand to strengthen the disciplinary force of self-containment. This reflexive strategy of containment, evidenced further by the ways radical/lesbian feminism sought to curb the influence of the impure other (all that is male-identified) by turning its rhetoric inwards, continually re-marked the boundaries of its own so-called liberatory goal. This strategy of reflexive containment might be better labeled a strategy of domestication. As the next section illustrates, not only did radical/lesbian feminists localize the political in predetermined identities and media, but also they defined liberation within the confines of an all too familiar location for women: the home.

Liberation Begins at Home

As the historical relegation of women to the private sphere has proved to be a formidable barrier for woman's/women's rights activists for over a century, the rhetorical importance of "home" in feminist rhetorics probably goes without saying. One might assume, for instance, that "home" for radical/ lesbian feminists would be identified primarily as the place of male identification and oppression. Indeed, there is some evidence for this assumption. Consider, for example, the ways in which radical/lesbian feminists further elaborated the claim made by "W-I-W" that "heterosexual structures" in the home bind women to male domination. Arguing that women should consider how living with men affected their personal lives, Martha Shelley wrote: "The lesbian, through her ability to obtain love and sexual satisfaction from other women, is freed of dependence on men for love, sex, and money. She does not have to do menial chores for them (at least at home), nor cater to their egos, nor submit to hasty and inept sexual encounters."[76] Similarly, others argued that a "woman who continues to relate to men has men in her home whom she may have to fear," and "although the lesbian like other women is oppressed by America's political structures . . . she does not have an individual 'oppressor' in her home."[77] While some simply asked women to consider the dangers of having men in their homes, others charged that heterosexual women who refused to leave men were taking advantage of the heterosexual privileges granted to them through male identification.[78]

A closer look into the radical/lesbian use of "home," however, highlights a much more complex use of the term, as it signified a place of both oppression and liberation. These woman-identified rhetorics contained liberation within distinct boundaries, as "home" functioned to domesticate politics and identities in particular ways. Mongoose, in her article "Liberation Begins at Home," expressed concern that feminists "can sit at a meeting and then go somewhere and allow ourselves to be oppressed by a male," observing "We are living examples of liberation that has not yet begun at home."[79] Similarly, Jill Johnston argued, "You can't fight the revolution from nine to five and then go home to a man."[80] These excerpts highlight a second, and possibly more important, function of "home" for radical/lesbian feminist discourse: to reinforce the collapse of the political into the personal, symbolically conjuring a personal place for political action.

Consider, for example, how the use of "house," like "home," seems to reinforce boundaries between man and woman identification. One author claimed that since she was a lesbian, she did not have to "deal with male chauvinism in [her] house."[81] Additionally, in *The Purple Star*, feminists argued that "since we were in an SDS collective and believed our personal and political lives should come together, we thought of living in a house with people we were working with would be important."[82] By positing that living in the same house represents the union of the personal with the political, they project a need to ground political action in personal living arrangements. Although in both of these instances the house is a literal and physical structure, Brown's use of "house" is meant more symbolically, to describe the movement itself: "Lesbianism will provide us with the individual and group skills for constructive confrontation for struggle, for progress. In other words, we need a foundation to build our house upon and this issue gives us our ideological and technical foundation."[83] Assuredly, Brown's description of lesbianism as the foundation on which to build the movement's "house" works consistently with that of others who argued that joining the group Radicalesbians meant not that they could finally come out in the movement but that they could "come home."[84]

At first glance, it may seem surprising that radical/lesbian feminists would, at times, rely on "home" metaphors to discuss women's liberation, and that they continued to contain liberation by strengthening its borders. More than ironic, it may appear that radical feminists, like the status quo, found it difficult to *identify* women outside of the home. This is precisely the predicament of identity commitments. To identify is not only to confine but also to "thematize differences . . . in terms of (the impossibility of their) sameness."[85] Identity, to put it another way, always depends on recognizability and/or intelligibility. The danger of politics premised on such recognizability is that conditions of possibility are eclipsed by whatever the status quo allows to emerge. On the one hand, while not particularly inventive, the use of "home" and "house" conjured a recognizable place—a woman's sphere of influence—that historically had been distinguished from the male public sphere. On the other hand, "home" worked paradoxically, as radical/lesbian feminists sought not only to challenge notions of woman bound to the home but also to identify a recognizable locale for the supposed liberated woman's birth. Most important, however, "home" may have worked in conjunction with woman identification to limit the possibilities of change, rhetorically and materially, to what was known in advance. By attempting to identify the conditions of social change at the outset, woman identification contained woman's liberation to an already established horizon of possibilities, to what was imaginable—to, merely, a new home.

Indeed, new "homes" were imagined and inhabited when radical/lesbian feminists turned to literal and figurative separation from the movement and the status quo. In a way that paralleled their exodus from the mainstream and New Left press, some radical/lesbian feminists by 1972 had begun to advocate separatism as a viable strategy for the movement and certain women within it. An editorial in *The Furies* declared:

> Separatism is a necessary strategy if women wish to become a political force with a power base strong enough to challenge male power. Women must stop nurturing individual men and feeding the institution of heterosexuality. That energy must be given to other women in order that we stop identifying with a male identity and become that political force with a female identity. To implement these women-identified politics we have, as Lesbian/Feminists, found it necessary to build our own movement and to develop a Lesbian/Feminist ideology. We have separated from the Women's Liberation movement which lacked a comprehensive analysis of sexism. It failed to create that analysis because it could not identify heterosexuality as one of the keys to male supremacy.[86]

Although this separatism took many forms, including radical/lesbian feminist collective living arrangements, it, in whatever form, contained women's liberation within very distinct boundaries, literal and figurative.

When it became apparent that separatism was a short-lived experiment (many separatist collectives survived for only a number of months), some radical/lesbian feminists began to publish their own reflections on the limitations of separatist practice.[87] Yet the grounds on which separatism was critiqued continued to reiterate a collapse of the personal into the political. Amidst feminist warnings that "to consider alliances without a clear basis for allying and to consider alliances with men before separatism has even been made a strong political force is crazy,"[88] Charlotte Bunch, in particular, sought to point out the dangers of the "purity" associated with separatism:

> Reasons for separatism are still valid. Increased consciousness about oppression through separatism developed strength and clarity among women in many ways. It has freed us from much dependence on men and helped us to start breaking the hierarchies of oppression and privilege that keep people in their place. . . . But we [have often slipped] into the purist assumption that if you aren't x, you can't be in our revolution[,] rather than stressing the development of x-consciousness whether you are x or not. . . . To avoid the dead ends of separatist purity, we must act on our belief that revolutionary consciousness is possible among all people.[89]

Bunch's comments seem to reveal a commitment to a revolutionary consciousness, above and beyond personal lifestyle choices; a rhetoric, in other words, that begins to turn away from the constitutive rhetorical wedding of consciousness effects laden with particular actions and practices.

Bunch's supposed critique is recuperated, however, in much the same way that "W-I-W" was so easily reiterated in terms of the necessity of a particular identity. Put simply, a notion of a revolutionary consciousness that is shared among all constituents relies on a faith in an authentic and essential being located outside the realm of male identification. This is why, despite her seeming openness, Bunch could write later: "Lesbian feminist politics is . . . a politics that combines the sexual aspect of lesbianism with a feminist perspective. It defines a certain direction for the future, for the kind of society we want to build."[90] Bringing us back to the importance of lesbian sexuality as the source of woman identification, Bunch and others, in their emphasis on securing a place for women's liberation, rhetorically confined liberated woman within the movement's predefined locales. Thus, these various locales of women's liberation—the home, lesbian / woman-identified identities, the alternative press, separatist communes—not only animate and amplify one another but also reveal a consistent mode of reflexive containment.

Containment and Identification

In *Gender Trouble,* Judith Butler warns of configuring a coalitional movement on an identity decided on at the outset, "because the articulation of an identity within available cultural terms instates a definition that forecloses in advance the emergence of new identity concepts in and through politically engaged actions."[91]Identity political movements are thus prohibitory, demanding that subjects conform to predetermined (recognizable) definitions and, sometimes, politically viable identifications. Butler's observations about the limitations inherent in identity commitments illuminate how feminist attempts to manage and support lesbian sexuality through rhetorics of containment are indicative of feminism's enduring commitment to identification. In the case of lesbian sexuality, feminism's identity commitments of the 1960s and 1970s responded to various threats in ways that limited and/or domesticated the movement's own potential and critique. More specifically, these identifications created disciplinary and bounded locales. These locales normalized and strengthened an apparent and supposed border between palatable feminists and man-haters, as well as between radical authenticity and the status quo. As a result, the commitments of feminism to identity (public and private) eclipsed its obligation to the lived experiences of many who saw themselves as women—credible, authentic, and/or otherwise.

Notably, liberal and radical feminism's varying commitments to identity—both public and personal—reinforced the constitutive link between sexuality and the truth of sex. Whether it be Friedan's dismissal of lesbians' concerns as a central task of the women's movement or some radical feminist groups' championing of lesbian practice as essential to a liberatory consciousness, sexuality circumscribed and contoured the sexed constituency of the movement. Like hegemonic negotiations of social dissent, feminism necessarily, even if unwittingly, engaged in disciplinary processes that limited change to the terms and structures of the status quo. What is at stake in these rhetorics is not simply a replication of any particular exclusionary practice but rather the reiteration of domesticating structures that unduly enclose and contain feminism within particular, currently available possibilities. Any persistent question of sex is circumvented, and the social order of sexed systems is preserved.

While feminism has, then, at some moments, engaged sex as inherently questionable, it also has assumed sexed identity as a necessary given. This compulsion to identify—to maintain itself as an identity-political movement—functions to limit feminism severely to the possibilities that are realizable, knowable, and recognizable by the very terms of the status quo. Put simply, this case of rhetorical containments reveals all too well that in its attempt to open up possibilities for women, feminism risks confining any notion of future possibilities to terms that domesticate and contain feminism from the start.

5

Questionable Engagements

SLUTWALKS AND BEYOND

IN JANUARY 2011 during a presentation about campus safety at York University, a Toronto police officer reportedly claimed that "women should avoid dressing like sluts in order not to be victimized."[1] This remark, characteristic of the way that women are often blamed for the violent acts perpetrated against them, sparked extraordinary controversy in the Toronto community. On April 3, 2011, an estimated three to four thousand people gathered in protest in the city and demanded accountability for the "common, persistent and documented victim-blaming within [Toronto] Police Services."[2] Calling their protest a SlutWalk, organizers sought to reappropriate the term "slut" to mean "someone—anyone—in charge of their own sexuality and unapologetic in the desire for consensual sex."[3] And while "slut" was conceptualized as an "attitude," not a "look," some protesters punctuated their message by wearing provocative, what some would consider "slutty," attire. Whether it be the provocatively dressed protesters, the audacious name, or the surprising turnout, SlutWalk Toronto received a lot of feminist and media attention and sparked a global wave of similar protests. Within less than a year after the Toronto march, an estimated eighty-five or more other affiliated SlutWalks took place in fourteen different countries, including nearly fifty in the United States alone.[4] "What began as reaction to one comment," write SlutWalk Toronto organizers, "a reaction that we had originally imagined only to include a handful of our closest friends, exploded into a movement that we never could have expected."[5]

Often described as a movement that "went viral," SlutWalk received a fair amount of both praise and criticism.[6] Well-known feminists like Jessica

Valenti, Gloria Steinem, and Katha Pollitt celebrated SlutWalks as collective feminist action. In Pollitt's words, "Here at last is that bold, original, do-it-yourself protest movement we've been waiting for, a rock-hard wall of female solidarity—an attack on one is an attack on all!—presented as media-savvy street theatre that connects the personal and the political and is as fresh as the latest political scandal."[7] And while Pollitt and others praised SlutWalk movements, others expressed concerns that ranged from questioning the marches' political efficacy to critiquing the blindness of the movement to issues faced by African American, transgender, Latina, and third-world communities, among others. Rebecca Traister, for example, wrote in the *New York Times*, "At a moment when questions of sex and power, blame and credibility, and gender and justice are so ubiquitous and so urgent, I have mostly felt irritation that stripping down to scivvies and calling ourselves a slut is passing for keen retort."[8] And in more pointed tones one blogger argued: "I do not want white English-speaking Global North women telling Spanish-speaking Global South women to 'reclaim' a word that is foreign to our own vocabulary. . . . We've got our own issues to deal with . . . we do not need to become poster children to try to make you feel better about yours."[9] A celebration of feminist collective action in a new media environment alongside serious questions about the composition of that collective and the methods of its proposed actions is a juxtaposition familiar to anyone who has paid attention to the debates among feminists about the "third wave" over the past twenty years and more. Who are these new feminists? Why do they care so much about sexuality? For what and for whom are they fighting? Will they actually be able to change anything that really matters to women's lives? Indeed, Martha Nussbaum's famous critique of Judith Butler has been rearticulated by some of the critics of SlutWalking: "Feminism demands more. Women deserve better."[10]

In the opening pages of this book, I characterized the resistance to contemporary feminist theory that questions sex as a critique that positioned feminism as a movement that was *necessarily* invested in the *fact of sex*. Arguing that feminism has long questioned sex, I have examined various moments in feminist history which demonstrate that feminists have engaged sex, not simply replicated it. Indeed, the contours of feminism's deepest commitment—the female subject, woman—changed in terms of various exigencies that surface in the movements' immediate and enduring rhetorical contexts. Whether it be Elizabeth Cady Stanton's arguably subtle critique of biological foundationalism or multicultural feminism's demand that we pay attention to various axes of identity and hegemonic relationships, sex, in the actual discursive practices of movements, is far from universal and stable. It is identified, re-identified, differentiated, and recognized variously over time. And while we may say that feminism has long rendered any specific view of sex as questionable, we might also conclude that, at any given moment, feminism operates as if the truth of sex can be known, identified, and recognized. Sojourner Truth *must* be a woman, self-examination offers a better understanding of sexed anatomy, lesbianism guarantees a more authentically sexed experience, and SlutWalks free sexual practices from an often sex-specific condemnation. Perhaps, then, feminism's relationship to sex is best described as deeply paradoxical, as it engages sex as questionable while insisting on its newly identified and recognized facticity. SlutWalk movements and discussions of them highlight this paradoxical relationship with sex in a way that asks us to consider the importance of understanding feminism's history for thinking about contemporary and future feminist practices.

To be more specific, SlutWalks have emerged in a distinctly anxious post-feminist moment with respect to feminism's historical relationship to sex (un)certainty. First, since the rise of multiculturalism in the 1980s, questions consistently surface regarding feminism's commitment to the material needs of women as those needs differ along lines of race, class, sexuality, and nationality. These questions are justified in that some feminist movements have a long history of white middle-class myopia. In response to these well-founded critiques, contemporary feminist movements are being asked to remember that the sexed subject is not just sexed. Second, the scholarly sex revolution of the 1990s made critiques of feminism's historically limited view of sex and its commitment to the sexed-female subject fairly commonplace. Consequently, feminism in recent years has been asked to pay more attention to intersexuality and transgenderism, both of which undermine the sanctity of a purely binary conceptualization of sex/gender difference. Finally, as feminist movements continue to emerge, they do so in a context in which feminism must be marketed, among other things, to counteract beliefs that: (1) the work of feminism is over and equality has been achieved, (2) sex difference does not figure in social practices, and (3) previous instantiations of feminism were antiquated and dogmatic, demanding that women deny their feminine specificity and (hetero)sexual desires. In light of these last concerns, it is not too surprising that, in the words of one 2011 discussion, the "most successful feminist action of the past 20 years" is a march in which activists fight the long-standing problem of sexual assault with a media-savvy strategy, proclaiming themselves not bra-burning prudes but lingerie-clad sluts.[11] Nor is it surprising that in this postfeminist context many ask, "Is this what feminism looks like?"

As one considers this anxious moment as it relates to SlutWalks, it is important to foreground the ways in which the marches and their reception necessarily circulate through memories of feminism. The question of feminism's current commitment to sex, however defined, is mediated in part through how one understands feminism's historical commitment to it. A closer look at SlutWalk discourse reveals quite clearly the movement's attempts to navigate a political context in which questions of sex and difference circulate through multiculturalism, transgenderism, and postfeminism. It also reveals how perceptions of feminism's past operate in public evaluations and judgments of current feminist practice. In this final chapter I explore the traces of these memories in SlutWalk discourse and reflect on what this book envisages as a questionable engagement with feminism's relationship to sex difference.

Before I turn my focus to SlutWalks, it is important to note that this analysis has also developed amidst considerable anxiety about feminism's relationship with sex, difference, and identity. After all, the scholarly sex revolution discussed in the opening pages of this book not only produced substantial attempts that undermined the facticity of sex but also helped spawn numerous critiques that pitted contemporary feminist theory against the materiality of sex and feminist movement activism. As a result, those who wish to consider questions of sex/gender in light of the work of Foucault, Butler, and others do so within a context that often dismisses such questions as purely conceptual and abstract, and in so doing, also damns those who do consider such questions as naïve, ignorant, or contemptuous of the hard, dirty work of real social change. As Carolyn Dever aptly writes: "In a feminist context, to be described as 'abstract' is usually a bad sign. The topic often arises in the charged context of accusation—if not of an outright character flaw, then of the perpetuation of an elitist, exclusionary mode of description, or of the failure to engage fully the matter of social justice."[12] This skeptical posture toward conceptual abstraction emerged in the feminist theories and practices in the 1970s and functions to reassert "the stakes of social change in all its concrete, material, and particular implications."[13] With the specter of being dismissed as abstract looming large, feminist scholars who question feminism and sex take on the responsibility of using these questions to offer something more than an exercise in intellectual prowess. In response to this anxiety, and perhaps even because of it, I attempt to show why questions of sex matter to current feminist practice. Although this project does not offer a political program or template that will guarantee social change, it does develop the value of a *questionable* mode of engagement with feminism—one that asks us to consider that matters of sex and feminism go beyond anatomical distinctions and bodily functions to include the very conditions through which any challenge to sex/gender politics can gain force. These final remarks concretize the stakes of such engagements.

Postfeminism and "Third Wave" Activism

SlutWalks have emerged in what has been described as a "postfeminist" context. "Postfeminism" is a term used variously to describe a historical and ideological moment in U.S. history. Appearing in lay discourse to "refer literally to the moment after feminism, a cultural moment in which feminism is (thought to be) no longer needed," the concept is one that, as Tasha N. Dubriwny writes, many feminist media scholars and social theorists present "as a more complex understanding of what Susan Faludi described as the 'backlash' against feminism."[14] According to many feminist media scholars, "postfeminism" describes a context in which mainstream media culture has subverted the supposed need for feminist political action, in part by implying that sexual equality has been achieved and feminism is thus hopelessly outdated.[15] This subversion of the need for collective political action, in turn, is buttressed by neoliberalism, whereby individualism and consumerism underpin the celebration of so-called liberated women, the choices they are freely able to make, and the products they are apt to purchase.[16] Characters such as Murphy Brown, Ally McBeal, and Carrie Bradshaw exemplify the postfeminist media context in which women's liberation is depicted as achieved, the product of individual choices, and characterized by professional, relational, and economic success. The problem with such formulation, in Bonnie J. Dow's terms, is that it "dismisses the fundamental insight of feminist ideology: Women operate within a sex/gender system that limits acceptable choices."[17]

Indeed, one of the most consistent criticisms of postfeminism is that it depoliticizes feminist critique and women's oppression. Although, as Ann Braithwaite observes some scholars use the terms "postfeminism" and "antifeminism" interchangeably, feminists are often careful to distinguish postfeminism from a simple rejection of feminism.[18] Postfeminism frequently acknowledges the gains of previous feminist generations and at times expresses gratitude for the advancements and achievements in the public sector that resulted from feminist organizing. This appreciation, however, is undermined by the simultaneous denial of the systemic nature of women's continuing subordination.[19] When considering this sometimes confusing celebration of women's empowered choices alongside the dismissal of the need for feminist activism, postfeminism, according to Sarah Projansky, "is by definition contradictory, simultaneously feminist and antifeminist, liberating and repressive, productive and obstructive of progressive political change."[20]

The confusion surrounding postfeminism is not confined to the nature of its supposed contradictory positions in relation to feminist and gender politics. Perhaps most perplexing is the number of phenomena that feminist scholars use the term to describe. Although feminist media scholars are most likely to define postfeminism in terms of a complex backlash against ("second wave") feminist activism that may or may not incorporate aspects of neoliberalism, others use the term variably (and strategically) to refer to a "conservative backlash, Girl Power, third wave feminism and postmodern/poststructuralist feminism."[21] Perhaps a term that is used to describe figures and groups as distinctive as Katie Roiphe and Judith Butler, Lara Croft and Murphy Brown, and the Spice Girls and the Riot Grrrls, suffers from such serious ambiguity that it fails to be useful for contemporary criticism. Such is the position of feminist media critic Susan Douglas, who uses the term "enlightened sexism" to describe how mainstream media capitalizes on feminism, simultaneously denying the need for feminist political action or critique.[22] In her words, postfeminism "has so many definitions that we don't know what [it] mean[s] anymore."[23]

Douglas's replacement of "postfeminism" with "enlightened sexism" to describe a media context that emphasizes individualism, consumerism, and female objectification is motivated in part by a desire to politicize a context that denies the need for collective feminist action. She rejects the term "postfeminism" because it "suggests that feminism is the root of this [media emphasis] when it isn't—it's good, old-fashioned, grade-A sexism that reinforces good, old-fashioned, grade-A patriarchy."[24] Douglas's distinction is an important one, especially when we consider further that contemporary—what some term "third wave"—feminist activity at times becomes conflated with postfeminism.[25] Helene A. Shugart's depiction of third wave feminists exemplifies the extent to which contemporary feminists are viewed as indistinguishable from those so-called postfeminist popular culture icons that have given rise to so many critiques. In what could double as a description of nearly every episode of *Sex and the City,* Shugart writes of "third wave" feminism:

> They are evident everywhere these days, and in no small number—confident, bold young women, self-identified feminists. You might see them at the local cigar bar, as likely to be describing their indignation at not being granted maternity leave as they are to be chastising a female colleague for filing a sexual harassment suit. They're educated, independent, assertive, and, often, unsettlingly conservative. In many respects they're a diverse lot; they are likelier than earlier feminists to count among them different classes, different races, different affectional orientations. . . . [T]hey seem united in their . . . exasperation with "traditional" feminist critiques of "male-defined sexuality" and "sexual objectification."[26]

As products of the postfeminist era, "third wavers acknowledge that they are the beneficiaries of those advances by the second wave," writes Kristy Maddux. "In contrast to their second wave foremothers," she continues, "third wave feminists are less invested in pursuing corporate change and more convinced that change now needs to be made by individuals exercising agency in their own situations."[27]

This bewildering similarity between postfeminism and "third wave" feminism might be best attributed to the fact that contemporary feminist movements emerge in a postfeminist context. This is the relationship that Maddux describes in her discussion of a "postfeminist world."[28] Arguing that the postfeminist "logic of individual empowerment further defines the primary avowed [third wave] feminist activism," Maddux also maintains that it is "postfeminism's vilification of the second wave" that renders unsurprising the attempts of "third wavers" to define themselves against their predecessors.[29] If postfeminism is the era that both proceeds chronologically from and sometimes rejects aspects of "second wave" feminism, then "third wave" feminism is perhaps inextricably defined by this overdetermining context.

The overdetermining features of this context serve as warrants for arguments that mark contemporary feminist activism as lacking. Stacy Gillis observes that "third wave feminism is excoriated by 'real' feminists for its apparent inability to politicise women."[30] Shugart, for example, argues that third wave feminism is not a "contemporary incarnation of feminism" but is best understood as a subculture of Generation X, exemplified in (postfeminist) figures such as Courtney Love and Alanis Morissette.[31] As the feminist literary critic Elaine Showalter puts it: "Third wave feminism is just another way of talking about the contemporary moment rather than calling it postfeminism. Third wave feminism implies a movement. . . . I am very dubious about the existence of a new feminist movement."[32] Although many self-identified third wavers reject any comparison of their advocacy with the tenets of post-feminism—as Rebecca Walker and Shannon Liss succinctly announced at a conference in New York in 1992, *"We are not postfeminist feminists. We are the third wave!"*—there is a perceived similarity between postfeminism and the "third wave" that is often highlighted in contemporary feminist discussions, and the public discourse about SlutWalks is no exception.[33]

Indeed, postfeminism and "third wave" feminism, as juxtaposed to "second wave" feminism, are important components of the rhetorical context from which SlutWalks emerged. If we take seriously the lessons from discussions of postfeminism, SlutWalkers are working against considerable ambivalence about feminist activism. And while supporters of SlutWalks attempt to distance the walks from postfeminism, others use postfeminism as grounds to understand and critique SlutWalks' shortcomings.[34] "Slutwalk is an essentially 'postfeminist' event, masquerading as a revolution," writes radical feminist blogger Ada Farrugia Conroy. "It is an event that assumes there is no patriarchal context . . . there is no subversion. this action is not a threat."[35] Under the heading "Post Feminism" on the blog The F Word, Meghan Murphy laments, "If [SlutWalk] is the future of feminism I am afraid";[36] and in her critique of SlutWalks, Gail Dines proclaims, "Feminism has been hijacked from women."[37] Perhaps what is at stake in the various understandings of postfeminism's relationship with contemporary feminist activism, SlutWalks or otherwise, is nothing less than the constitution of *feminism* itself—how we understand its goals, ideas, constituents, and methods, in short, the grounds on which we can identify and recognize *true* "feminism" at all. Nicole Wilson puts it bluntly: "SlutWalkers are the *real* third-wave feminists! I chide. If the third-wave requires women to conform to a male-directed image to protest about masculine-inflicted pain, that is *not* actually any sort of feminism."[38]

These critiques of "third wave" feminism and SlutWalks reiterate not only the terms through which we understand contemporary contexts and activism but also how we remember and consider feminism's past. I have yet to read an article or a book that attempts to explain what "postfeminism" or "third wave feminism" is without some reference to or description of previous feminist movements, most often the "second wave." For example, Stéphanie Genz and Benjamin A. Brabon's *Postfeminism: Cultural Texts and Theories*—a book committed to demonstrating postfeminism's "compelling and provocative" features—repeatedly juxtaposes post- and "third wave" feminism with "second wave" feminism's "reliance on separatism and collectivism."[39] And Helene A. Shugart, Catherine Egley Waggoner, and D. Lynn O'Brien Hallstein state outright that "so-called third-wave feminism . . . is strikingly different from the second-wave feminism of Gloria Steinem." For example, "third wavers seek to embrace sexual desire and expression, freeing it from . . . what they perceive to be the anti-sex sensibilities of second-wave feminism." Moreover, empowerment for third wavers is not conceptualized in the "collective terms, as with the second wave, but in very individualistic terms."[40] These brief examples underscore particular aspects of "second wave" feminism: its anti-sex stance, its very clear goals, its separatist impulses, and its commitment to collective political struggle.

Anyone who knows much about feminist movement history, including the authors just mentioned, would likely argue that this list of "second wave" feminist features is fair and representative of how the "second wave" is most often perceived; at the same time, however, those characteristics are an oversimplified shorthand for the complex conglomeration of groups, advocacies, goals, and personalities that made up feminist activities of the 1960s and 1970s. While I have no interest in correcting any thumbnail version of the "second wave" here, of central importance to this consideration of SlutWalk discourse is the fact that contemporary feminist activism and its postfeminist cultural context are repeatedly represented in terms of their differences from the features of earlier feminist activity. Indeed, certain features of earlier "waves" of feminism constitute the terms of what feminism is really about, and thus become the criteria for evaluating any current self-identified "feminist" movement's goals, methods, and constituents. The terms we use to frame feminism's past thus have a direct influence on how we discuss, theorize, and evaluate feminism's present and future.

Memories of Sex and Feminism

In discussions about SlutWalks, memories of feminism's past are used both to celebrate and to censure the movement. What is most exciting about Slut-Walks, it seems, is the fact that they use a recognizable method of achieving social change: collective protest that is highly visible and publicized. Emily Nussbaum wrote in *New York Magazine* that SlutWalk NYC reminded her of those "second wave" protests of the late 1960s and 1970s that she had read about: "These events weren't polite demands for legislative change; they were raw and sloppy theatrical displays, ecstatic bonding experiences that managed to be at once satirical and celebratory, alienating and illuminating. Not coincidentally, they were also the kind of protest that was hard to ignore, since they were designed to capture the camera's (and the media's, a.k.a. my) eye. And SlutWalk is more public still: Even as we march, it is being tweeted and filmed and Tumblr'd, a way of alerting the press and a way of bypassing the press."[41] Jessica Valenti made the same comparison in the *Washington Post:* "More than 40 years after feminists tossed their bras and high heels into a trash can at the 1968 Miss America pageant—kicking off the bra-burning myth that will never die—some young women are taking to the streets to protest sexual assault, wearing not much more than what their foremothers once dubbed 'objects of female oppression' in marches called SlutWalks. . . . In a feminist movement that is often fighting simply to hold ground, Slut-Walks stand out as a reminder of feminism's more grass-roots past and point to what the future could look like."[42] The celebration of SlutWalk as grass-roots activism is significant, as it challenges the idea that collective feminist movements are a thing of the past. For some, at least, SlutWalks are refreshing reiterations of those social movement features that make the walks recognizably feminist.[43] Moreover, Valenti's description of SlutWalking warrants a closer look, because embedded within it are assumptions about feminist movements of the sixties and seventies, sex, and feminism that go beyond the celebration of grassroots efforts. Note, for example, that Valenti contrasts the liberatory gestures of earlier feminists who tossed away bras and heels with the practices of SlutWalkers who wear those same "objects of *female* oppression" in their public protest. Such a comparison highlights what is often referred to as the anti-sex, prudish, and even humorless aspects of feminism's past while projecting the sex-positivity of contemporary feminist activism.

In her discussion of SlutWalks, Amanda Marcotte in *Slate* characterizes the current context of feminist activism as one in which "the image of the pinch-mouthed feminist scold telling the fun-loving boys to keep it down has quickly become a dinosaur, replaced now by the image of the knuckle-rapping church ladies telling third-wave feminists to roll up their stockings and tone down the dirty jokes on their ironically named blogs." For Marcotte, SlutWalks demonstrate that "it's the sexists who are clutching their pearls in horror at the lack of ladylike decorum on the left, and the feminists who are embracing nose-thumbing humor as their primary weapon."[44] Others, however, are less enthusiastic about the sex-positivity and absence of prudishness that run through SlutWalks. Noting that the "second wave" was a "collective project of liberation demanding wide-sweeping transformation," radical-lesbian feminist blogger Kathy Miriam writes, "Slutwalk is a Third-wave phenomenon, given that it finds its object of protest not in rape-culture but at best, individual empowerment in the form of sexual and satirical 'self-expression,' and at worst, slut-as-identity." She continues, "Rather than the power relations at stake in victim-blaming and rape," Slut-Walks' main focus becomes the promotion of "some Madison Ave brand of female pleasure and sexuality."[45] From Valenti to Miriam, what is explicitly remembered about feminism in the past is its commitment to collective political action, its systemic analysis of women's oppression, and its wariness of using the so-called master's tools (in this case sexualized expression) to dismantle patriarchal norms and conventions. At stake for this discussion is what is subtly implied in these comparisons about feminist history and sex. Or to be more precise, the question raised here is: If memories about previous waves of feminism circulate in the reception of "third wave" feminist activism, what is remembered and reiterated about feminism's relationship to sex (and) difference?

There seem to be at least two predominant memories about sex, difference, and feminism that move through feminist discussions of SlutWalks. The first is that feminism always has been and continues to be a movement largely, if not exclusively, composed of women committed to helping other women. Valenti, for example, recalls earlier feminists who threw away their bras and heels in an effort to shed those tools of "female" oppression, depicting feminism as concerned primarily with those things that harm female bodies. Meanwhile, those who are critical of the sex-positivity of the "third wave" seem to be concerned with the departure from previous generations' focus on the systemic use of female bodies to render "woman" an object of male desire. Embedded within these memories are reiterations of feminism's historical reluctance to embrace certain forms of female sexual expression as purely liberatory, and its preference for those whose gender identity matched sexed characteristics. For example, Emily Nussbaum, writing about the new media environment through which SlutWalks emerged, argues:

> While seventies feminists had little truck with matrimony, feminist bloggers lobbied for gay marriage. There were deconstructions of modern media sexism, including skeptical responses to the "concern-trolling" of older women who made a living denouncing the "hookup epidemic." There was new terminology: "slut-shaming," "body-snarking," "cisgender." And there were other cultural shifts as well: an acceptance (and sometimes a celebration) of porn, an interest in fashion, and the rise of the transgendered-rights movement, once seen as a threat, now viewed as a crucial part of sexual diversity.[46]

Although I do think that Nussbaum's description of 1970s feminism and the current feminist blogging environment is a fairly accurate one, it risks reinforcing the perception that earlier feminists had a fairly uncomplicated view

of sex difference, and that they simply reiterated the cultural norms of a binary sex/gender system.

The second memory about feminism's past with regard to sex and difference is that white feminists tended to suffer from white middle-class myopia,
attending exclusively to the needs of privileged Anglo women in the United
States. In "An Open Letter from Black Women to the SlutWalk," a number of
women argued:

> As Black women, we do not have the privilege or the space to call ourselves
> "slut" without validating the already historically entrenched ideology and re-
> curring messages about what and who the Black woman is. . . . For us the
> trivialization of rape and the absence of justice are viciously intertwined with
> narratives of sexual surveillance, legal access and availability to our person-
> hood. It is tied to institutionalized ideology about our bodies as sexualized
> objects of property, as spectacles and deviant sexual desire. . . . We know the
> SlutWalk is a call to action and we have heard you. Yet we struggle with the
> decision to answer this call by joining with or supporting something that even
> in name exemplifies the ways in which mainstream women's movements have
> repeatedly excluded Black women even in spaces where our participation is
> most critical.[47]

The issue of whiteness and the movement became even more pronounced
when a young white woman at SlutWalk NYC carried a sign quoting John
Lennon: "Woman is the nigger of the world." In their response to the sign and
other trends in SlutWalk movements, the Crunk Feminist Collective wrote:

> If we thought of the history of feminist movement building as a battle over
> terms, what we found is that every major battle over terms and the rights
> and identities attached to them have always had the same damn problem: the
> racial politics, like the Black women implicated in them, have been fucked.
> "Suffrage" did not include all women. (Just ask Ida B. Wells how she felt
> marching in the back of the 1913 suffrage march.) "Woman" is not a universal
> experience. (Sojourner Truth anyone?) "Nigger" is not a catchall term for op-
> pression. (Ask Pearl Cleage.) Feminism is not a universal organizing category.
> (Ask bell hooks, Audre Lorde, Barbara Smith, Fran Beale, and on and on.)
> And "slut" is not the anchor point of a universal movement around female
> sexuality, no matter how much global resonance it has. (Ask a Hip Hop Gen-
> eration Feminist.)[48]

Both of these examples highlight the naïvely racist assumptions about some
of the terms that circulate in various SlutWalks, and the critiques are punctuated with the reminder that such racism is familiar, a part of the legacy of
many women's movements. Moreover, it is here that some feminists consider
how female identities differ along lines of race, while also reminding readers

that feminist movements have long ignored the fact that race is a difference that matters in the constitution of sex/gender identity.

Looking, then, at feminist responses to SlutWalks, one finds that previous feminist generations are remembered primarily as having had a rather narrow vision of sex/gender difference. Undoubtedly, feminist movements, through both explicit and implicit actions, have excluded many who might self-identify as "woman," socially, biologically, psychologically, or any combination thereof. These critiques of feminism's past are as important and necessary as they are pressing and relevant to how we engage current feminist practices. What is problematic, however, is that these critiques represent the only ways feminism, sex, and difference are remembered in the discourse about SlutWalks. As a result, many of the ways in which SlutWalks, like the actions of other feminist generations, participate in and question political and rhetorical traditions of sex differentiation are largely ignored.

SlutWalks' Questionable Engagement

What is ignored in much current criticism is that SlutWalks emerge not only within the postfeminist context I have described but also within a setting in which various advocacy groups are aiming to proliferate sex/gender categories. With more and more attention being devoted to transgenderism, intersexuality, and queer advocacy in mainstream and academic communities, a simple reiteration of binary sex/gender norms would potentially lose traction among activists. Additionally, SlutWalks' attention to sexual abuse occurs in the wake of recent controversies that center on sex, power, and the abuse of men and boys, not just women and girls. These controversies include the systematic cover-up of recurrent sexual molestation of young boys by Catholic clergy, the sexualized torture and abuse of male prisoners at Abu Ghraib, highly publicized instances in which female secondary school teachers were convicted of rape because of their sexual "relationships" with their young male students, and the sexual assault of men by other men in male-dominated contexts such as prisons and the U.S. military. Indeed, by 2011, in the public's eye the problem of sexual assault and abuse was no longer confined to girls and women.

The increased attention to male survivors of sexual assault is particularly interesting, in light of statistics which show that women and girls are far more likely to be sexually assaulted and abused than men and boys.[49] And while this is not to say that attention should not be paid to male victims, the confluence of high rates of sexual assault against women with increased attention to sexual abuse of men creates a perplexing context for activists fighting sexual violence. First, SlutWalk activists must respond to the need for public recognition of the sexual abuse of men and boys as well as the public's ignorance about the use of power and sexual violence against women and girls. Second, they must contend with a number of rhetorics, described earlier, which suggest that there is no longer any need for feminist activism (as we have typically known it), either because systemic sexism against women is a thing of the past or because feminism has blindly privileged a category that ignores the complexity of identity-based oppression. Arguably, then, while sexual violence is a problem that disproportionately affects those who typically are identified as women, efforts to fight this problem must address the fact that *woman* marks a difference that is irrelevant, outdated, and even dangerously oversimplified.

A quick glance at SlutWalks' promotional discourse reveals a recognition of this situation. If we recall that it was a remark about women's attire that sparked the first protest, it is telling that many of the SlutWalk organizations focus on victim-blaming more broadly and explicitly frame their protest as one for people of "any gender-identification."[50] As the SlutWalk Chicago website declares: "Women are most often the targets and men are most often the perpetrators, but all genders are affected. SlutWalk recognizes all gender expressions as those that have been negatively impacted. *All genders* can be sluts or allies."[51] Similarly, after acknowledging that "slut" is a term most often aimed at women, the organizers of SlutWalk Toronto, for example, describe their movement this way:

> We are a movement demanding that our voices be heard. . . . We want to feel that we will be respected and protected should we ever need them [public authorities], but more importantly, be certain that those charged with our safety have a true understanding of what it is to be a survivor of sexual assault—slut or otherwise. . . . WE ARE COMING TOGETHER. Not only as women, but as people from all gender expressions and orientations, all walks of life, levels of employment and education, all races, ages, abilities, and backgrounds, from all points of this city and elsewhere.[52]

Here, spokespersons for SlutWalk Toronto seem careful to recognize the problem of sexual assault for women while at the same time not let *woman* overdetermine the movement's focus.[53] "People from all gender expressions" will march and are part of the interpellated "we" that defines not only those who are working toward change but also those who are "tired of being oppressed by slut-shaming."[54]

There is, in other words, a clear sense of strategic ambiguity in the manifestos of SlutWalk movements. Does "slut," a recognized slur used against women, function in SlutWalk Toronto's rhetoric to refer to women, or does it refer to any survivor of sexual assault? Some SlutWalks ignored the assumed sexed/gendered specificity of the term and refrained from marking gender in any way. The mission statement for SlutWalk D.C. states: "We are asking you to join us for SlutWalk, to make a unified statement about sexual assault and victims' rights and to demand respect for all. You needn't claim the word slut for yourself; whether a fellow slut or simply an ally, you don't have to wear your sexual proclivities on your sleeve, we just ask that you come. Any gender-identification, any age. Singles, couples, parents, sisters, brothers, children, friends. Come walk of roll or strut or holler or stomp with us."[55] Others acknowledged the assumed sex specificity of the term "slut" but worked implicitly and explicitly to assert that "all genders can be sluts or allies."[56] SlutWalk Lubbock, for instance, claimed that "the word 'slut' is used primarily against women, but men experience shaming in similar ways as well. By using the word 'slut' in the name of our walk, we directly challenge the use of shame as a weapon and 'sluttiness' as a justification of victimization."[57] The ambiguity surrounding the term "slut," its varied uses among SlutWalkers, and its relation to survivors of sexual assault and women may be directly related to the paradoxical rhetorical scene of SlutWalking protests: A context in which sex/gender identities have on occasion proliferated beyond the binary man/woman or male/female and at the same time are undermined as categories that matter (by assertions that we are all equal). A scene that demands recognition of difference (intersections of race, class, sexuality, nation, etc.) and yet yearns for productive coalitions.[58] A situation in which the problem of sexual assault and abuse (and its relevance) traverses sexed and gendered categories but also has different entailments for different communities. Indeed, SlutWalkers face a problem of identity and difference—which differences matter and which do not.

Kenyon Farrow's remarks at SlutWalk NYC in 2011 are emblematic of the struggles over identity and difference that circulate in rhetorics from and about SlutWalk:

> I am a slut. And I have always been a slut. Some of you might find this tongue-in-cheek, or even annoying coming from a male-identified person, right? Because when men call themselves sluts or ho's, or players or whatever, it doesn't carry the same social stigmas that it carries for women, particularly women of color. I understand that. But I am not here to make fun of sexual violence, street harassment or any other form of nonconsensual behavior, often visited on the bodies of women. Nor am I here to try to displace the impact of gen-

dered forms of violence against women, including transgender women, have
to face, by doing what people with whatever relative form of privilege try to
do when they want to justify being in spaces not deemed for them—to claim
that they too, suffer forms of oppression. And then proceed to take over and
displace the most impacted voices. But I am here because . . . I am well aware
of the ways in which I am marked, my gender, the sex I have (or am imagined
to be having), and my physical body, as a problem. . . . I have come to embrace
the fact that yes, I am a slut too.[59]

Farrow's remarks highlight a keen awareness of our current identity-political moment, when attention to differences matters as much as, if not more
than, a shared identity through which disparate groups can build productive coalitions. The very fact that Farrow, a black gay man, was called upon
to speak, however, also directs attention to the way contemporary feminist
sex politics demand that attention be paid to the problems of an expansive
constituency. Indeed, what is most ironic about the SlutWalks is that despite
the presumed sex-specificity of their title, many of the marches explicitly
distanced themselves from an exclusive focus on the sexed and/or (hetero)
sexualized female subject.

The fact that SlutWalks attempted to assert the problem of sexual assault for
women while at the same time expanding their attention beyond the male/fe-
male binary was largely ignored by bloggers and the mainstream press. Those
who celebrated the walks did so on the grounds of what women were doing
for other women—the feminist dream of female solidarity and action. As Valenti wrote: "SlutWalks have cropped up organically, in city after city, fueled by
the raw emotional and political energy of young women. And that's the real
reason SlutWalks have struck me as the future of feminism. . . . One woman's
anger begins online but takes to the street, when a local step makes global
waves and when one feminist action can spark debate, controversy and activism that will have lasting effects on the movement."[60] Similarly, many of those
who criticized SlutWalks' attempt to reclaim "slut" as naïve at best reasserted
the significance of the term for women. Gail Dines and Wendy J. Murphy argued: "Women need to find ways to create their own authentic sexuality, outside of male-defined terms like slut. . . . Women need to take to the streets—
but not for the right to be called 'slut'. Women should be fighting for liberation
from culturally imposed myths about their sexuality that encourage gendered
violence. Our daughters—and our sons—have the right to love in a world
that celebrates equally women's sexual freedom and bodily integrity."[61] The
problem with these comments is that they confine feminism and SlutWalks
to questions of womanhood, not to questions of sex and difference. In other

words, if feminists continue to argue exclusively about the propriety of *women* marching as *sluts* for other women, we miss the opportunity to consider and evaluate SlutWalks' engagement with the relationship between feminism and that sexed subject, and what appears to be feminism's recurring struggle to identify, recognize, and delineate the importance of difference.

In sum, rather than viewing SlutWalk exclusively in terms of a *remembered* feminism's myopic commitment to privileged white women, as we currently understand that identity, we ought to examine SlutWalk discourse as one that struggles with identities and difference, especially as those identifications travel through sexed/gendered categories. When feminism is remembered as a movement for the sexed woman-as-we-know-(have-always-known)-her, SlutWalk advocacy is always already framed and critiqued in terms of this (pre)identified female subject, despite explicit attempts by the movement to broaden feminism's purview. The problem with this framing and understanding of SlutWalks is not that they misidentify the movements' strengths and weaknesses, for critics have highlighted aspects of SlutWalks that ought to be (re)examined; rather, the problem is that these understandings address SlutWalks exclusively in terms of what is remembered as feminism's legacy of engaging the "woman problem," failing to consider its engagement not just with *woman* but with systems of sex, difference, and identity.

Finally, while the reception of SlutWalks clearly shows that memories and histories of feminist movements matter to our understanding of contemporary activism, SlutWalks themselves also remind us that the material manifestations of oppression (in this case sexual violence) and the movements that address these problems cannot be examined some attention paid to discursive systems of identity and difference that shape those material realities. SlutWalks, like those movements that came before them, are enmeshed in the politics of sex differentiation, but the question remaining for feminist critics ought not to be centered on comparing SlutWalks to prevailing understandings of feminist movements of the past, and specifically their relation to sex and difference. Instead, it must take into account a much more varied and complex understanding of feminism's history, considering feminism's relationship with sex difference as fundamentally contingent and rhetorical.

Feminism 's Sex Legacy

I began this book by reflecting on a number of noteworthy turns in feminist theory that began to surface most clearly in the early 1990s. These turns questioned the "nature" and ontological stability of sex and reinvigorated debates about gender, the body, and feminism's most fundamental commitments. Over the course of this book, I have focused on the ways feminist movements, too, have questioned sex, engaging systems of sex differentiation over time, and in so doing I have suggested that it is the questionability, not the certainty, of sex which functions as a central feature of feminism's legacy. This claim is at once a response to those who have suggested that the scholarly sex revolution had little to do with movement politics and feminism's "real world" commitments, and at the same time a demonstration of the value of a rhetorical orientation toward how we understand feminism's ongoing relationship with sex, identity, and difference. To be more precise, the foregoing analyses have highlighted something that theories of the questionability of sex have neglected to illustrate clearly: that feminist commitments to the materiality of sex politics do not simply amplify sex as an ontological and/or biological category, nor do they throw out the materiality of sex altogether. Feminist questionings of sex are, at their very core, invested in sex's contingency. This investment exists not in spite of feminism's commitments to the social and material conditions of women's real lives but precisely because of them.

More specifically, a closer look at the interaction between multicultural anxiety and feminist uses and critiques of Sojourner Truth's "A——'t I a Woman?" suggests that when feminists engage the politics of sex differentiation, they do so by asserting which differences matter and which do not. Elizabeth Cady Stanton's early rhetoric serves as an exemplar of this tendency by illustrating how difference within a citizenry is simultaneously effaced and recognized in enlightened liberal political contexts. Cady Stanton's response to the prevailing rhetorical scene was to minimize the biological foundations of sex and race differences—questioning, to some extent, the corporeal matters of identity—while amplifying the importance of sociological difference among citizens. Cady Stanton theorized difference in a way that undermined sex as a difference that mattered, all the while positioning race as one that did.

Her extracorporeal view of sex (and race) difference, however, is not one that has been uniformly shared or deployed by feminist movements over time. Just as she responded to a specific immediate and enduring context, so too did feminists who followed her. Feminist women's health activists of the "second wave" focused precisely on the corporeal features of sex difference, and they worked within and against the psycho-medical context of the time to help transform women's health care. Although this movement's engagement with sex appears simply to reiterate biological sex-as-we-know-it, a closer look at its rhetoric reveals a recognition of the multiple ways in which sex is produced, as well as the material consequences of those productions. Indeed, many feminist groups of the "second wave" had a keen awareness of the contexts from which their advocacies emerged as they sought to strategize the relationship between public sex identities and the efficacy of the movement. Although different groups diverged on many issues from media strategy to the possibilities offered through lesbian sexual identifications and practices, "second wave" movements were often united in their commitment to identification itself—a commitment that domesticated the radical potential of their critique and blinded them to the very possibilities opened up by their questioning of sex.

These blind spots are of serious concern as we continue to think about the relationship between sex and feminism. Assuredly, it appears that feminist movements question sex while at the same time asserting its stability, and it is the rhetorical force of this latter move that may be responsible for the insistence on the *fact* of sex for feminism's past, present, and future. Nevertheless, as feminism faces an increasingly complex situation of sex politics, we ought to remember, not forget, feminism's longtime tendency to radically, skillfully, and strategically engage sex contexts variously, with unforeseen consequences. If we do so, we can proliferate the ways in which we critically respond to and assess contemporary movements like SlutWalk and promote an understanding of feminist movements that pivots on neither pure abstraction nor materiality but on rhetoricity.

Taken together, then, the case studies in this book present a nuanced portrait of feminist movements by illustrating feminist engagements with sex as rhetorical animations of emerging anxieties and steadfast commitments to both identity and difference. They demonstrate that for feminists (and others), sex is not a static ontological category but an identity and a system of differentiation that relies on the constitutive force of a number of rhetorical practices, including visual, medical, media, sexual, political, and corporeal ones. While feminism's historical questioning of sex was *necessarily* tied to bodily matters—for feminist responses emerged through bodies, were about bodies and their role in the distribution of rights, and, perhaps most important, were provoked by violence and other actions that put bodies at risk—the link between the body and feminism's intervention in sex is not an assertion of sex's corporeal certitude. Indeed, the case studies presented here highlight the active role of bodies in feminist rhetorical acts and contexts, but they also point to the fact that the ways in which those same bodies are *activated* and *differentiated* along lines of sex, race, sexuality, etc. vary substantially. The context for feminist activism, yesterday, today, and tomorrow, consistently demands that feminists contend with difference—those differences that matter in terms of importance and those differences that are thought to be grounded, and indeed surface, in the matter of human bodies. And when we consider how feminist movements have variously engaged these activations, we are reminded not of the necessity of sexed corporeality or specificity for feminism but rather of the material importance of a number of differentiated specificities at every turn.

Arguably, then, the questionable engagements promoted and demonstrated in this book ought not to be dismissed as academic exercises that get us no closer to the materiality of social movements than other philosophies of sex, gender, and/or difference. SlutWalks, as well as the other cases studied here, demonstrate that when feminist activists attempt to change the material conditions of "women's" lives, they address the enduring (and oftentimes abstract) traditions and contexts through which any view of sex/gender gains material and rhetorical force. In doing so, feminist movements, not just feminist theorists and academics, aptly blur the line between the abstract and material conditions of sex difference, because the ways in which sex materializes—the idioms, practices, and contexts through which we identify *female* and/or *woman*—are of primary concern for how movements act. Put simply, it is precisely in feminist attempts to make the "real world" a better place that we can see a feminist legacy of rhetorically engaging "sex." And this legacy ought to serve as a reminder that questions of sex, difference, and identity not only are a conceit for feminist theory but also are, and perhaps always have been, at the center of feminist activism.

Notes

Introduction

1. Michele L. Hammers, "Talking about 'Down There': The Politics of Publicizing the Female Body through *The Vagina Monologues*," *Women's Studies in Communication* 29, no. 2 (2006): 221; "The Vagina Monologues: About the Book," www.randomhouse.com.

2. "The Vagina Monologues: Q&A," www.randomhouse.com.

3. Hammers, "Talking about 'Down There,'" 221; "Vday: A Global Movement to End Violence against Women and Girls," www.vday.org.

4. Thomas Laqueur, *Making Sex: Body and Gender from the Greeks to Freud* (Cambridge: Harvard University Press, 1990).

5. Anne Fausto-Sterling, "The Five Sexes: Why Male and Female Are Not Enough," *The Sciences* 33 (March/April 1993): 20–24.

6. Judith Butler, *Gender Trouble: Feminism and the Subversion of Identity* (1990; New York: Routledge, 1999).

7. Nathan Stormer, "A Vexing Relationship: Gender and Contemporary Rhetorical Theory," in *The Sage Handbook of Gender and Communication*, ed. Bonnie J. Dow and Julia T. Wood (Thousand Oaks, Calif.: Sage, 2006), 252.

8. John M. Sloop, *Disciplining Gender: Rhetorics of Sex Identity in Contemporary U.S. Culture* (Amherst: University of Massachusetts Press, 2004), 2.

9. See, for example, Shannon L. Holland, "The Dangers of Playing Dress-Up: Popular Representations of Jessica Lynch and the Controversy Regarding Women in Combat," *Quarterly Journal of Speech* 92, no. 1 (2006): 27–50; Sloop, *Disciplining Gender*.

10. Jenae S., "More Than a Vagina: A Critique of the Vagina Monologues," February 2011, http://thefbomb.org. See also Hammers, "Talking about 'Down There.'"

11. Teresa L. Ebert, *Ludic Feminism and After: Postmodernism, Desire, and Labor in Late Capitalism* (Ann Arbor: University of Michigan Press, 1996).

12. Martha C. Nussbaum, "The Professor of Parody," *New Republic* 220, no. 8 (February 22, 1999): 45.

13. Tania Modleski, *Feminism without Women: Culture and Criticism in a "Postfeminist" Age* (New York: Routledge, 1991).

14. Samuel Chambers offers a nice summary and reading of the problem of materiality, sex, and gender for Butler's critics. He argues that at its core, these critics' concern can be summed up by the question: "If sex is really gender 'all the way down,' then is there no such thing as sex?" See Samuel A. Chambers, "'Sex' and the Problem of the Body: Reconstructing Judith Butler's Theory of Sex/Gender," *Body & Society* 13, no. 4 (2007): 49.

15. Judith Butler, *Bodies That Matter: On the Discursive Limits of Sex* (New York: Routledge, 1993), 28.

16. Anne Fausto-Sterling, *Sexing the Body: Gender Politics and the Construction of Sexuality* (New York: Basic Books, 2000), 3–4.

17. John Muckelbauer, *The Future of Invention: Rhetoric, Postmodernism, and the Problem of Change* (Albany: State University of New York Press, 2008), 100.

18. Ibid., 99.

19. Lloyd F. Bitzer, "The Rhetorical Situation," *Philosophy and Rhetoric* 1, no. 1 (1968): 3.

20. John Poulakos, "Toward a Sophistic Definition of Rhetoric," *Philosophy and Rhetoric* 16, no. 1 (1983): 42.

21. David Zarefsky, "History of Public Discourse Studies," in *The Sage Handbook of Rhetorical Studies,* ed. Andrea A. Lunsford (Thousand Oaks, Calif.: Sage, 2009), 433.

22. Muckelbauer, *The Future of Invention,* 99.

23. Maurice Charland, "Constitutive Rhetoric: The Case of the *Peuple Québécois,*" *Quarterly Journal of Speech* 73, no. 2 (1987): 134.

24. Ibid., 148.

25. Karlyn Kohrs Campbell, *Man Cannot Speak for Her: A Critical Study of Early Feminist Rhetoric,* 2 vols. (New York: Praeger, 1989), 1:10.

26. See, for example, Suzanne M. Daughton, "The Fine Texture of Enactment: Iconicity as Empowerment in Angela Grimke's Pennsylvania Hall Address," *Women's Studies in Communication* 18, no. 1 (1995): 19–43; Diane Helene Miller, "From One Voice a Chorus: Elizabeth Cady Stanton's 1860 Address to the New York State Legislature," *Women's Studies in Communication* 22, no. 2 (1999): 152–89; E. Michele Ramsey, "Inventing Citizens during World War I: Suffrage Cartoons in *The Woman Citizen,*" *Western Journal of Communication* 64, no. 2 (2000): 113–47; Angela G. Ray, "The Rhetorical Ritual of Citizenship: Women's Voting as Public Performance, 1868–1875," *Quarterly Journal of Speech* 93, no. 1 (2007): 375–402.

27. Campbell, *Man Cannot Speak for Her.*

28. Susan Zaeske, *Signatures of Citizenship: Petitioning, Antislavery, and Women's Political Identity* (Chapel Hill: University of North Carolina Press, 2003), 6.

29. James Jasinski, "Instrumentalism, Contextualism, and Interpretation in Rhetorical Criticism," in *Rhetorical Hermeneutics: Invention and Interpretation in the Age of Science,* ed. Alan G. Gross and William M. Keith (Albany: State University of New York Press, 1997), 196–97.

30. Ibid., 200.

31. John M. Murphy, "Critical Rhetoric as Political Discourse" *Argumentation and Advocacy* 32, no. 1 (1995): 11.

32. Jasinski, "Instrumentalism," 212–14; Murphy, "Critical Rhetoric," 11.

33. Michel Foucault, *The History of Sexuality: An Introduction,* vol. 1, trans. Robert Hurley (New York: Vintage Books, 1978). For examples of those who follow Foucault's lead, see Laqueur, *Making Sex;* Butler, *Bodies That Matter;* Butler, *Gender Trouble;* Sloop, *Disciplining Gender.*

34. Nussbaum, "The Professor of Parody," 40, 45.

35. Barbara A. Biesecker and John Louis Lucaites, "Introduction," in *Rhetoric, Materiality, and Politics,* ed. Barbara A. Biesecker and John Louis Lucaites (New York: Peter Lang, 2009), 1.

36. Butler, *Gender Trouble,* 11.

37. Ibid.

38. Chambers, " 'Sex' and the Problem of the Body," 63.

39. Foucault, *The History of Sexuality,* 151–52.

40. See the interview with Butler in Vicki Kirby, *Judith Butler: Live Theory* (London: Continuum, 2006), 145. For a similar argument, see Butler, *Bodies That Matter,* 10.

41. Fausto-Sterling, *Sexing the Body,* 4.

42. Butler, *Bodies That Matter,* 32. Vicki Kirby discusses Butler's choice of matter over substance and urges a conceptualization of performativity that takes seriously the Derridean notion of *différance.* Kirby develops this argument to substantiate further her critique of the

reliance of Butler's theory on the Lacanian notion of *lack* which Butler attempts to resist. A similar critique of Butler and lack is the backbone of Jeffrey Nealon's book *Alterity Politics*. These critiques are important ones that urge critics not think of linguistic practices as inevitable failures to represent the essence of the referent. In this discussion, such a claim might resemble one that insists that there may be truths about sexed anatomy that *exceed* the signification of that anatomy. See Kirby, *Judith Butler*, 82–107; Jeffrey T. Nealon, *Alterity Politics: Ethics and Performative Subjectivity* (Durham: Duke University Press, 1998).

43. See, for example, Karlyn Kohrs Campbell, "Femininity and Feminism: To Be or Not to Be a Woman," *Communication Quarterly* 31, no. 2 (1983): 101–8; Campbell, "Gender and Genre: Loci of Invention and Contradiction in the Earliest Speeches by U.S. Women," *Quarterly Journal of Speech* 81, no. 4 (1995): 479–95; Bonnie J. Dow, "The 'Womanhood' Rationale in the Woman Suffrage Rhetoric of Frances E. Willard," *Southern Communication Journal* 56, no. 4 (1991): 298–307; Elizabeth Galewski, "The Strange Case for Women's Capacity to Reason: Judith Sargent Murray's Use of Irony in 'On the Equality of Sexes' (1790)," *Quarterly Journal of Speech* 93, no. 1 (2007): 84–108; Cindy L. Griffin, "Rhetoricizing Alienation: Mary Wollstonecraft and the Rhetorical Construction of Women's Oppression," *Quarterly Journal of Speech* 80, no. 3 (1994): 293–312; Carmen Heider, "Suffrage, Self-Determination, and the Women's Christian Temperance Union in Nebraska, 1879–1882," *Rhetoric & Public Affairs* 8, no. 1 (2005): 85–108; Sheryl Hurner, "Discursive Identity Formation of Suffrage Women: Reframing the 'Cult of True Womanhood' through Song," *Western Journal of Communication* 70, no. 3 (2006): 234–60; Phyllis M. Japp, "Esther or Isaiah? The Abolitionist-Feminist Rhetoric of Angelina Grimké," *Quarterly Journal of Speech* 71, no. 3 (1985): 335–48; Miller, "From One Voice a Chorus"; Ray, "Rhetorical Ritual."

44. See, for example, Hammers, "Talking about 'Down There'"; Holland, "Dangers of Playing Dress-Up"; Kristy Maddux, "*The Da Vinci Code* and the Regressive Gender Politics of Celebrating Women," *Critical Studies in Media Communication* 25, no. 3 (2008): 225–48.

45. Some notable exceptions include Joshua Gunn, "On Speech and Public Release," *Rhetoric & Public Affairs* 13, no. 2 (2010): 175–215; Jordynn Jack, "Gender Copia: Feminist Rhetorical Perspectives on an Autistic Concept of Sex/Gender," *Women's Studies in Communication* 35, no. 1 (2012): 1–17.

46. Butler, *Bodies That Matter*, xi.

47. Holland, "The Dangers of Playing Dress-Up," 29.

48. Chambers, "'Sex' and the Problem of the Body," 59.

49. Ibid., 60.

50. Karen Barad, "Posthumanist Performativity: Toward an Understanding of How Matter Comes to Matter," *Signs* 28, no. 3 (2003): 810.

51. Ibid., 823.

52. Chambers, "'Sex' and the Problem of the Body," 64, emphasis added.

53. Mary Wollstonecraft, *A Vindication of the Rights of Woman* ([Sandy, Utah]: Quiet Vision Publishing, 2003).

54. At times throughout this book I use the terms "first wave," "second wave," and "third wave." These terms are generally used to describe the surges of feminist activism that emerged between 1848 and 1920, 1966 and 1982, and 1990 and beyond, respectively. In recent years, the wave metaphor to describe feminist scrutiny has come under critique. While the terms themselves are useful shorthand, they fail to describe aptly how women's movements continually emerge in U.S. history. In Ednie Kaeh Garrison's terms, the problem with the wave metaphor is that it "limits our ability to recognize difference and to adequately represent shifts in feminist ideological and movement formations over the last half of the twentieth century"; it "constructs certain kinds of historical narratives of women's movements and feminism, narratives which continue to reproduce exclusions and obfuscations." Ednie Kaeh Garrison, "Are We on a Wavelength Yet? On Feminist Oceanography, Radios, and Third Wave Feminism," in *Different Wavelengths: Studies of the Contemporary Women's Movement*, ed. Jo Reger (New York:

Routledge, 2005), 238, 239. As this project challenges certain unified notions of feminism's development, I think that Garrison's argument is an important one. Thus, in the analyses that follow, I often refrain from using "wave" terms, and when I do write of feminism's "waves," I frequently place the term in quotes to indicate the problems associated with it. I still find it useful to use the shorthand term for a period of time, but I also want to mark my wariness about what kinds of activism (and for whom) typically gets included and excluded with the metaphor. See also Linda Nicholson, "Feminism in 'Waves': Useful Metaphor or Not," *New Politics* 13, no. 48 (2010), http://newpol.org; Natalie Fixmer and Julia T. Wood, "The Personal Is *Still* Political: Embodied Politics in Third Wave Feminism," *Women's Studies in Communication* 28, no. 2 (2005): 235–57.

55. Butler, *Gender Trouble*, 182.

1. Recognizing Sex

1. See, for example, Eleanor Flexner and Ellen Fitzpatrick, *Century of Struggle: The Woman's Rights Movement in the United States,* enlarged ed. (Cambridge: Belknap Press, 1996), 84–86.

2. Angela Y. Davis, *Women, Race, and Class* (New York: Vintage Books, 1981), 60.

3. Stephanie M. H. Camp, "Ar'n't I a Woman? In the Vanguard of the History of Race and Sex in the United States," *Journal of Women's History* 19, no. 2 (2007): 147. See also Nell Irvin Painter, "Representing Truth: Sojourner Truth's Knowing and Becoming Known," *Journal of American History* 81, no. 2 (1994): 461–92.

4. See, for example, Nell Irvin Painter, *Sojourner Truth: A Life, a Symbol* (New York: Norton, 1996), 164–78; Roseann M. Mandziuk and Suzanne Pullon Fitch, "The Rhetorical Construction of Sojourner Truth," *Southern Communication Journal* 66, no. 2 (2001): 120–38; Carleton Mabee and Susan Mabee Newhouse, *Sojourner Truth: Slave, Prophet, Legend* (New York: New York University Press, 1993), 67–82.

5. Karlyn Kohrs Campbell, "Agency: Promiscuous and Protean," *Communication and Critical/Cultural Studies* 2, no. 1 (2005): 12.

6. Teresa C. Zackodnik, "'I Don't Know How You Will Feel When I Get Through': Racial Difference, Woman's Rights, and Sojourner Truth," *Feminist Studies* 30, no. 1 (2004): 53–54; Painter, "Representing Truth," 477–78; Carleton Mabee and Susan Mabee Newhouse look at stylistic features of Gage's text and compare them to other samples of Gage's writing to provide further insight into the invention of the transcript. See Mabee and Newhouse, *Sojourner Truth*, 77.

7. Zackodnik, "'I Don't Know How You Will Feel,'" 49–73; Painter, "Representing Truth," 477–79.

8. Painter, "Representing Truth," 480, emphasis added.

9. Painter, *Sojourner Truth*, 287.

10. Davis, *Women, Race, and Class,* 61. Although I am using Angela Davis's words as an example of this interpretation of Truth's speech, it is important to emphasize that Davis also discusses the black feminist interpretation of the speech. As she notes, "Sojourner Truth's 'Ain't I a Woman?' address had deeper implications, for it was also, it seems, a comment on the racist attitudes of the same white women who later praised their Black sister" (62).

11. Zackodnik, "'I Don't Know How You Will Feel,'" 58.

12. Ibid., 61.

13. Ibid., 70.

14. Ibid., 59.

15. Although Truth collaborated with Olive Gilbert, since Truth was illiterate, she had no direct editorial control over written narratives about her. Truth's illiteracy, combined with her seeming reluctance to contradict obvious factual discrepancies about her life in published works, has posed a number of obstacles to the authentication of various narratives about her. Nell Irvin Painter discusses the problem explicitly in her 1994 article about Truth in the

Journal of American History. There she pushes historians to "develop means of knowing our subjects, and adapt to our subjects' ways of making themselves known, that look beyond the written word." See Painter, "Representing Truth," 462.

16. Nell Irvin Painter, "Introduction," in *Narrative of Sojourner Truth; a Bondswoman of Olden Time, with a History of Her Labors and Correspondence Drawn from Her Book of Life,* ed. Nell Irvin Painter (New York: Penguin, 1998), xviii.

17. Roseann M. Mandziuk, "Commemorating Sojourner Truth: Negotiating the Politics of Race and Gender in the Spaces of Public Memory," *Western Journal of Communication* 67, no. 3 (2003): 275.

18. Mandziuk and Fitch, "The Rhetorical Construction of Sojourner Truth."

19. Painter points out that the ex-slave narrative genre emerged most prominently in the 1840s. By the time Truth's *Narrative* was published, other narratives by Frederick Douglass, William Wells Brown, and Henry Bibb had become best-sellers. These other accounts contributed to the reception of Truth's narrative because they had established certain generic expectations. Painter, "Representing Truth," 472.

20. Painter, "Introduction," xiv.

21. Ibid., xii; Naomi Greyser, "Affective Geographies: Sojourner Truth's *Narrative,* Feminism, and the Ethical Bind of Sentimentalism," *American Literature* 79, no. 2 (2007): 287.

22. Greyser, "Affective Geographies," 287.

23. Ibid. See also Mandziuk and Fitch, "The Rhetorical Construction of Sojourner Truth," 124–25.

24. Mandziuk and Fitch, "The Rhetorical Construction of Sojourner Truth," 124–28.

25. Ibid., 128.

26. Painter, "Representing Truth," 476. Stowe published an earlier version of the article in the *Independent* in 1860, but "The Libyan Sybil" is the story that most scholars cite as the pivotal one. Moreover, although Stowe doesn't acknowledge the piece as a work of fiction, there is a good deal of evidence to suggest that much of the narrative, if not all of it, was a product of Stowe's creative talents as a writer of *fiction.* See Mabee and Newhouse, *Sojourner Truth,* 83–86.

27. Painter, "Representing Truth," 475–77.

28. Ibid., 475–78. For another discussion of Stowe's influence on Gage's text, see Mabee and Newhouse, *Sojourner Truth,* 80.

29. Painter, "Representing Truth," 479; Mabee and Newhouse, *Sojourner Truth,* 79.

30. Painter, "Representing Truth," 479. For a more extensive account of the ways Truth was made into a symbol as a result of several publications, see Painter, *Sojourner Truth;* Mandziuk and Fitch, "The Rhetorical Construction of Sojourner Truth."

31. Zackodnik, "'I Don't Know How You Will Feel,'" 56. It is important to note that while this reading is common, it is not as simple as Zackodnik may have us believe. Although many critics have relayed this reading, they don't always offer it as one that suggests, in Zackodnik's terms, that Truth was advocating *"solely"* for gender equality. In fact, a quick look at Zackodnik's footnotes reveals that the very sources she cites often acknowledge that Truth's speech was also an address about racial inequalities and a critique of feminism itself. What follows, then, are examples of readings that at times *emphasize* Truth as a woman's rights advocate and neglect to *make explicit* that she is also critiquing first wave white feminists. Most, however, do recognize that Truth is also calling attention to the particularly dire situation of black/slave women, thus not ignoring race, and in some cases making a clear argument about the intersection of race and gender. See Karlyn Kohrs Campbell, *Man Cannot Speak for Her: A Critical Study of Early Feminist Rhetoric,* 2 vols. (New York: Praeger, 1989), 1:19–22; Deborah Gray White, *Ar/N/T I a Woman: Female Slaves in the Plantation South* (1985; New York: Norton, 1999), 13–16; Flexner and Fitzpatrick, *Century of Struggle,* 85; bell hooks, *Ain't I a Woman: Black Women and Feminism* (Cambridge: South End Press, 1981), 159–61; Gerard A. Wagner, "Sojourner Truth: God's Appointed Apostle of Reform," *Southern Communication Journal*

28, no. 2 (1962): 126–28; Phyllis Marynick Palmer, "White Women / Black Women: The Dualism of Female Identity and Experience in the United States," *Feminist Studies* 9, no. 1 (1983): 151–53; Campbell, "Agency," 9–11; Elizabeth Fox-Genovese, *Within the Plantation Household: Black and White Women of the Old South* (Chapel Hill: University of North Carolina Press, 1988), 50–51.

32. Zackodnik, " 'I Don't Know How You Will Feel,' " 50.

33. Ibid., 57.

34. Mandziuk, "Commemorating Sojourner Truth," 279. While Zackodnik divides the two common interpretations between those that argue solely for gender equality and those that discuss the intersection of race and gender, it is more instructive for my purposes to consider how feminists "read" Truth's speech and the audience to which the question is directed. As a result, I discuss the division in terms of Truth as a woman's rights advocate versus Truth as a black feminist. I do this not only because such a division better resonates with my rhetorical perspective, but also because I think it better accounts for the overlap between what we now would label "black feminism" and woman's rights advocacy. Zackodnik's division is a difficult one to maintain, since, as I have discussed, many who position Truth primarily as woman's rights advocate do so in a way that also emphasizes the intersection of race and gender. Additionally, it is important to note that not all of the following citations explicitly posit Truth as a black feminist who both critiques white feminism and calls attention to the intersection of race and gender. For instance, notice that I have cited hooks as one whose reading of the speech highlights it exclusively as one that argues against gender inequality, failing to render Truth's speech explicitly as a critique of white feminism. Yet hooks uses the question as the framing title of her germinal book on black women and feminism, where she, among other things, points to the various ways racism has emerged in white feminist movements. Moreover, only paragraphs after offering her reading of Gage's text, hooks writes about white female racism in the first wave. I therefore think it is safe to say that hooks implicitly positions Truth as an emblematic figure of black feminism, although she never explicitly suggests that "A——'t I a Woman?" is a pivotal black feminist text. The sources cited here, then, are ones that both explicitly and implicitly render Truth as an emblematic black feminist, who not only emphasizes the importance of the intersection of race and gender but also critiques the racism of nineteenth-century white feminists. See hooks, *Ain't I a Woman*, 159–61; Sara M. Evans, *Born for Liberty: A History of Women in America* (New York: Free Press Paperbacks, 1989), 104; Davis, *Women, Race, and Class*, 61–64; Painter, *Sojourner Truth*, 171; Painter, "Representing Truth," 464; Camp, "Ar'n't I a Woman?" 147.

35. Zackodnik, " 'I Don't Know How You Will Feel,' " 58.

36. For a brief discussion of how Truth's question is used as a sign of unity, see Donna Haraway, "Ecce Homo, Ain't (Ar'n't) I a Woman, and Inappropriate/d Others: The Human in a Post-Humanist Landscape," in *Feminists Theorize the Political*, ed. Judith Butler and Joan W. Scott (New York: Routledge, 1992), 92.

37. Truth as figure of unity may in fact be even more prevalent outside feminist circles. Roseann Mandziuk has examined three contemporary commemorations of Sojourner Truth, finding that Truth has not only been figured as an ardent black feminist reformer, but also has been rendered as a benign figure of unity and women's capacity to be man's civic equal. When Truth gets memorialized outside of feminism, her racial defiance is ignored, and in its place a conciliatory religious servant emerges. See Mandziuk, "Commemorating Sojourner Truth," 281–89.

38. "Editorial," *Ain't I a Woman?* June 26, 1970, 2.

39. Zackodnik, " 'I Don't Know How You Will Feel,' " 59.

40. Ibid., 70.

41. Camp, "Ar'n't I a Woman?," 147. See also Campbell, "Agency," 13.

42. Mandziuk and Fitch trace the various ways Truth has been used as symbol to meet various needs. Their argument that Truth gets transfigured into "the" black feminist by people

like hooks implies a stance similar to the one I take here—that a certain kind of multiculturalism forms a backdrop for many contemporary discussions of Truth. Mandziuk and Fitch,
however, make a move similar to that of Zackodnik, arguing that the rhetorical transforma-
tions of Truth erase the specific complexities of her life and advocacy. And while Mandziuk
and Fitch lament that "Truth has become *merely* a vessel for the rhetoric of others," they
neglect to reflect on how calling for more accurate representations is also a rhetorical deployment of Truth, possibly toward the same multicultural end. See Mandziuk and Fitch, "The
Rhetorical Construction of Sojourner Truth," 133–36, quotation 135.

43. Jeffrey T. Nealon, *Alterity Politics: Ethics and Performative Subjectivity* (Durham: Duke
University Press, 1998), 1.

44. Ibid.

45. Judith Butler, *Gender Trouble: Feminism and the Subversion of Identity* (1990; New York:
Routledge, 1999), 182; Nealon, *Alterity Politics*, 2.

46. Davis, *Women, Race, and Class*, 63–64.

47. Ibid., 7.

48. Ibid., 6–7.

49. Haraway, "Ecce Homo," 93.

50. Frances Dana Gage, "Sojourner Truth" (1863), in *Sojourner Truth as Orator: Wit, Story,
and Song*, ed. Suzanne Pullon Fitch and Roseann M. Mandziuk (Westport: Greenwood Press,
1997), 105.

51. Ibid.

52. Donna Haraway argues that when Truth was forced to bare her breasts at a speaking
event, her difference was reduced to her anatomy. While I agree with Haraway, I also believe that the same is true when one answers her question. Haraway's comment is important,
however, as it begins to position the question of sex and difference away from anatomy. See
Haraway, "Ecce Homo," 92.

53. Ibid.

54. Ibid., 86.

55. Ibid., 87.

56. Ibid., 86.

57. Ibid.

58. Nealon, *Alterity Politics*, 4.

59. Haraway, "Ecce Homo," 92.

60. Ibid., 95.

61. Ibid., 97–98.

62. Ibid., 97.

63. Quoted in Zackodnik, "'I Don't Know How You Will Feel,'" 66.

64. Ibid., 69.

65. Gloria Anzaldúa, *Borderlands/La Frontera: The New Mestiza* (San Francisco: Spin-
sters/Aunt Lute, 1987), 78.

66. Ibid.

67. Ibid., 84–86.

68. Zackodnik, "'I Don't Know How You Will Feel,'" 51.

69. Haraway, "Ecce Homo," 97.

70. Judith Butler, *Giving an Account of Oneself* (New York: Fordham University Press,
2005), 121–22.

71. Judith, Butler, *Undoing Gender* (New York: Routledge, 2004), 35.

72. My use of "risky" is meant to echo a conversation about recognition, response, rhetoric, and alterity that appeared in *Philosophy and Rhetoric*. More specifically, John Muckelbauer engages the question of practical responses to the Other as one that inevitably involves,
among other things, risk and violence. See Diane Davis, "Addressing Alterity: Rhetoric,
Hermeneutics, and the Nonappropriative Relation," *Philosophy and Rhetoric* 38, no. 3 (2005):

191–212; John Muckelbauer, "Rhetoric, Asignification, and the Other: A Response to Diane Davis," *Philosophy and Rhetoric* 40, no. 2 (2007): 238–47.

73. Erik Doxtader, "Is There a Question of Rhetorical/Theory?" 3, paper presented at "Rhetorical Questions: The South Carolina Conference on Rhetorical Theory," Columbia, S.C., 2009.

2. Matters of Sex and Race

1. Elizabeth Cady Stanton, "This Is the Negro's Hour," in *The Selected Papers of Elizabeth Cady Stanton and Susan B. Anthony*, vol. 1, *In the School of Anti-Slavery, 1840–1866*, ed. Ann D. Gordon (New Brunswick: Rutgers University Press, 1997), 564.

2. Eleanor Flexner and Ellen Fitzpatrick, *Century of Struggle: The Woman's Rights Movement in the United States* (1959), enlarged ed. (Cambridge: Belknap Press, 1975), 136; Ellen Carol Dubois, *Feminism and Suffrage: The Emergence of an Independent Women's Movement in America, 1848–1869* (Ithaca: Cornell University Press, 1978), 164.

3. Flexner and Fitzpatrick, *Century of Struggle*, 139.

4. Ibid., 138–39. Dubois, *Feminism and Suffrage*, 71–72.

5. Angela Y. Davis, *Women, Race, and Class* (New York: Vintage Books, 1981), 71.

6. Susan B. Anthony was one of Cady Stanton's closet allies, and the two of them are often noted as examples of those who were willing to maintain racist positions to help gain momentum for woman suffrage. Ironically, it was Anthony who championed the cause of black women as evidence of the need for universal, not manhood, suffrage, despite the fact that later, along with Cady Stanton, she would solicit financial support for woman suffrage from the well-known white supremacist George Francis Train and ask black women to march behind white women in the nation's largest woman suffrage march. In other words, Cady Stanton's letter is just one of countless examples of racism among some of feminism's earliest known activists. See Dubois, *Feminism and Suffrage*, 162–202. Davis, *Women, Race, and Class*, 70–86; Aileen S. Kraditor, *The Ideas of the Woman Suffrage Movement, 1890–1920* (New York: Norton, 1981), 163–218.

7. Suzanne M. Marilley, *Woman Suffrage and the Origins of Liberal Feminism in the United States, 1820–1920* (Cambridge: Harvard University Press, 1996), 159, emphasis added. See also Flexner and Fitzpatrick, *Century of Struggle*, 136–41; Dubois, *Feminism and Suffrage*, 174.

8. Kraditor, *Ideas of the Woman Suffrage Movement*, 163–218.

9. William Leach, *True Love and Perfect Union: The Feminist Reform of Sex and Society* (New York: Basic Books, 1980), 143. See also Beth M. Waggenspack, *The Search for Self-Sovereignty: The Oratory of Elizabeth Cady Stanton* (New York: Greenwood Press, 1989), 89. For the comparison to Wollstonecraft and de Beauvoir, see Vivian Gornick, *The Solitude of Self: Thinking about Elizabeth Cady Stanton* (New York: Farrar, Straus and Giroux, 2005), 9.

10. Marilley, *Woman Suffrage and the Origins of Liberal Feminism*, 7.

11. Karlyn Kohrs Campbell, *Man Cannot Speak for Her: A Critical Study of Early Feminist Rhetoric*, vol. 1 (New York: Praeger, 1989), 133.

12. Limiting the texts to these dates facilitates a focus on the immediate rhetorical situation as well as a more expansive context of sexual identity politics. In particular, 1870 is an obvious year to end with since it was not only the year when the Fifteenth Amendment was ratified, enfranchising black men but not women, but also the year when Cady Stanton and Anthony temporarily shifted their focus away from winning the ballot via a federal constitutional amendment toward developing strategies aimed at using the judiciary to enfranchise women.

13. Alice S. Rossi, "A Feminist Friendship: Elizabeth Cady Stanton and Susan B. Anthony," in *One Woman, One Vote: Rediscovering the Woman Suffrage Movement*, ed. Marjorie Spruill Wheeler (Troutdale, Ore.: New Sage Press, 1995), 51. See also Campbell, *Man Cannot Speak for Her*, 59–63.

14. "The Solitude of Self" remains Cady Stanton's most canonical work. Much of the philo-

sophical underpinnings of and contributions to her thought is evident in this speech. To a certain extent, my reading of her earlier work is framed by understandings of "Solitude."

15. Campbell, *Man Cannot Speak for Her*, 142. See also Nathan Stormer, "Embodied Humanism: Performative Argument for Natural Rights in "The Solitude of Self," *Argumentation and Advocacy* 36, no. 2 (1999): 55.

16. William Leach, *True Love and Perfect Union: The Feminist Reform of Sex and Society* (New York: Basic Books, 1980), 147. See also Kathi Kern, *Mrs. Cady Stanton's Bible* (Ithaca: Cornell University Press, 2001), 55; Laura L. Behling, *The Masculine Woman in America, 1980–1935* (Urbana: University of Illinois Press, 2001), 35.

17. Kern, *Mrs. Cady Stanton's Bible*, 55.

18. Thomas Laqueur, *Making Sex: Body and Gender from the Greeks to Freud* (Cambridge: Harvard University Press, 1990), 149.

19. Ibid., 10.

20. Ibid., 34.

21. Ibid., 149.

22. Ibid., 153.

23. Ibid., 151–52.

24. Catherine H. Palczewski, "The Male Madonna and the Feminine Uncle Sam: Visual Argument, Icons, and Ideographs in 1909 Anti–Woman Suffrage Postcards," *Quarterly Journal of Speech* 91, no. 4 (2005): 375–76. See also Kraditor, *Ideas of the Woman Suffrage Movement*, 28.

25. Linda Nicholson, "Interpreting Gender," *Signs* 20, no. 1 (1994): 85.

26. Laqueur, *Making Sex*, 155; Nicholson, "Interpreting Gender," 85.

27. Laqueur, *Making Sex*, 155.

28. Marilley, *Woman Suffrage and the Origins of Liberal Feminism*, 3.

29. Laqueur, *Making Sex*, 156–57; Marilley, *Woman Suffrage and the Origins of Liberal Feminism*, 3; Nicholson, "Interpreting Gender," 83–85. See also Carole Pateman, *The Sexual Contract* (Stanford: Stanford University Press, 1988).

30. Pateman, *The Sexual Contract*, 94–101.

31. Laqueur, *Making Sex*, 157.

32. Ibid., 152; Marilley, *Woman Suffrage and the Origins of Liberal Feminism*, 4.

33. Kraditor, *Ideas of the Woman Suffrage Movement*, 43–74.

34. One of the first ways women's roles as citizens were articulated was in terms of "republican motherhood," whereby women's duties primarily included educating their sons to be good citizens. For discussions of republican motherhood, see Sara M. Evans, *Born for Liberty: A History of Women in America* (New York: Free Press Paperbacks, 1989), 57–66; Linda Kerber, *Women of the Republic: Intellect and Ideology in Revolutionary America* (Chapel Hill: University of North Carolina Press, 1980), 265–88; Marilley, *Woman Suffrage and the Origins of Liberal Feminism*, 5–6, 20–22. For descriptions and analyses of the relationship between liberal theory and women's changing political identities or identities as citizens, see Campbell, *Man Cannot Speak for Her*, 10–12, 106–19; Josephine Donovan, *Feminist Theory: The Intellectual Traditions of American Feminism* (New York: Continuum Publishing, 1985), 17–46; Kraditor, *Ideas of the Woman Suffrage Movement*, 52–74; and Marilley, *Woman Suffrage and the Origins of Liberal Feminism*, 22–65.

35. Campbell, *Man Cannot Speak for Her*, 14, emphasis added. See also Karlyn Kohrs Campbell, "Femininity and Feminism: To Be or Not to Be a Woman," *Communication Quarterly* 31, no. 2 (1983): 102.

36. Marilley, *Woman Suffrage and the Origins of Liberal Feminism*, 103.

37. Evans, *Born for Liberty*, 57–66.

38. Donovan, *Feminist Theory*, 5.

39. Elizabeth Cady Stanton, "Address by ECS on Woman's Rights," in *Selected Papers*, 1:99.

40. Donovan, *Feminist Theory*, 2, 5.

41. Cady Stanton, "Address by ECS on Woman's Rights," 98. For explications of similar performative strategies in early woman's rights rhetoric, see Campbell, *Man Cannot Speak for Her*, 17–69; Suzanne M. Daughton, "The Fine Texture of Enactment: Iconicity as Empowerment in Angela Grimke's Pennsylvania Hall Address," *Women's Studies in Communication* 18, no. 1 (1995): 19–43; Susan Zaeske, *Signatures of Citizenship: Petitioning, Antislavery, and Women's Political Identity* (Chapel Hill: University of North Carolina Press, 2003), 115–23.

42. See Cady Stanton, "Address by ECS on Woman's Rights," 104; Elizabeth Cady Stanton, "Elizabeth Cady Stanton for Congress," in *Selected Papers*, 1:593; Elizabeth Cady Stanton, "To the Women of the Republic," in *Selected Papers*, 1:483; Elizabeth Cady Stanton, "Universal Suffrage," in *Selected Papers*, 1:551; Elizabeth Cady Stanton, "Manhood Suffrage," in *The Selected Papers of Elizabeth Cady Stanton and Susan B. Anthony*, vol. 2, *Against an Aristocracy of Sex, 1866–1873*, ed. Ann D. Gordon (New Brunswick: Rutgers University Press, 1997), 194; Elizabeth Cady Stanton, "Speech by ECS in Burlington, Kansas," in *Selected Papers*, 2:98.

43. Cady Stanton, "Elizabeth Cady Stanton for Congress," 593–94.

44. Campbell, *Man Cannot Speak for Her*, 133.

45. Elizabeth Cady Stanton, "Paper by ECS for the Yearly Meeting of the Friends of Human Progress," in *Selected Papers*, 1:344.

46. Cady Stanton, "Address by ECS on Woman's Rights," 108.

47. Elizabeth Cady Stanton, "Constitutional Convention," in *Selected Papers*, 2:84. For a similar use of Hamilton, see Elizabeth Cady Stanton, "John Stuart Mill," in *Selected Papers*, 2:262.

48. Campbell, *Man Cannot Speak for Her*, 143, emphasis added.

49. For examples of Cady Stanton's championing of education, see Elizabeth Cady Stanton, "Douglass and Johnson," in *Selected Papers*, 1:577; and Elizabeth Cady Stanton, "Miss Becker on the Difference in Sex," in *Selected Papers*, 2:180.

50. Wollstonecraft writes, " 'Moralists' have unanimously agreed, that unless virtue be nursed by liberty, it will never attain due strength—and what they say of man I extend to mankind, insisting, that in all cases morals must be fixed on immutable principles; and that being cannot be termed rational or virtuous, who obey any authority but that of reason." Mary Wollstonecraft, *A Vindication of the Rights of Woman* ([Sandy, Utah]: Quiet Vision Publishing, 2003), 157. For analysis of Wollstonecraft's views on education and reason, see Donovan, *Feminist Theory*, 8–11.

51. Donovan, *Feminist Theory*, 8.

52. Arguably, Cady Stanton was influenced by (and benefited from) a number of widely read reformers, such as Judith Sargent Murray and Mary Wollstonecraft, who also advocated female classical education. As Elizabeth Galewski makes clear, however, it was not just those whom we now would label "feminists" who advocated for female education; in fact, a number of promoters of women's intellectual capacity grounded their arguments not in appeals to sex equality but in distinct sexual and political difference. Echoing Linda Kerber, Galewski writes, "More desirable than a frivolous beauty . . . was a *knowledgeable* republican mother who could pass on the fledgling nation's values to her sons and daughters." Elizabeth Galewski, "The Strange Case for Women's Capacity to Reason: Judith Sargent Murray's Use of Irony in 'On the Equality of Sexes' (1790)," *Quarterly Journal of Speech* 93, no. 1 (2007): 92, emphasis added. Ironically, then, the efficacy of Cady Stanton's arguments surrounding women's capacity to reason as evidence of woman's and man's ontological similarity may have benefited from earlier arguments that articulated women's reason in terms of men's and women's different roles as citizens.

53. Campbell, *Man Cannot Speak for Her*, 61. See also Marilley, *Woman Suffrage and the Origins of Liberal Feminism*, 159–78; Kern, *Mrs. Cady Stanton's Bible*, 106–16; Dubois, *Feminism and Suffrage*, 174–79.

54. Elizabeth Cady Stanton, "Address by ECS to the Legislature of New York," in *Selected Papers*, 1:241–42.

55. Cady Stanton, "This Is the Negro's Hour," 564.

56. Cady Stanton, "Manhood Suffrage," 195–96.

57. See Marilley, *Woman Suffrage and the Origins of Liberal Feminism*, 159–78; Kern, *Mrs. Cady Stanton's Bible*, 106–16; and Dubois, *Feminism and Suffrage*, 174–79.

58. Cady Stanton, "Manhood Suffrage," 194. See also Elizabeth Cady Stanton, "The Sixteenth Amendment," in *Selected Papers*, 2:237.

59. Stormer, "Embodied Humanism," 55.

60. Elizabeth Cady Stanton, "Address by ECS to the Eighth National Woman's Rights Convention," in *Selected Papers*, 1:369; Elizabeth Cady Stanton, "Appeal by ECS," in *Selected Papers*, 1:285. See also Cady Stanton, "Address by ECS to the Legislature of New York," 244; Cady Stanton, "Address by ECS on Woman's Rights," 96.

61. Cady Stanton, "Miss Becker on the Difference in Sex," 178.

62. Cady Stanton, "Manhood Suffrage," 195.

63. For other appeals to fair representation, see Cady Stanton, "The Sixteenth Amendment," 237; Cady Stanton, "Universal Suffrage," 550–51; Elizabeth Cady Stanton, "Stand by Your Guns, Mr Julian," in *Selected Papers*, 2:202.

64. Cady Stanton, "Manhood Suffrage," 194. See also Cady Stanton, "Miss Becker on the Difference in Sex," 182.

65. Cady Stanton, "Manhood Suffrage," 197.

66. Cady Stanton, "Miss Becker on the Difference in Sex," 181.

67. Cady Stanton, "Address by ECS on Woman's Rights," 104–5.

68. For a view which suggests that Cady Stanton's thoughts on sex are an entirely social phenomenon, see Rossi, "A Feminist Friendship," 51.

69. Cady Stanton, "Address by ECS on Woman's Rights," 102.

70. Elizabeth Cady Stanton, "Mrs. Swisshelm," in *Selected Papers*, 1:184–85.

71. Cady Stanton, "Miss Becker on the Difference in Sex," 177.

72. Wollstonecraft, *Vindication of the Rights of Woman*, 157, 58, 158.

73. Cady Stanton, "Stand by Your Guns, Mr. Julian," 202.

74. Cady Stanton, "Paper by ECS for the Yearly Meeting of the Friends of Human Progress," 342.

75. Elizabeth Cady Stanton, "I Have All the Rights I Want," in *Selected Papers*, 1:402.

76. Elizabeth Cady Stanton, "Woman's Dress," in *Selected Papers*, 2:253.

77. Laqueur, *Making Sex*, 154.

78. E. Michele Ramsey, "Addressing Issues of Context in Historical Women's Public Address," *Women's Studies in Communication* 27, no. 3 (2004): 354, 353.

3. Visions of Sex

1. Michelle Murphy, "Immodest Witnessing: The Epistemology of Vaginal Self-Examination in the U.S. Feminist Self-Help Movement," *Feminist Studies* 30, no. 1 (2004): 115.

2. Ibid., 116.

3. Quoted in Sandra Morgen, *Into Our Own Hands: The Women's Health Movement in the United States, 1969–1990* (New Brunswick: Rutgers University Press, 2002), 23.

4. Ibid., 22.

5. Ruth Rosen, *The World Split Open: How the Modern Women's Movement Changed America* (New York: Penguin, 2000), 177.

6. Morgen, *Into Our Own Hands*, 22.

7. Ibid. See also Wendy Kline, *Bodies of Knowledge: Sexuality, Reproduction, and Women's Health in the Second Wave* (Chicago: University of Chicago Press, 2010).

8. Murphy, "Immodest Witnessing," 128. See also Susan E. Reverby and Susan B. Bell, "Vaginal Politics: Tensions and Possibilities in *The Vagina Monologues*," *Women's Studies International Forum* 28, no. 5 (2005): 434–37.

9. Reverby and Bell, "Vaginal Politics," 438, emphasis added.

10. Rosen, *The World Split Open*, 175, 79.

11. Cultural/difference feminists, such as Mary Daly, Marilyn French, and Carol Gilligan, are most often the targets of this charge. Arguably they, like feminists of the FFWHC, articulate a much more complex point than simple biological essentialism—one that still attends to social factors of gender development. For critiques of feminist uses of biology, see Kristy Maddux, *The Faithful Citizen: Popular Christian Media and Gendered Civic Identities* (Waco, Tex.: Baylor University Press, 2010), 155–79; Michele L. Hammers, "Talking about "Down There": The Politics of Publicizing the Female Body through *the Vagina Monologues*," *Women's Studies in Communication* 29, no. 2 (2006): 220–43; Rosemarie Putnam Tong, *Feminist Thought: A More Comprehensive Introduction* (Boulder: Westview Press, 1998), 45–93.

12. Kathy Davis, *The Making of Our Bodies, Ourselves: How Feminism Travels across Borders* (Durham: Duke University Press, 2007), 124.

13. For example, see Federation of Feminist Women's Health Centers (FFWHC), *How to Stay Out of the Gynecologist's Office* (Culver City, Calif.: Peace Press, 1981), 1–3; FFWHC, *A New View of a Woman's Body: A Fully Illustrated Guide by the Federation of Feminist Women's Health Centers* (Los Angeles: Feminist Health Press, 1991), 17–18.

14. FFWHC, *New View*, 17.

15. Ibid.

16. Kate Millett, *Sexual Politics* (New York: Avon Books, 1969), 178.

17. Jane Gerhard, *Desiring Revolution: Second-Wave Feminism and the Rewriting of American Sexual Thought, 1920 to 1982* (New York: Columbia University Press, 2001), 52. See also Mari Jo Buhle, *Feminism and Its Discontents: A Century of Struggle with Psychoanalysis* (Cambridge: Harvard University Press, 1998), 207; Josephine Donovan, *Feminist Theory: The Intellectual Traditions of American Feminism* (New York: Continuum Publishing, 1985), 101.

18. Gerhard, *Desiring Revolution*, 99.

19. Anne Koedt, "The Myth of the Vaginal Orgasm," in *Radical Feminism: A Documentary Reader*, ed. Barbara A. Crow (1973; New York: New York University Press, 2000), 371.

20. Ibid., 372.

21. Donovan, *Feminist Theory*, 101.

22. FFWHC, *A New View*, 34, 46.

23. Donovan, *Feminist Theory*, 101–3. For extensive discussion of second wave feminist critiques of Freud, see Buhle, *Feminism and Its Discontents*, 206–20; Gerhard, *Desiring Revolution*.

24. Luce Irigaray, *This Sex Which Is Not One* (1977; Ithaca: Cornell University Press, 1985), 39. All italics are in the original except for the added emphasis on "sight."

25. Terri Kapsalis, *Public Privates: Performing Gynecology from Both Ends of the Speculum* (Durham: Duke University Press, 1997), 88, emphasis added.

26. Sigmund Freud, "Some Psychical Consequences of the Anatomical Distinction between the Sexes" (1925), in *The Standard Edition of the Complete Psychological Works of Sigmund Freud*, ed. James Strachey, vol. 19 (London: Hogarth Press, 1961), 252, emphasis added.

27. Ibid.

28. Millett, *Sexual Politics*, 181.

29. Germaine Greer, *The Female Eunuch* (New York: Farrar, Straus and Giroux, 1971), 44.

30. FFWHC, *Stay Out*, 1.

31. Morgen, *Into Our Own Hands*, 73; Kapsalis, *Public Privates*, 4; FFWHC, *Stay Out*, 5; Rosemary Pringle, *Sex and Medicine: Gender, Power and Authority in the Medical Profession* (Cambridge: Cambridge University Press, 1998), 203.

32. Boston Women's Health Book Collective (BWHBC), *Our Bodies, Ourselves: A Book by and for Women* (New York Simon and Schuster, 1973), 241; Morgen, *Into Our Own Hands*, 124.

33. Morgen, *Into Our Own Hands*, 73; FFWHC, *New View*, 21; FFWHC, *Stay Out*, 5.

34. BWHBC, *Our Bodies, Ourselves*, 237–38; Morgen, *Into Our Own Hands*, 73, 122–24; FFWHC, *Stay Out*, 5; Pringle, *Sex and Medicine*, 203.

35. Kapsalis, *Public Privates*, 31.

36. Ibid., 34.

37. For a discussion of the public campaign against midwifery, see Barbara Ehrenreich and Deirdre English, *For Her Own Good: 150 Years of the Experts' Advice to Women* (Garden City, N.Y.: Anchor Press, 1978).

38. Morgen, *Into Our Own Hands*, 122.

39. Ibid., 124.

40. Carolyn Herbst Lewis, "Waking Sleeping Beauty: The Premarital Pelvic Exam and Heterosexuality during the Cold War," *Journal of Women's History* 17, no. 4 (2005): 86–110; FFWHC, *Stay Out*, 6; Angela Y. Davis, *Women, Race, and Class* (New York: Vintage Books, 1981), 215–21.

41. Kapsalis, *Public Privates*, 61–79; Kline, *Bodies of Knowledge*.

42. Morgen, *Into Our Own Hands*, 124. See also Pringle, *Sex and Medicine*, 203.

43. Kapsalis, *Public Privates*, 5.

44. Ibid., 99–100.

45. Quoted ibid., 37.

46. Ibid., 32.

47. Ibid., 99–100.

48. Ibid., 100.

49. Ibid., 93.

50. Ibid., 96.

51. FFWHC, *New View*, 18.

52. For examples of images and or imagery of sexed-female anatomy in *Ms.* in the 1970s, see Barbara Seaman, "The Liberated Orgasm," *Ms.*, August 1972, 67; Erica Jong, "Gardener," *Ms.*, March 1973, 79; Jamaica Kinkaid, "Arts: Erotica!" *Ms.*, January 1975, 31–32; April Kingsley, "Art: The I-Hate-to-Cook 'Dinner Party,'" *Ms.*, June 1979, 30–31. For similar examples in *off our backs*, see Pam Kalishman, "Cancer-Causing Hormone," *off our backs*, October 1972, 22; Pam Kalishman, "Herpes-Deadly Vd," *off our backs*, April 1973, 22; Mary Quinn, "Make Waves on the Waves," *off our backs*, April 1973, 10; Chris Hobbs, review of *Our Bodies, Ourselves, off our backs*, May 1973, 29; Maryse Holder, "Another Cuntree: At Last, a Mainstream Feminist Art Movement," *off our backs*, September 1973, 11–17.

53. *New View* was reprinted in 1991 by the Feminist Health Press.

54. *Women's Health in Women's Hands* was too large for mass publication at a reasonable price. *New View* was considered to be a "picture book" of sorts, and the feminists of the FFWHC believed that it would be first to break new ground since *Our Bodies, Ourselves*. See FFWHC, *New View*, 20.

55. Conventional medical professionals typically use a speculum with the bills up, handles extending downward. Such a use is for the professional's "convenience" but is not practical for self-examination. See FFWHC, *New View*, 23.

56. Ibid., 17–18.

57. Ibid., 21.

58. FFWHC, *Stay Out*, 1.

59. Gerhard, *Desiring Revolution*.

60. FFWHC, *New View*, 22.

61. The same is true for *Stay Out*. Three of the four opening images are of women engaging in cervical self-examination. The fourth is a photographic image of the cervix itself.

62. The original appeared in *Sister*, a feminist publication of the L.A. Women's Center. Reprints can be found in Kline, *Bodies of Knowledge*, 75; Donna Haraway, *Modest_Witness@ Second Millennium. Femaleman©_ Meets_Oncomouse™* (New York: Routledge, 1997), 194.

63. FFWHC, *New View,* 20.

64. James Jasinski, *Sourcebook on Rhetoric: Key Concepts in Contemporary Rhetorical Studies* (Thousand Oaks, Calif.: Sage, 2001), 12.

65. FFWHC, *New View,* 33.

66. FFWHC, *Stay Out,* 3.

67. Ibid., 2. See also FFWHC, *New View,* 37–39.

68. FFWHC, *New View,* 67.

69. FFWHC, *Stay Out,* 12, 33, 35. Reading the text that accompanies this last image, one learns that cervical cysts are fairly common and normal.

70. This section appears between pages 128 and 129 of FFWHC, *New View,* but is not itself paginated.

71. FFWHC, *Stay Out,* 128.

72. FFWHC, *New View,* unpaginated.

73. Ibid.

74. Ibid.

75. Ibid.

76. Ibid., 128.

77. Ibid., 50.

78. FFWHC, *Stay Out,* 1. See also FFWHC, *New View,* 152.

79. FFWHC, *Stay Out,* 87–89.

80. FFWHC, *New View,* 123–26, 30.

81. Ibid., 26, 36, 44–45, 68–69; FFWHC, *Stay Out,* 1, 65, 83, 89.

82. FFWHC, *New View,* 27–31; FFWHC, *Stay Out,* 86.

83. FFWHC, *New View,* 98–99; FFWHC, *Stay Out,* 40–42.

84. FFWHC, *New View,* 112–13.

85. Ibid., 124–26; FFWHC, *Stay Out,* 89.

86. FFWHC, *New View,* 50.

87. Ibid., 50–53.

88. Ibid., 34–35, 50–53, 126, second page of photo inset.

89. Ibid., 22–24, 27, 44–45, 68, 112–13, 26.

90. FFWHC, *Stay Out,* 65.

91. Kapsalis, *Public Privates,* 133.

92. See also Kline, *Bodies of Knowledge.*

4. Sexing Woman

1. Judith Butler, *Bodies That Matter: On the Discursive Limits of Sex* (New York: Routledge, 1993), 15.

2. Jane Gerhard, *Desiring Revolution: Second-Wave Feminism and the Rewriting of American Sexual Thought, 1920 to 1982* (New York: Columbia University Press, 2001), 2, 3.

3. Quoted in Alice Echols, *Daring to Be Bad: Radical Feminism in America, 1967–1975* (Minneapolis: University of Minnesota Press, 1989), 164. See also Gerhard, *Desiring Revolution,* 109–10.

4. Echols, *Daring to Be Bad,* 165.

5. Quoted ibid., 238, 173. As Echols makes clear, Atkinson's initial denunciation of heterosexual and homosexual practices was characteristic of the group she founded, The Feminists.

6. Gerhard, *Desiring Revolution,* 3.

7. For a good description of the difference between liberal feminism's commitment to equality and radical feminism's commitment to liberation, see Sara Evans, *Tidal Wave: How Women Changed America at Century's End* (New York: Free Press, 2003), 24.

8. Miriam Schneir, ed., *Feminism in Our Time: The Essential Writings, World War II to the*

Present (New York: Vintage Books, 1994), 95. See also Patricia Bradley, *Mass Media and the Shaping of American Feminism, 1963–1975* (Jackson: University Press of Mississippi, 2003), 29–33; Bernadette Barker-Plummer, "News as a Political Resource: Media Strategies and Political Identity in the U.S. Women's Movement, 1966–1975," *Critical Studies in Mass Communication* 12, no. 3 (1995): 306–24. Although I have chosen to discuss the history of liberal feminism through the history of NOW specifically, I want to emphasize that NOW was not the only liberal feminist organization of its time. Other organizations included the Women's Equity Action League (WEAL) and the National Women's Political Caucus (NWPC). While there were some differences between these groups, NOW was seen as the most prominent force of the liberal branch of the woman's movement.

9. Flora Davis, *Moving the Mountain: The Women's Movement in America since 1960* (New York: Simon and Schuster, 1999), 51–68; Evans, *Tidal Wave*, 24–26; Ruth Rosen, *The World Split Open: How the Modern Women's Movement Changed America* (New York: Penguin, 2000), 78–84.

10. Patricia Bradley, "Mass Communication and the Shaping of Us Feminism," in *News, Gender, and Power*, ed. Gill Branston, Cynthia Carter, and Stuart Allan (London: Routledge, 1998), 160–73.

11. Ibid., 164. See also Barker-Plummer, "News as a Political Resource"; Bernadette Barker-Plummer, "Producing Public Voice: Resource Mobilization and Media Access in the National Organization for Women," *Journalism and Mass Communication Quarterly* 79, no. 1 (2002): 188–205.

12. Bradley, "Mass Communication and the Shaping of Us Feminism"; Bradley, *Mass Media and the Shaping of American Feminism*.

13. Barker-Plummer, "News as a Political Resource," 315.

14. Davis, *Moving the Mountain*.

15. Sidney Abbott and Barbara Love, *Sappho Was a Right-On Woman: A Liberated View of Lesbianism* (New York: Stein and Day, 1972); Karla Jay, *Tales of the Lavender Menace: A Memoir of Liberation* (New York: Basic Books, 1999).

16. Echols, *Daring to Be Bad*.

17. Davis, *Moving the Mountain*; Rosen, *The World Split Open*.

18. Echols, *Daring to Be Bad*; Marcia Cohen, *The Sisterhood: The True Story of the Women Who Changed the World* (New York: Simon and Schuster, 1988); Davis, *Moving the Mountain*.

19. "Who's Come a Long Way, Baby?" *Time*, August 31, 1970, 16; "Women's Lib: A Second Look," *Time*, December 14, 1970.

20. Kristan Poirot, "Mediating a Movement, Authorizing Discourse: Sexual Politics, Kate Millett, and Feminism's Second Wave," *Women's Studies in Communication* 27 (2004): 204–35.

21. Betty Friedan, *"It Changed My Life": Writings on the Women's Movement* (New York: Penguin, 1976).

22. Susan Brownmiller, "'Sisterhood Is Powerful': A Member of the Women's Liberation Movement Explains What It's All About," *New York Times Magazine*, March 15, 1970, 140.

23. See, for example, "It Was a Great Day for Women on the March," *New York Times*, August 30, 1970; Betty Friedan, "We Don't Have to Be That Independent," *McCall's*, January 1973; Enid Nemy, "The Movement . . . Is Big Enough to Roll with All These Punches," *New York Times*, October 2, 1972.

24. Judy Klemesrud, "The Disciples of Sappho, Updated," *New York Times Magazine*, March 28, 1971, 50, emphasis added.

25. Midge Decter, "The Liberated Woman," *Commentary*, October 1970, 33–44.

26. Friedan, "We Don't Have to Be That Independent," 21.

27. Betty Friedan, letter to the editor, "Betty Friedan Replies," *New York Times Magazine*, March 25, 1973, 50, 147.

28. Betty Friedan, "Up from the Kitchen Floor," *New York Times Magazine*, March 4, 1973, 33, 34. "Zap" is a term used by "second wave" radical feminists to describe a kind of public protest that is designed to raise awareness about an issue. "Zaps" were often designed to shock or offend the audience. See Echols, *Daring to be Bad*, 70, 94.

29. Ibid.

30. Robin Morgan, letter to the editor, "Sisters under Each Other's Skin," *New York Times Magazine*, March 25, 1973, 16.

31. Friedan, "Up From the Kitchen Floor," 33.

32. Ibid. Years later Friedan's fear had apparently not dissipated, as the *New York Times* reported that "[Friedan] warned feminists from becoming anti-male and said they must move away from negative thinking to a 'new yes' spirit. 'With the Watergate revelations—how the C.I.A. has manipulated and infiltrated, and usually under the guise of pushing, like an agent provocateur, a radical or pseudo-radical in every other movement to render it ineffective— one can assume that the same thing has been happening in the women's movement.'" See Betty Friedan Fears C.I.A. Movement Role," *New York Times*, July 23, 1975.

33. Pauli Murray, letter to the editor, "What's the Hubbub?," *New York Times Magazine*, March 25, 1973, 109.

34. Morgan, "Sisters under Each Other's Skin," 16.

35. Ginny Vida and Jean O'Leary, letter to the editor, "End Lesbian Oppression!," *New York Times Magazine*, March 25, 1973, 16, 20.

36. Mim Kelber, letter to the editor, "Solipsism Decried," *New York Times Magazine*, March 25, 1973, 20.

37. Jill Johnston, letter to the editor, "Unwilling Gladiator of a Modern Male State," *New York Times Magazine*, March 25, 1973, 22, 29.

38. Ti-Grace Atkinson, letter to the editor, "Outrage," *New York Times Magazine*, March 25, 1973, 108.

39. Tony Carabillo, letter to the editor, "History Now," *New York Times Magazine*, March 25, 1973, 108.

40. Friedan, "We Don't Have to Be That Independent," 108–9.

41. Judy Klemesrud, "The Lesbian Issue and Women's Lib," *New York Times*, December 18, 1970; Lyn Tornabene, "The Liberation of Betty Friedan," *McCall's*, May 1971, 136; "Feminist Marchers Brave Icy Rain," *New York Times*, December 13, 1970.

42. Karrin Vasby Anderson, "Rhymes with Rich: "Bitch" as a Tool of Containment in Contemporary American Politics," *Rhetoric and Public Affairs* 2, no. 4 (1999): 599–623.

43. John M. Murphy, "Domesticating Dissent: The Kennedys and the Freedom Rides," *Communication Monographs* 59, no. 1 (1992): 74.

44. Ibid., 64.

45. Susan Douglas, *Where the Girls Are: Growing up Female with the Mass Media* (New York: Random House, 1994), 186, 191.

46. Echols, *Daring to Be Bad*; Sara Evans, *Personal Politics: The Roots of Women's Liberation in the Civil Rights Movement and the New Left* (New York: Vintage Books, 1979); Rosen, *The World Split Open*.

47. "Editorial," *Ain't I a Woman?* June 26, 1970, 2.

48. Judith Hole and Ellen Levine, *Rebirth of Feminism* (New York: Quadrangle Books, 1971). See also David Armstrong, *A Trumpet to Arms: Alternative Media in America* (Los Angeles: J. P. Tarcher, 1981); Barker-Plummer, "News as a Political Resource."

49. Barbara Burris, "What Is Women's Liberation?" *It Ain't Me Babe*, February 1970, 2; See also Rita Mae Brown, "Coitus Interruptus or Stop Your Fucking Around," *RAT*, February 6, 1970, 12, 20; "Toward the Liberation for Women: A Struggle for Identity," *It Ain't Me Babe*, January 29, 1970, 2.

50. Rita Mae Brown, "Say It Isn't So," *RAT*, March 7, 1970, 18.

51. See "Women's Liberation Is a Lesbian Plot! Congress to Unite Women?" *RAT,* May 8, 1970, 3; "Rambling on Women-Identified Women," *Ain't I a Woman?* February 19, 1971, 13; "So We Put It On," *Ain't I a Woman?* February 19, 1971, 3; "The Lavender T-Shirt Fit," *Ain't I a Woman?* February 19, 1971, 3; "Sisters," *RAT,* July 1, 1970, 21.

52. "Our Response," *It Ain't Me Babe,* December 1, 1970, 14; Loretta Ulmschneider, "Bisexuality," *The Furies,* March–April 1973, 2. See also "C.L.I.T. Statement #2," *off our backs,* July 31, 1974, 11.

53. "Washington to Watcher One Way," *Ain't I a Woman?* April 2, 1971, 11; Rita Mae Brown, "Letter to the Editor," *Ain't I a Woman?* June 4, 1971, 2.

54. Helen Tate, "The Ideological Effects of a Failed Constitutive Rhetoric: The Co-option of the Rhetoric of White Lesbian Feminism," *Women's Studies in Communication* 28, no. 1 (2005): 12. See also Shane Phelan, *Identity Politics: Lesbian Feminism and the Limits of Community* (Philadelphia: Temple University Press, 1989).

55. Radicalesbians, "The Woman-Identified-Woman," in *Radical Feminism: A Documentary Reader,* ed. B. A. Crow (1970; New York: New York University Press, 2000), 236, 237.

56. Cathy Nelson, "Untitled," *Lavender Woman,* November 1971, 6. See also Charlotte Bunch, "Lesbian Feminist Politics," *off our backs,* April 30, 1973, 17.

57. Charlotte Bunch, "Lesbians in Revolt," *The Furies,* January 1972, 9.

58. See interview with Jill Johnston in Maedell Dulaney, "Jill Johnston," *off our backs,* August 31, 1973, 14. See also Bunch, "Lesbian Feminist Politics"; Francis Chapman, "The Soul Selects: A New Separate Way," *off our backs,* January 31, 1972, 7; editorial, *The Furies,* March–April 1973, 5–6; "Rambling on Women-Identified Women"; Ulmschneider, "Bisexuality."

59. Bunch, "Lesbians in Revolt," 8; "This Is for Straight, Bisexual, and Lesbian Women Who Won't Let Go of Men," *Ain't I a Woman?,* July 20, 1973, 4; Brooke, "Women-Get It Together," *Lesbians Fight Back,* July 1972, 3.

60. Tate, "The Ideological Effects of a Failed Constitutive Rhetoric," 9, emphasis added.

61. "Out of the Closets & into the Streets," *Ain't I a Woman?* July 10, 1970, 11.

62. "C.L.I.T. Statement #2." See also Ulmschneider, "Bisexuality."

63. Pat Buchanan, "The Living Contradiction," *The Lesbian Tide,* May–June 1973, 6.

64. Equally problematic for radical/lesbian feminists was that "not all lesbians are consciously woman-identified." Rita A. Goldberger, "Get It Straight!" *The Lesbian Tide,* May 1972, 7. See also Bunch, "Lesbians in Revolt."

65. Chapman, "The Soul Selects," unpaginated; Rita Mae Brown, "Roxeanne Dunbar: How a Female Heterosexual Serves the Interests of Male Supremacy," *The Furies,* January 1972, 14–15; Bunch, "Lesbian Feminist Politics"; Goldberger, "Get It Straight!"; Marychild, "Calling All Dykes . . . Come in Please," *off our backs,* July 31, 1974, 16.

66. Rita Mae Brown, "Take a Lesbian to Lunch," *The Ladder,* April–May 1972, 17.

67. "The Lavender T-Shirt Fit," 3.

68. Radicalesbians, "The Woman-Identified-Woman," 236.

69. Martha Shelley, "Step in Fetch It Woman," *Ain't I a Woman?* September 11, 1970, 2.

70. Rita Mae Brown, "Hanoi to Hoboken, a Round Trip Ticket," *Ain't I a Woman?* April 2, 1971, 11.

71. Ulmschneider, "Bisexuality," 2. See also Bunch, "Lesbian Feminist Politics"; Adrienne Rich, "Compulsory Heterosexuality and Lesbian Existence," in *The Lesbian and Gay Studies Reader,* ed. Henry Abelove, Michele Aina Barale, and David M. Halperin (1980; New York: Routledge, 1993), 227–54.

72. Phelan, *Identity Politics,* 47.

73. Bunch, "Lesbian Feminist Politics," unpaginated, emphasis added.

74. Bonnie J. Dow, *Prime-Time Feminism: Television, Media Culture, and the Women's Movement since 1970* (Philadelphia: University of Pennsylvania Press, 1996), 207. Dow's articulation of the way popular television reduces feminist politics to feminist identity is par-

ticularly apt for this discussion. Although I think that she is correct that, generally speaking, feminism's adage about the personal being political "was meant to describe *patriarchy,* not *feminism,*" I would also add that popular television's *problematic* tendency to transform "a set of political ideas and practices . . . into a set of attitudes and lifestyle choices" (ibid.) is also applicable to radical/lesbian feminism.

75. "Lesbian Demands," *Ain't I a Woman?* October 9, 1970, 5.

76. Shelley, "Step in Fetch It Woman," 2.

77. "This Is for Straight, Bisexual, and Lesbian Women," 4; Rita Mae Brown, "Women Who Love Men Hate Them: Male Supremacy versus Sexism," *The Furies,* Fall 1972, 14.

78. See "C.L.I.T. Statement #2."; "Out of the Closets & into the Streets"; Ulmschneider, "Bisexuality."

79. Mongoose, "Liberation Begins at Home," *Goodbye to All That,* September 15, 1970, 6.

80. See interview with Jill Johnston in Dulaney, "Jill Johnston," unpaginated.

81. Judy, "Lesbians as Women," *It Ain't Me Babe,* May 21, 1970, 7.

82. "Up from SDS—Why We Split," *The Purple Star,* Spring 1971, 13.

83. Brown, "Hanoi to Hoboken, a Round Trip Ticket," 11.

84. "Radicalesbians: Coming Out vs. Coming Home," *Awake & Move,* March 1971, 4.

85. Jeffrey T. Nealon, *Alterity Politics: Ethics and Performative Subjectivity* (Durham: Duke University Press, 1998), 6.

86. Editorial, *The Furies,* 5. See also Brown, "Take a Lesbian to Lunch"; Chapman, "The Soul Selects"; Rosina Richter, letter to the editor, *The Furies,* March–April 1973, 5.

87. See Charlotte Bunch, "Perseverance Furthers: Separatism and Our Future," *The Furies,* Fall 1972, 3–5; "Painful Times," *Ain't I a Woman?* March 12, 1971, 2.

88. Richter, letter to the editor, 5.

89. Bunch, "Perseverance Furthers," 3.

90. Bunch, "Lesbian Feminist Politics," unpaginated.

91. Judith Butler, *Gender Trouble: Feminism and the Subversion of Identity* (1990; New York: Routledge, 1999), 21.

5. Questionable Engagements

1. SlutWalk Toronto, "Why?" www.slutwalktoronto.com.

2. SlutWalk Toronto, "How?" www.slutwalktoronto.com.

3. SlutWalk Toronto, "Slutwalk Toronto (Facebook Event)," www.facebook.com.

4. Numbers based on the compilation of satellite SlutWalks listed on SlutWalk Toronto's webpage. See SlutWalk Toronto, "Satellites List," http://slutwalktoronto.com.

5. SlutWalk Toronto, "How?"

6. For examples of viral description, see Patty Henetz, "Viral Slutwalk Protest Hits Salt Lake City," *Salt Lake Tribune,* July 30, 2011; Salamishah Tillet, "What to Wear to a Slutwalk," *The Nation,* September 28, 2011; Jessica Valenti, "Slutwalks and the Future of Feminism," *Washington Post,* June 3, 2011.

7. Katha Pollitt, "Talk the Talk, Walk the Slutwalk," *The Nation,* July 18–25, 2011, 9. For other celebrations of SlutWalks, see Chloe Angyal, "Slutwalk Protests: A Dress Is Not a Yes," *Christian Science Monitor,* June 13, 2011; Libby Purves, "Lay Off the Bitching Sisters! Just Be Nice," *The Times* (London), June 13, 2011; Christie Thompson, "Taking *Slut* for a Walk," *Ms.* 21, no. 3 (Summer 2011): 14; "Slutwalks: Women Reclaim the Streets . . . and Language," October 18, 2011, www.permanentrevolution.net.

8. Rebecca Traister, "Ladies, We Have a Problem," *New York Times,* July 24, 2011. See also Jill, "Toronto Activists Take Back the Slut," March 31, 2011, http://blog.iblamethepatriarchy.com; "Dear Feminists, Will You Also Be Marching in N***Erwalk?" October 4, 2011, www .peopleofcolororganize.com; Laura Woodhouse, "Slutwalk London," April 30, 2011, www .thefword.org.uk.

9. Aura Blogando, "Slutwalk: A Stroll through White Supremacy," May 13, 2011, http://tothecurb.wordpress.com. See also Mahendra Ved, "'Slut' Puts Off Many from Protest Walk in Delhi," *New Straits Times* (Malaysia), August 8, 2011.

10. Martha C. Nussbaum, "The Professor of Parody," *New Republic* 220, no. 8 (February 22, 1999): 45.

11. Valenti, "Slutwalks and the Future of Feminism."

12. Carolyn Dever, *Skeptical Feminism: Activist Theory, Activist Practice* (Minneapolis: University of Minnesota Press, 2004), xi.

13. Ibid.

14. Tasha Dubriwny, *The Vulnerable Empowered Woman: Feminism, Postfeminism, and Women's Health* (New Brunswick: Rutgers University Press, 2013), 22.

15. See, for example, Bonnie J. Dow, *Prime-Time Feminism: Television, Media Culture, and the Women's Movement since 1970* (Philadelphia: University of Pennsylvania Press, 1996), 92–93; Angela McRobbie, "Post-Feminism and Popular Culture," *Feminist Media Studies* 4, no. 3 (2004): 255; Kristy Maddux, "Winning the Right to Vote in 2004: *Iron Jawed Angels* and the Retrospective Framing of Feminism," *Feminist Media Studies* 9, no. 1 (2009): 80.

16. Dubriwny, *The Vulnerable Empowered Woman*; Stéphanie Genz and Benjamin A. Brabon, *Postfeminism: Cultural Texts and Theories* (Edinburgh: Edinburgh University Press, 2009), 5, 24; Yvonne Tasker and Diane Negra, eds., *Interrogating Postfeminism: Gender and the Politics of Popular Culture* (Durham: Duke University Press, 2007), 1–13.

17. Dow, *Prime-Time Feminism*, 96.

18. Ann Braithwaite, "The Personal, the Political, Third-Wave and Postfeminisms," *Feminist Theory* 3, no. 3 (2002): 336.

19. Dow, *Prime-Time Feminism*, 92. See also Braithwaite "The Personal, the Political," 338; McRobbie, "Post-Feminism and Popular Culture," 255.

20. Sarah Projansky, "Mass Magazine Cover Girls: Some Reflections on Postfeminist Girls and Postfeminism's Daughters," in Tasker and Negra, *Interrogating Postfeminism*, 68. Similar conclusions about postfeminism can be found in Dow, *Prime-Time Feminism*; Dubriwny, *The Vulnerable Empowered Woman*; Genz and Brabon, *Postfeminism*.

21. Genz and Brabon, *Postfeminism*, 1.

22. Susan Douglas, *Enlightened Sexism: The Seductive Message That Feminism's Work Is Done* (New York: Times Books, 2010); Hye Jin Lee and Wen Huike, "Where the Girls Are in the Age of New Sexism: An Interview with Susan Douglas," *Journal of Communication Inquiry* 33, no. 2 (2009): 93–103.

23. Quoted in Lee and Huike, "Where the Girls Are," 93.

24. Douglas, *Enlightened Sexism*, 10.

25. For descriptions of the conflation of postfeminism and third wave feminism, see Leslie Heywood and Jennifer Drake, ed., *Third Wave Agenda: Being Feminist, Doing Feminism* (Minneapolis: University of Minnesota Press, 1997), 1. See also Ednie Kaeh Garrison, "Contests for the Meaning of Third Wave Feminism: Feminism and Popular Consciousness," in *Third-Wave Feminism: A Critical Exploration,* ed. Stacy Gillis, Gillian Howie, and Rebecca Munford (New York: Palgrave, 2004), 30–31; Kristyn Gorton, "(Un)Fashionable Feminists: The Media and *Ally McBeal*," in Gillis, Howie, and Munford, *Third-Wave Feminism*, 160.

26. Helene A. Shugart, "Isn't It Ironic? The Intersection of Third-Wave Feminism and Generation X," *Women's Studies in Communication* 24, no. 2 (2001): 131.

27. Maddux, "Winning the Right to Vote in 2004," 81. See also Genz and Brabon, *Postfeminism*, 162; Rebecca Munford, "'Wake up and Smell the Lipgloss': Gender, Generation, and the (a)Politics of Girl Power," in Gillis, Howie, and Munford, *Third-Wave Feminism*, 144.

28. Maddux, "Winning the Right to Vote in 2004," 80.

29. Ibid., 81.

30. Stacy Gillis, "Neither Cyborg nor Goddess: The (Im)Possibilities of Cyberfeminism," in Gillis, Howie, and Munford, *Third-Wave Feminism*, 187. See also Braithwaite, "The Personal,

the Political," 336; Rebecca Walker, *To Be Real: Telling the Truth and Changing the Face of Feminism* (New York: Anchor Books, 1995), xxix–xi; and Helene A. Shugart, Catherine Egley Waggoner, and D. Lynn O'Brien Hallstein, "Mediating Third-Wave Feminism: Appropriation as Postmodern Media Practice," *Critical Studies in Media Communication* 18, no. 2 (2001): 194–210.

31. Shugart, "Isn't It Ironic?" 134.

32. Stacy Gills and Rebecca Munford, "Interview with Elaine Showalter," in Gillis, Howie, and Munford, *Third-Wave Feminism*, 60.

33. Quoted in Deborah Siegel, *Sisterhood Interrupted: From Radical Women to Grrls Gone Wild* (New York: Palgrave, 2007), 128.

34. Connie Wang and Lexi Nisita, "Tavi Discusses Sluts, Activism, and Why the Fashion Industry Has a Ways to Go," www.refinery29.com; "Slutwalk New Orleans 2011," July 13, 2011, http://womenempoweredandlovinglife.weebly.com.

35. Ada Farrugia Conroy, "More Thoughts on Slutwalk," May 1, 2011, http://the-broken-arted .blogspot.com. See also Mary-Ellen Lynn, comment on "Slutwalk Is Out-of-Context Feminism", June 8, 2011, http://intentious.com.

36. Meghan Murphy, "Slutwalks, Sex Work, and the Future of Feminism," The F Word: Feminist Media Collective, May 7, 2011, www.feminisms.org (no longer available). Murphy's essay can currently be found at Meghan Murphy, "Slutwalks, Sex Work, and the Future of Feminism," June 8, 2011, http://feministcurrent.com.

37. "'Slut Walks' and Modern Feminism," *The Agenda with Steve Paikin*, podcast, May 6, 2011, http://castroller.com.

38. Nicole Wilson, "*Slutwalk Philadelphia:* Intention and Image," August 14, 2011, http:// the-st-claire.com.

39. Genz and Brabon, *Postfeminism*, 25.

40. Shugart, "Mediating Third-Wave Feminism," 194, 195.

41. Emily Nussbaum, "The Rebirth of the Feminist Manifesto," *New York Magazine*, November 7, 2011, 44.

42. Valenti, "Slutwalks and the Future of Feminism."

43. Not surprisingly, the public protest features of SlutWalk that recall feminism's past also become the grounds on which SlutWalk is criticized. For examples of anti-feminist challenges to SlutWalk that compare it to previous generations of activism, see "Slutwalks: Women Reclaim the Streets"; Janice Shaw Crouse, "Slutwalking Our Way to Gomorrah; Reclaiming a Naughty Word Can't Change Reality," *Washington Times*, June 8, 2011; Charlotte Allen, "When Women Dress as Halloween Candy," *Los Angeles Times*, October 30, 2111; Beatriz Foster, "Fractured Feminist Positions," October 5, 2011, www.thecowl.com; Margaret Wente, "Embrace Your Inner Slut? Um, Maybe Not," *Toronto Globe and Mail*, May 12, 2011.

44. Amanda Marcotte, "Slutwalks and the New Political Incorrectness," *Slate*, April 21, 2011, www.slate.com.

45. Kathy Miriam, "Branding Feminism," Dialectical Spin: Radical Feminism in Other-Land, October 23, 2011, http://kmiriam.wordpress.com. For other examples of self-proclaimed feminists critiquing SlutWalks as not being truly "feminist," see Victoria Coren, "Frocks Are Not a Feminist Issue: The Fight for Women's Rights Is Being Waylaid by Needless Talk about What Women Wear," *The Observer*, June 19, 2011; Wendy Kaminer, "Is Sluttishness a Feminist Statement?" *Free Inquiry*, August–September 2011; Minette Marrin, "With Every Step Slutwalkers Betray the Liberty of Women," *The Sunday Times*, May 15, 2011; Kirsten Powers, "'Slut Walk': Feminist Folly," *New York Post*, May 11, 2011; Jennifer Selway, "This Silly Feminist Protest," *The Express*, May 14, 2011.

46. Nussbaum, "Rebirth of the Feminist Manifesto," 45.

47. "An Open Letter from Black Women to the Slutwalk," September 23, 2011, www .blackwomensblueprint.org. See also Briana, "After a Lot of Time and Consideration, I've Decided to Leave Slutwalk," October 15, 2011, http://confessionsofaformerslutwalker

.blogspot.com; Ernesto, "Four Brief Critiques of Slutwalk's Whiteness, Privilege, and Un-examined Power Dynamics," May 16, 2011, www.peopleofcolororganize.com; TJ, "A Response to Slut Walk!" April 28, 2011, www.musingsandmoans.com; Harsha Walia, "Slutwalk: To March or Not to March," May 18, 2011, http://rabble.ca; Monica Roberts, "Dear White Women, You Never Fail to Disappoint Me," October 11, 2011, http://transgriot.blogspot.com.

48. Crunk Feminist Collective, "I Saw the Sign but Did We Really Need a Sign? Slutwalk and Racism," October 6, 2011, www.crunkfeministcollective.com. For SlutWalk Toronto's official response to what happened at SlutWalk NYC, see Heather Jarvis, "Racism and Anti-Racism: Why They Matter to Slutwalks," October 31, 2011, www.slutwalktoronto.com.

49. For a compilation of sexual assault statistics by sex/gender, see "Who Are the Vicitms?" www.rainn.org.

50. SlutWalk Toronto, "How?"

51. "Slutwalk Chicago's Mission," www.slutwalkchicago.org.

52. SlutWalk Toronto, "Why?"

53. Although the SlutWalks that emerged in other cities subsequent to the SlutWalk Toronto march were independently in control of their message, some recirculated much of the rhetoric found on SlutWalk Toronto's Web page. In fact, SlutWalk Toronto's statement, quoted here, was also found on the Facebook information pages of SlutWalk San Francisco Bay, SlutWalk Tampa, and SlutWalk Los Angeles.

54. SlutWalk Toronto, "Why?"

55. SlutWalk D.C., "Basic Information," www.facebook.com. Other examples of SlutWalks that refrained from discussing the assumed sexed connotation of the term "slut," and that explicitly expanded the term to refer to more than just women, include SlutWalk Tucson, "Basic Information," www.facebook.com; SlutWalk Omaha, "Basic Information," www.facebook.com; SlutWalk NYC, "Mission Statement," http://slutwalknyc.com; SlutWalk Philadelphia, "Basic Information," www.facebook.com.

56. SlutWalk LA, "Basic Information," www.facebook.com.

57. SlutWalk Lubbock, "Basic Information," www.facebook.com. See also SlutWalk Seattle, "About the Walk," slutwalkseattle.com; SlutWalk Toronto, "Why?"; SlutWalk SF Bay, "Basic Information," www.facebook.com; SlutWalk Tampa, "Information," www.facebook.com; SlutWalk Baltimore, "Basic Information," www.facebook.com; SlutWalk Spokane, "Basic Information," www.facebook.com.

58. A good example of the desire to recognize intersection identity and difference while building productive coalitions appears in a discussion about SlutWalks on a socialist organization's website in which one writer argues, "We cannot tackle the oppression of women generally without linking our struggle to the wider class struggle, the fight against racism, for LGBT rights, and against all the divide-and-conquer tactics used to maintain capitalism." Kelly Bellin, "Dismantling Rape Culture, Dismantling Capitalism: Minneapolis Forum Discusses Way Forward for Women's Liberation," www.socialistalternative.org.

59. Kenyon Farrow, "My Remarks for SlutWalk NYC," October 2, 2011, http://kenyonfarrow.com.

60. Valenti, "Slutwalks and the Future of Feminism." See also Rachel Friedlander, "'Slutwalks' Sparking an Important Conversation about Sexual Assaults," *Journal of Gender, Race, and Justice,* October 24, 2011, http://blogs.law.uiowa.edu, 522; Nussbaum, "Rebirth of the Feminist Manifesto"; Pollitt, "Talk the Talk."

61. Gail Dines and Wendy J. Murphy, "Slutwalk Is Not Sexual Liberation," May 8, 2011, www.guardian.co.uk. See also "Open Letter from Black Women"; Jill, "Toronto Activists"; "'Dear Feminists, Will You Also Be Marching in N***Erwalk?'; Woodhouse, "Slutwalk London."

Index

abolition, 22, 27–28, 30, 40, 44–45
abortion, 64, 71, 74, 79–80, 82, 89
"Ain't I a Woman?" *See under* Truth, Sojourner
alterity, 18, 24–25, 31, 40–41, 135–36n72
amplification strategies, 77–81
Anderson, Karin Vasby, 95
Anthony, Susan B., 50, 136n6
Anzaldúa, Gloria, 38–39
arguments from expediency, 44, 50
arguments from justice, 49, 50, 61
Aristotle, 7, 47–48
Atkinson, Ti-Grace, 88, 93–94, 97, 142n5
audience. *See under* rhetoric

Barad, Karen, 15–16
Barker-Plummer, Bernadette, 90. *See also* media pragmatism; media subversion
biological determinism, 13, 55, 59, 68
biological foundationalism, 18–19, 33–35, 49–51, 55–56, 60–61, 110
bisexuality, 99, 100, 103
black feminism, 22–24, 28–30, 39, 134n34
body: as discourse vs. as matter, 4, 12–16, 85–86, 127; and liberal theory, 46–51, 61; and race, 33–35, 38, 48, 55–56, 61–63; and science, 47–48. *See also* sex: and anatomy; feminism: and the body
Boston Women's Health Collective, 68, 76
breasts, 66, 72, 81; exams, 82–83; and Sojourner Truth, 34, 135n52
Brown, Rita Mae, 90, 99, 101–2, 105
Brownmiller, Susan, 91
Bunch, Charlotte, 100, 102–3, 106–7
Burke, Kenneth, 8, 37, 99
Butler, Judith, 2, 33, 41, 112, 114, 129n14; critiques of, 4, 11–13, 110, 130–31n42; and identity politics, 18, 31, 107; and matter, 12–15, 58, 130n42; and performativity, 13, 15–16, 130–31n42

Cady Stanton, Elizabeth, 18–19, 110; and Civil War amendments, 43–45, 54–56; and education, 54–56, 59–61; and immigration, 19, 44, 51, 55–56; as liberal theorist, 18–19, 45–46, 49–51, 52–53, 56–59, 61–63, 126; as opportunistic, 19, 44, 46, 55, 62; and racism, 43–46, 54–56, 62–63, 123, 136n6; and "Solitude of Self," 46, 53, 56–57, 136–37n14
Campbell, Karlyn Kohrs, 9, 23, 46, 50, 53, 54
Cell 16, 88
cervix, 72, 78–79, 142n69; and self-examination, 64–66, 74–76, 81–83, 85, 141n61
citizenship: and education, 54, 61; and natural rights, 18, 46, 48–52; and rationality, 52–54; and women, 9, 48–51, 137n34, 138n52
civil rights movements, 95, 97
Civil War amendments. *See* Cady Stanton, Elizabeth: and Civil War amendments
clitoris, 66, 68–69, 74–81, 83–84
Comte, Auguste, 46
consciousness-raising. *See under* second wave feminism
constitutive rhetoric, 6–11, 16, 99, 106, 127
containment strategies. *See* domestication strategies
corporeality. *See* body
cult of true womanhood, 9, 33–34
cultural feminism, 17, 140n11

Daly, Mary, 140n11
Daughters of Bilitis, 90
Davis, Angela, 32–33, 44
différance, 130–31n42
Dines, Gail, 116, 124
domestication strategies, 94–98, 100, 103–8
domesticity, 9–10, 33–34, 48, 50
Douglas, Susan, 94, 96, 114
Dow, Bonnie J., 113, 145n74
Downer, Carol, 64–66, 85

KRISTAN POIROT is an assistant professor at Texas A&M University. Her research has been recognized by the Organization for Research on Women and Communication and the National Communication Association. She earned a PhD from the University of Georgia, and currently lives in College Station with her husband and their three children.